Asian American Literature and the Environment

I0591486

"*Asian American Literature and the Environment* is a book I have long waited to see in print. It is a groundbreaking contribution to ecocritical inquiry and Asian American literary studies and will help define the fields for years to come." —*Robert T. Hayashi, Amherst College, USA*

"A wide-ranging and ground-breaking study that expands our understanding of Asian-American culture, environmental literature, and the connections between them. This should be required reading in ecocriticism, environmental studies, and multi-cultural studies." —*David Landis Barnhill, University of Wisconsin Oshkosh, USA*

"By collecting essays that focus on connections between environmental thought and Asian American literary productions, this book presents a new and exciting approach to two fields that have rarely been in dialogue with each other and moves the field of Asian American studies in new directions." —*Claudia Sadowski-Smith, Arizona State University, USA*

This book is a ground-breaking transnational study of representations of the environment in Asian American literature. Extending and renewing Asian American studies and ecocriticism by drawing the two fields into deeper dialogue, it brings Asian American writers to the center of ecocritical studies. This collection demonstrates the distinctiveness of Asian American writers' positions on topics of major concern today: environmental justice, identity and the land, war environments, consumption, urban environments, and the environment and creativity. Represented authors include Amy Tan, Maxine Hong Kingston, Ruth Ozeki, Ha Jin, Fae Myenne Ng, Le Ly Hayslip, Lan Cao, Mitsuye Yamada, Lawson Fusao Inada, Jeanne Wakatsuki Houston, Milton Murayama, Don Lee, and Hisaye Yamamoto. These writers provide a range of perspectives on the historical, social, psychological, economic, philosophical, and aesthetic responses of Asian Americans to the environment conceived in relation to labor, racism, immigration, domesticity, global capitalism, relocation, pollution, violence, and religion. Contributors apply a diversity of critical frameworks, including critical radical race studies, counter-memory studies, ecofeminism, and geomantic criticism. The book presents a compelling and timely "green" perspective through which to understand key works of Asian American literature and leads the field of ecocriticism into neglected terrain.

Lorna Fitzsimmons is Associate Professor and Coordinator of Humanities at California State University Dominguez Hills, USA.

Youngsuk Chae is Associate Professor of English at the University of North Carolina, Pembroke, USA.

Bella Adams is Lecturer in English at Liverpool John Moores University, UK.

Routledge Interdisciplinary Perspectives on Literature

For a full list of titles in this series, please visit www.routledge.com

Asian American Literature and the Environment

Edited by Lorna Fitzsimmons,
Youngsuk Chae, and Bella Adams

Routledge
Taylor & Francis Group

LONDON AND NEW YORK

First published 2015
by Routledge

2 Park Square, Milton Park, Abingdon, Oxfordshire OX14 4RN
711 Third Avenue, New York, NY 10017

*Routledge is an imprint of the Taylor & Francis Group,
an informa business*

First issued in paperback 2018

Library of Congress Cataloging-in-Publication Data

Asian American literature and the environment / edited
  by Lorna Fitzsimmons, Youngsuk Chae, Bella Adams.
     pages cm. — (Routledge interdisciplinary perspectives on literature)
   Includes bibliographical references and index.
  1. American literature—Asian American authors—History and criticism.
2. Environmental protection in literature.   3. Ecology in literature.
4. Ecocriticism.   I. Fitzsimmons, Lorna, 1957– editor.   II. Chae,
Youngsuk, editor.   III. Adams, Bella, editor.
   PS153.A84A74 2014
   810.9'895—dc23
   2014021460

ISBN: 978-0-415-71323-8 (hbk)
ISBN: 978-1-138-54784-1 (pbk)

Typeset in Sabon
by Apex CoVantage, LLC

Contents

PART II
The Environment and Violence

PART III
The Environment and Philosophy

Figures

Foreword

Joni Adamson

Anyone who has searched a forest floor for highly prized mushrooms in the spring or autumn knows that in the midst of a seeming absence, something that sprouts from networks that have been growing for a very long time, something just out of sight, might await. *Asian American Literature and the Environment* signals an auspicious moment not only in the field of ecocriticism but the long intertwined fields of American Studies and ethnic studies. This satisfyingly complex book focuses on Asian American cultures and literary production and makes clear the ways in which all of these fields, entangled in complicated ways, are now bearing fruit.

Scholars are increasingly suggesting the rhizome as a metaphor for thinking about interdisciplinarity.[1] Gilles Deleuze and Felix Guattari were among the first to see the beauty of root structures that supply nutrients to trees as a metaphor for research that allows for multiple, non-hierarchal entry and exit points for representation and interpretation.[2] Leading anthropologist Anna Tsing, who studies the matsutake mushroom, has also been cited as an inspiration for describing interdisciplinary work as "rhizomatic." Tsing writes compellingly about the global cultural, scientific, and commercial networks surrounding this valued fruit, and her work has become a model for research that explores entangled intellectual, cultural, and natural systems. This research suggests why the more visible and symbolic tree, with its branched and canopied "hierarchies," might no longer be the best metaphor for field histories of what is coming to be known as the "environmental humanities." And the more you know about this mushroom, the more apparent the reason for a shift away from metaphors associated with strict hierarchical chronologies and towards those associated with systems that have been growing and spreading over long periods, often out of sight, but which contribute to long-term social and ecosystemic health. The trees most associated with the matsutake grow in the bare, nutrient-deficient soils of industrial tree plantations or well-used forests where the soils are poor. In bare mineral soils, the matsutake's underground fungal networks make nutrients available to the trees from which they, in return, take nourishment. In short, trees, mushrooms, and rhizomes cannot do without each other, and the extensive systems below the ground are responsible for the recuperation of nutrients and the resilience of forest systems. Moreover, matsutake "cultures" contribute to the economic and nutritional health of diverse human communities around the globe. The matsutake is harvested by people on the margins of the industrial economy, Tsing observes, and supports the livelihoods of 600,000 diverse people from Oregon to Japan to China.[3]

Viewed from a more "rhizomatic" perspective, the field of ecocriticism, or its history, starts to look very different. The field is often said to have emerged after the 1990s, spurred most dramatically by the emerging fields of environmental history and environmental literary criticism that were taking root in American Studies. However, as Kimberly N. Ruffin and I have recently argued, Lawrence Buell's *The Environmental Imagination*, which takes the work of Thoreau as its touchstone and is itself a touchstone for the field of ecocriticism, begins to look more like a mushroom, or a single fruit sprouting from a long growing network, that actually began to take root, and grow rhizomatically, from the 1940s forward.[4] Long before the appearance of *The Environmental Imagination,* there was a deeply rooted tradition of scholarly humanities research into individual and collective identity, cultural landscapes and memory, and human relationships to the natural world.[5] Many scholars have noted that early work in both American Studies and ecocriticism provided far-reaching accounts of environmental perception and the place of nature in Western thought, but too often failed to account for the diversity of non-Western cultures and ecological lifeways both inside and outside U.S. borders. In previous work, I have mapped the blind spots of American Studies research (with an environmental focus) that clearly promoted nationalist objectives and questionable assumptions about European and American "discoverers" who move from cities or urban areas, often to the unsettled "wilderness."[6] Robert T. Hayashi has also rightly called the nationalized and racialized discourses and essentialism inherent in some early American Studies and ecocritical work into question. Hayashi's *Haunted by Waters* might be thought of as one of the first monograph-length works to signal an "emergent interdisciplinarity" between American Studies, Asian American Studies, and ecocriticism focused on race, place, labor, and ecology, which began growing in the 1940s, then more broadly and deeply in the 1970s and 1980s, until it became unmistakably visible in the first decade of the twenty-first century.[7]

Asian American Literature and the Environment is the first and most robust anthology on some of the newly appearing field histories that account for more diverse genres and forms of environmentalism beyond the dominant Western Euro-American focus in ecocriticism. The contributors to *Asian American Literature and the Environment* build on environmental justice, postcolonial, critical race, counter-memory, and eco-feminist frameworks and concerns as they provide a sweeping and deeply thought-provoking range of perspectives on the historical, social, psychological, economic, philosophical, and aesthetic responses of Asian Americans to the environment conceived in relation to labor, racism, immigration, domesticity, global capitalism, relocation, pollution, violence, and religion.

Contributors work with a range of trans-Pacific genres, including war memoirs, poetry, and fiction, that defy notions of American Studies as a field that works only with topics set inside U.S. borders. The book might be thought of as the emergence of a long-developing network of transnational study of representations of the environment in Asian American and Asian literature that has been taking root and growing for many decades both inside and outside of the U.S. Contributors address an illuminating range of issues and topics, including urban space of San Francisco's Chinatown, discursive traditions surrounding Japanese American internment camps during World War II, Cambodian American memoirs focusing on Pol Pot's reign from 1976–79, destruction of land in Vietnam by munitions and chemical agents, and Japanese American engagement with agricultural industry prior to internment. Many of the chapters affirm that ecocritical work continues to be deeply influenced by the abolition, civil rights, and labor movements in the United States, by the environmental justice movement of the 1980s, and by innovative movements for social and environmental justice taking root around the world.

Like the largely unseen fungal networks supporting the fruiting body referred to as the "mushroom," a rich variety of cultural and ecology lifeways emerge all across matsutake's paths, as Tsing documents. *Asian American Literature and the Environment* might also be seen to be doing something very much like "documenting a rich variety of cultural and ecology lifeways" across very wide-ranging trans-Pacific paths. As I mentioned above, the book is auspicious, because it is appearing just at the same moment when there is suddenly much excitement and activity in Asian and Asian American literary studies and ecocriticism around the globe. Indeed, in my travels to many ecocritical conferences in Asia over the last decade, I have had the pleasure and honor of speaking with and working with scholars from Taiwan, Korea, India, Japan, China, the U.S., U.K., and Australia who have long been laboring to develop a field that may have been just out of sight (to U.S. audiences) but which has long been visible in Asian communities and now is becoming much more visible on the international stage. For example, Karen Laura Thornber's *Ecoambiguity: Environmental Crises and East Asian Literatures* is opening new portals of inquiry in East Asian ecocriticism.[8] *Ecoambiguity* is the first book to analyze the complexities of Chinese, Japanese, Korean, and Taiwanese literary treatments of damaged ecosystems. While many scholars in the past have over-simplified Asian literatures as celebrating the beauties of nature and romanticizing Asians themselves as intimately connected with the natural world, Thornber shows how East Asian writers themselves challenge this depiction. Their literary works portray inconsistent human attitudes, behaviors, and a long history of transforming and exploiting nature.

Other anthologies, newly published, also illuminate the import of *Asian American Literature and the Environment* and show it to be a part of a growing global field. *East Asian Ecocriticisms: A Critical Reader,* edited by Simon C. Estok and Won-Chung Kim, brings together original essays by speakers of Chinese, Korean, Japanese, and Taiwanese, who write compellingly in English.⁹ It reveals the specific geopolitical and cultural situations that are shaping the aesthetics of the literatures in Asia. Another collection, *Ecoambiguity, Community, and Development: Toward a Politicized Ecocriticism,* edited by Scott Slovic, Swarnalatha Rangarajan, and Vidya Sarveswaran decisively outlines why environmental justice and postcolonial theories are taking hold among the many ecocritics at work in China, Japan, and India, among other nations.¹⁰ Scholars in it, picking up on Thornber's work, confront the paradoxical, "ecoambiguous" tendencies of selective cultural appreciation and destruction found in some of the globe's most discussed "developing nations." At the same time, many ecocritical studies are appearing in Asian languages all around the world. As noted, the current energy in this field is quite astonishing and bodes well for ecocriticism as an international field and practice.

Asian American Literature and the Environment, and other critical works with trans-Pacific literary, cultural, and ecological foci, all appearing in the same moment, give a sense of how nearly two decades of scholarship has powerfully shifted the global environmental humanities in necessary and important ways. This is a book that will have a long and lasting influence. And perhaps most importantly, it evidences the networked relations of trans-Pacific peoples who are building socially and ecologically resilient cultures that offer important insights to a world increasingly in need of innovative ways to think about our environmental past, present, and future.

NOTES

1. See Dianne Rocheleau and Robin Roth, "Rooted Networks, Relational Webs and Powers of Connection: Rethinking Human and Political Ecologies," *Geoforum* 38 (2007): 433–37, and Anna Tsing, "Unruly Edges: Mushrooms as Companion Species," *Environmental Humanities* 1.1 (2012): 141–54.
2. Gilles Deleuze and Felix Guattari, *A Thousand Plateaus: Capitalism and Schizophrenia* (Minneapolis: University of Minnesota Press, 1987), 19.
3. See "Matsutake Worlds Live," http://matsutakeworlds.org (accessed April 3, 2014).
4. See Joni Adamson and Kimberly N. Ruffin, introduction to *American Studies, Ecocriticism and Citizenship: Thinking and Acting in the Local and Global Commons,* ed. Joni Adamson and Kimberley N. Ruffin (New York: Routledge, 2013), 1–17.
5. Ibid.
6. See Joni Adamson, "Literature-and-Environment Studies and the Influence of the Environmental Justice Movement," in *A Companion to American Literature and Culture,* ed. Paul Lauter (New York: Wiley-Blackwell, 2010), 593–607, and Joni Adamson and Scott Slovic, "The Shoulders We Stand On: An

Introduction to Ethnicity and Ecocriticism," *MELUS: Multi-Ethnic Literature of the United States* 34.2 (2009): 5–24.
7. Robert T. Hayashi, *Haunted by Waters: A Journey through Race and Place in the American West* (Iowa City: University of Iowa Press, 2011), and "Beyond Walden Pond: Asian American Literature and the Limits of Ecocriticism," in *Coming into Contact: Explorations in Ecocritical Theory and Practice,* ed. Annie Merrill Ingram, Ian Marshall, Daniel J. Philippon, and Adam W. Sweeting (Athens: University of Georgia Press, 2007), 58–75.
8. Karen Laura Thornber, *Ecoambiguity: Environmental Crises and East Asian Literatures* (Ann Arbor: University of Michigan Press, 2012).
9. Simon Estok and Won-Chung Kim, eds., *East Asian Ecocriticisms: A Critical Reader* (New York: Palgrave-MacMillan, 2013).
10. Scott Slovic, Swarnalatha Rangarajan, and Vidya Sarveswaran, eds., *Ecoambiguity, Community, and Development: Toward a Politicized Ecocriticism* (New York: Lexington Books, 2014).

BIBLIOGRAPHY

Adamson, Joni. "Literature-and-Environment Studies and the Influence of the Environmental Justice Movement." In *A Companion to American Literature and Culture*, edited by Paul Lauter, 593–607. New York: Wiley-Blackwell, 2010.
———— and Kimberly N. Ruffin. Introduction to *American Studies, Ecocriticism and Citizenship: Thinking and Acting in the Local and Global Commons*, edited by Joni Adamson and Kimberly N. Ruffin, 1–17. New York: Routledge, 2013.
———— and Scott Slovic. "The Shoulders We Stand On: An Introduction to Ethnicity and Ecocriticism." *MELUS: Multi-Ethnic Literature of the United States* 34.2 (2009): 5–24.
Deleuze, Gilles and Felix Guattari. *A Thousand Plateaus: Capitalism and Schizophrenia*. Minneapolis: University of Minnesota Press, 1987.
DeLoughrey, Elizabeth and George Handley, eds. *Postcolonial Ecologies: Literature of the Environment*. New York: Oxford University Press, 2011.
Estok, Simon and Won-Chung Kim, eds. *East Asian Ecocriticisms: A Critical Reader*. New York: Palgrave-MacMillan, 2013.
Hayashi, Robert T. "Beyond Walden Pond: Asian American Literature and the Limits of Ecocriticism." In *Coming into Contact: Explorations in Ecocritical Theory and Practice*, edited by Annie Merrill Ingram, Ian Marshall, Daniel J. Philippon, and Adam W. Sweeting, 58–75. Athens: University of Georgia Press, 2007.
————. *Haunted by Waters: A Journey through Race and Place in the American West*. Iowa City: University of Iowa Press, 2011.
"Matsutake Worlds Live." http://matsutakeworlds.org (accessed April 3, 2014).
Thornber, Karen Laura. *Ecoambiguity: Environmental Crises and East Asian Literatures*. Ann Arbor, MI: University of Michigan Press, 2012.
Slovic, Scott, Swarnalatha Rangarajan, and Vidya Sarveswaran, eds. *Ecoambiguity, Community, and Development: Toward a Politicized Ecocriticism*. New York: Lexington Books, 2014.
Rocheleau, Dianne and Robin Roth. "Rooted Networks, Relational Webs and Powers of Connection: Rethinking Human and Political Ecologies." *Geoforum* 38 (2007): 433–37.
Tsing, Anna. "Unruly Edges: Mushrooms as Companion Species." *Environmental Humanities* 1.1 (2012): 141–54.

Preface

Paul Outka

It is hard to imagine a more timely or important set of topics than the ones this book takes up. A badly needed contribution to the so-called third wave of ecocritical scholarship, *Asian American Literature and the Environment* extends the field's recent engagement with critical race theory and globalism to the neglected histories of Asian American environmental experience both in the United States and throughout the Pacific. In doing so, it expands yet again our sense of what counts as nature and, inevitably, what counts as America and American as well.

Building on ongoing work that has broadened ecocriticism's early focus on North American wilderness and a concomitant, if often unconscious, naturalization of a privileged white, male, and heteronormative perspective on that wilderness, this volume insists on the importance of Asian American history and culture to environmental history and politics in North America and globally. It thereby rejects the silence and invisibility of America's "model minority" and reclaims the transcontinental railroad, the internment camps, the Chinatowns, and the remembered landscapes of trauma and beauty in the East as part of the nature we all (should) share.

It does so, moreover, without rendering Asian and Asian American experiences monolithic, without creating some universal and essentialist Asian American natural subject. The perspectives here are as diverse as the environments they inhabit and create. Divided into three broad sections—The Environment and Labor, The Environment and Violence, The Environment and Philosophy—the organization of the book itself speaks to how environment is a place as much made as found, a landscape composed not just of nonhuman animals, plants, and geographic features, but of work, suffering, and philosophical and aesthetic contemplation. Labor, violence, and thought are at once highly individual categories of experience, and ones profoundly shaped by histories of racism, oppression, craft, and imagination. Both landscapes and people are in these ways similarly constructed.

And they are not just similarly constructed, but *mutually* constructed. For literature and environment studies to move beyond circular disagreements between what we might call the "wilderness" or the deep ecology position that emphasizes the preservation of nonhuman nature, and what might be called the social ecology position that focuses on how environments both reflect and create human suffering, we must start with an insistence on that mutual construction, an insistence that since both sides are right, neither is, at least, in isolation. Since Homo sapiens are always already manifestations of the environment and utterly dependent on nonhuman nature for the possibility of their happiness—if not, indeed, their basic survival—the preservation of that nonhuman nature cannot be dismissed as nothing more than a preoccupation of the privileged. Just as vitally, the intrinsically misanthropic—and in practice often racist, classist, ableist, heteronormative, and patriarchal—tendencies of a focus on wilderness preservation are not only pernicious in themselves, but they also block the very possibility of forging the sort of diverse green political alliance that might actually make a difference to the fate of the various human and nonhuman inhabitants of our planet. When we are presented with a choice between nonhuman nature and human needs, between poor loggers and the spotted owl, for instance, we should first ask who is forcing us to choose, what they stand to gain from this either/or frame, what possibilities are foreclosed if we accept that binary as defining the possible forms of environmental politics in which we might engage. If such a choice is occasionally necessary in certain limited and temporary circumstances, we should not accede to it generally, and never without the profoundest suspicion and fiercest resistance. Otherwise we are back fighting each other while the world burns and people suffer, and while that fire and misery enhance the power of the individuals and institutions that we should be dealing with together.

While most significant contemporary work in the environmental humanities is built on an assumption of a profound imbrication of human and nonhuman nature, every study will engage with these intersecting concerns with a different emphasis. Although each essay in *Asian American Literature and the Environment* approaches these questions of emphasis variously, on the whole, the volume is more concerned with social ecology, critical race environmentalism, and environmental justice than with an explicit valuation of the nonhuman natural. Appropriately so: as the book demonstrates so well, Asian American experience has historically been more often an experience of degradation than the sort of liberatory sublimity that has marked white representations of nature. From the chilling re-description of the mid-century Japanese internment camps in the green-washed language of nineteenth-century frontier ideology, to the callous exploitation of Chinese laborers in building the nation's railroad lines, to explicit and implicit policies of urban segregation and immigration policies based in the pseudo-science of Social Darwinism, Asian experiences in the United States demonstrate again and again how readily environmental discourse can be coopted to racist and oppressive ends.

That history of cooption still makes mainstream environmentalism deeply uncomfortable, and has contributed, I think, to the relative silence about Asian American environmental history in ecocriticism. In breaking that silence, not only does this book do vitally important work in Asian American literary study, but it encourages the larger field of environmental humanities to pay greater attention to its own historical blind spots, including the frequent neglect of environmental labor; the unhappy historical connections between the construction of race, citizenship, and natural experience; and the Orientalism and nationalism that have, at least unconsciously, often shaped United States ecocritical inquiry.

Just as important, however, is that this volume refuses a too-sweeping association of nature and oppression in favor of a nuanced understanding of how the environment also has provided refuge and solace to a range of Asian Americans, a literal and figurative outside to that oppression and a source of beauty and inspiration in its own right. While the landscape has often been made to signify nation and citizen, it of course is not these things intrinsically; the same place can be a different place too and exemplify a range of environmental traditions and subjects. In insisting on this more salutary environmental history, a much longer tradition of Eastern environmental thought promises to become more available to Western scholars, and with a greater possibility of genuine transnational and transcultural environmental conversation and activism. This book, in short, not only teaches us what we have done; it teaches us what we might do.

Acknowledgements

Poems by Mitsuye Yamada used with permission from Mitsuye Yamada and Rutgers University Press.
Poems by Lawson Fusao used cited with permission from Coffee House Press.

Introduction
Ecocriticism and Asian American Literature

John Gamber

The question we have to ask ourselves in considering a book of ecocritical essays about Asian American literature is not "why now?" but rather, "what took so long?" Asian American literature is replete with narratives that focus on ecological connections. From early texts set amidst agricultural labor (Carlos Bulosan's *America Is in the Heart* might be the most obvious example) to recent texts with environmentalist threads running throughout them (such as Ruth Ozeki's *My Year of Meats* and Karen Tei Yamashita's *Through the Arc of the Rain Forest*), the canon of Asian American Literature brims with narratives containing clearly identifiable ecological foci. Of course, there is nothing surprising about these correlations. As readers of this collection are no doubt well aware, early Asian immigration to the United States was to a large extent related to agricultural as well as manual labor. Literature growing out of populations engaged in such labor practices inevitably includes representation of the other-than-human. But more than that, immigrant and transnational narratives (indeed, immigrant and transnational subjectivities) understandably abound with concerns of space and place. Moreover, the literature produced by the succeeding generations of Asian Americans continues these trends. When we relocate we notice differences in our new physical environments. Sometimes these representations of spatial difference manifest in descriptions of trees and plants and in birds and other animals. Sometimes they do so by detailing the ways we engage with urban landscapes, different styles of buildings, different sights, sounds, and smells at street level.[1] Any and all of these representations should be seen to fall under the umbrella of ecocriticism.

To support such an assertion, of course, we need to determine what we mean when we say *ecocriticism*. All too often, scholars within and without ecocriticism define the term and the field as a study of nature-writing or environmental/ist literary study, rather than the study of the relationships between the human and other-than-human in literature. These definitions fall short not only for their limitations but also for their theoretical shortcomings. Many ecocritics focus their work on nature-writing. Nature-writing often comes in the form of creative nonfiction, as in Henry David Thoreau's *Walden*, John Muir's *My First Summer in the Sierra*, Edward

Abbey's *Desert Solitaire*, Annie Dillard's *Pilgrim at Tinker Creek,* and Greta Ehrlich's *The Solace of Open Spaces*. All of these represent narratives of white people leaving the hustle and bustle of modern existence to seek the comfort of more "natural" environs. These texts generally privilege individualism, a sense within their autobiographical first-person narrators that they feel little responsibility to the human communities they have left behind. Of course, such a movement back and forth between the realms so often represented as polar opposites (the town and the country in Raymond Williams' parlance) generally stems from dwelling first and foremost in a position of class privilege. Not everyone gets to escape the supposed ills of civilization; not everyone wants to.

While nature-writing is valuable to ecocriticism, it has never been the only thing that ecocritics value. Similarly, ecocritics have always engaged with environmentally-focused/environmentalist literature. These books easily lend themselves to ecocritical analysis—in some ways they are an ecocritic's low-hanging fruit. Texts that overtly treat environmentalist issues open themselves to readings of their specific environmentalisms: are they preservationist? Conservationist? Activists for environmental justice? Do they privilege rural spaces? Wilderness spaces? What forms of activism do they advocate? What mainstream values do they challenge and which do they uphold or bolster? Among the most widely taught texts of this mode are Abbey's *Monkey Wrench Gang*, Seuss's *The Lorax*, T.C. Boyle's *Tortilla Curtain*, Yamashita's *Through the Arc of the Rain Forest*, and Ozeki's *My Year of Meats*. Of course, some of these texts take environmentalists to task for ignoring social issues in their quest to protect other species.

Along with these overtly environmentalist texts, we often find those set in rural and wilderness landscapes ripe for ecocritical approaches. Much of Romantic poetry finds its way into the ecocritical canon through this venue, as do the works of Gary Snyder, Ralph Waldo Emerson, and Walt Whitman.[2] With their treatises on human relationships to other-than-human space and species through farming, Wendell Berry and Aldo Leopold fall into this camp as well. Some of these texts focus on journeys over water: Melville's oeuvre, especially *Moby Dick*, Steinbeck's *The Log from the Sea of Cortez*, and Mark Twain's river narratives serve as obvious examples. Finally, I include within this category, texts of environmental catastrophe, cautionary tales of toxicity, overpopulation, climate change, and myriad other forms of ecological degradation. Don DeLillo's *White Noise*, Octavia Butler's *Parable of the Sower*, Cynthia Kadohata's *In the Heart of the Valley of Love*, Alejandro Morales' *The Rag Doll Plagues*, indeed much of speculative fiction's dystopic literature contains such representations.

Cheryll Glotfelty asserts, "Simply put, ecocriticism is the study of the relationship between literature and the physical environment."[3] The term *ecocriticism* implies a focus on interrelationality. This interrelationality is often imagined within ecocriticism to come in the form of the ways the other-than-human interacts with the human. But, perhaps the recognition of connection that ecology demonstrates can come in the form of understanding that the very distinction between the human and the other-than-human represents a false dichotomy. Perhaps ecocriticism's most important work comes in the form of dispelling the myth of that dichotomy.

Our field addresses representations of the world in and with which we exist. I would elaborate that ecocriticism resists anthropocentrism and human exceptionalism, always recognizing that humans exist as parts of all ecosystems, in complex interrelationships with all other species, and never understood in isolation. As such, ecocriticism must address elements that are not exclusively human, but I suspect it would prove difficult to locate texts devoid of such elements. Other species, diseases, weather, geology, the materials we use to clothe and shelter ourselves, our tools, our food, all of these represent elements of the other-than-human. Even human beings cannot be understood as a species in isolation, teeming as we are with other species in and on us all of the time. As such, there are likely no texts at all that fall outside of the scope of ecocriticism.

Nonetheless, as Robert T. Hayashi points out,

> The absence of Asian American authors from the field of ecocriticism is part of the field's more general inability to address seriously issues of race and class, as has been pointed out by other scholars. Despite the fresh perspective ecocritical inquiry has offered, its reliance on canonical authors—Willa Cather, John Muir, Aldo Leopold, Annie Dillard, and of course Henry David Thoreau—continues to limit its discoveries and its relevance.[4]

Has ecocriticism proven particularly reluctant to engage with Asian American literature? I think it has. But this oversight (or shortsightedness) is not constrained to the limits of Asian American literature. Rather, mainstream ecocriticism (and I would argue that as a field we can now speak of ecocriticism as having a mainstream, and even of being mainstream) has historically proven reluctant to engage with literature by minority writers broadly speaking. This is not to say that it has failed to do so entirely. Although the field was born out of nature-writing and cut its teeth on a deeply European and Euro-American canon, ecocriticism has outgrown its initial provincialism.

Recent research includes a number of texts that address issues of race and ethnicity broadly, as well as Asian American literature specifically, as they intersect with ecocriticism. *MELUS*' special issue on ecocriticism edited by Joni Adamson and Scott Slovic is one example. Essays within that collection examine the work of David Mas Masumoto and Ruth Ozeki as well as other neglected authors. Ozeki's work likewise finds its way into Allison Carruth's *Global Appetites: American Power and the Literature of Food*. John

Beck examines narratives of Japanese American internment in *Dirty Wars: Landscape, Power, and Waste in Western American Literature*. Other texts examined in this book, such as Don Lee's *Wrack and Ruin*, have, unfortunately, received very little critical attention.

Indeed, we have plenty of examples of recently published comparative ethnic ecocriticisms. Jeffrey Myers' 2005 text, *Converging Stories: Race, Ecology, and Environmental Justice in American Literature* points out that the bulk of ecocriticism dealing overtly with issues of race has focused on American Indian writers and, to a lesser degree, African American authors. Until quite recently very little work had been done with Asian American or Latina/o authored texts. However, in recent years, ecocriticism's paucity of studies on texts by minority authors has undergone a rapid and welcome change. Lawrence Buell and Ursula K. Heise represent two of the major scholars to address issues of race, ethnicity, and nation in ecocriticism. Other examples include Joni Adamson's *American Indian Literature, Environmental Justice, and Ecocriticism: The Middle Place* (2001), Alison Deming and Lauret Savoy's *The Colors of Nature: Culture, Identity, and the Natural World* (2002), Lee Schweninger's *Listening to the Land: Native American Literary Responses to the Landscape* (2008), Tom Lynch's *Xerophilia: Ecocritical Explorations in Southwestern Literature* (2008), Lindsey Claire Smith's *Indians, Environment, and Identity on the Borders of American Literature: From Faulkner and Morrison to Walker and Silko* (2008), Paul Outka's *Race and Nature from Transcendentalism to the Harlem Renaissance* (2008), Ian Finseth's *Shades of Green: Visions of Nature in the Literature of American Slavery, 1770–1860* (2009), Anissa J. Wardi's *Water and African American Memory: An Ecocritical Perspective* (2011), and Elizabeth DeLoughrey and George B. Handley's *Postcolonial Ecologies: Literatures of the Environment* (2011). Again, we recognize the ecocritical trend of focusing on Native American literature. Native people remain (quite falsely, of course) associated with rural spaces, especially those of reservations. By contrast, Latina/os and Asian Americans are more commonly associated with urban spaces, and urban spaces are seen to fall outside of the purview of ecocriticism.

Ecocriticism's primary intellectual organization, the Association for the Study of Literature and Environment (ASLE), has made strides to diversify. By placing its biennial conference in Boston in 2003, ASLE attempted to increase its visibility to scholars interested in urban-based communities. It seemed that the representation of scholars researching minority writers increased during that particular meeting, as well as at subsequent conferences. ASLE does have a commitment emblematized by its Diversity Caucus. Nonetheless, all of six arguably Asian American authors are named in ASLE's last biennial conference program: Yamashita, Ozeki, Masumoto, Myung Mi Kim, Amitav Ghosh, and Sohaila Abdulali. But, of course, this is a two-way street. If ecocritics have been reluctant to address Asian American literature, Asian American literature scholars have likewise been reluctant to adopt ecocritical approaches. Fortunately, the scholars in this collection work to overturn these gaps within both ecocriticism and Asian American literary studies.

To that end, Andrea Aebersold begins this book with her examination of Maxine Hong Kingston's *China Men* and Milton Murayama's *All I Asking for Is My Body*. Aebersold demonstrates one of the causes of ecocriticism's reluctance to engage with Asian American literature, specifically the erasure of Asian immigrants from the dominant story of the Western United States throughout its history. She further links a broad refusal to engage with Hawaii as an important part of that Western narrative, crafting a chapter intended to correct this geographical oversight and demonstrating the role of agricultural labor and gardening in establishing a deep relationship to space and place.

Wenying Xu's chapter focuses on Fae Myenne Ng's novels *Bone* and *Steer toward Rock,* particularly the role of the urban space of San Francisco's Chinatown. This piece analyzes the legal mandates of immigration and naturalization that structured Chinatown's bachelor society and paper families. As Xu demonstrates, our relationships to urban spaces shape our narratives just as much as do our relationships to rural spaces. As such, we should recognize urban-set texts as reasonably and integrally falling under the purview of ecocritical analysis.

In Chapter 3, Bella Adams investigates Don Lee's novel *Wrack and Ruin* as a re-envisioning of the pastoral tradition. Adams expresses the importance of this approach on two fronts. First, the pastoral tradition within the United States has largely written minorities out of itself, privileging instead white narratives of the middle place between "nature" and "civilization." Second, Asian American Studies has engaged first and foremost in an anthropocentric materialist political movement in which it has allowed little space for a discourse of ecological relationality. Adams points to *Wrack and Ruin* as a counter example to both of these fronts, while also placing Lee's discourse on Asian American masculinity as an outgrowth of engagement with the other-than-human.

Zhou Xiaojing's chapter focuses on the discursive traditions surrounding Japanese American concentration camps during World War II, particularly in terms of the frontier ideologies that frame and inform those traditions. According to Zhou, this frontier ideology manifests itself in the works projects fostered within the camps. For Zhou, who draws upon the work of George Lipsitz, the writings of the internees, including Mitsuye Yamada, Lawson Fusao Inada, and Jeanne Wakatsuki Houston, represent a counter-memory to triumphalist constructions of westward expansion and manifest destiny, crafting a parallel between Japanese American internment and Native American displacement and relocation as effects of the United States' imperial impulses.

Helena Grice draws our attention to Cambodian American memoirs focusing on Pol Pot's reign as prime minister of Kampuchea from 1976–79.

Running counter to the privileging of rural spaces in U.S. ecocriticism, these narratives present the horrors of Khmer Rouge agrarian reforms. Rather than spaces into which urban and suburban dwellers can flee, seeking refuge from the ills of urban overcrowding and pollution, these individuals find themselves dragged into the killing fields. Cities, then, serve as idealized locations while farms and fields become not only the sites of forced labor and reeducation, but also the systems by which Cambodia's economy and infrastructure were ravaged by the devaluing of professional education. The valorization of the rural destroys not only the lives of thousands of laborers, but also the national culture.

Chapter 6 moves to Cathy J. Schlund-Vials' reading of Vietnamese American texts, specifically those of Le Ly Hayslip and Lan Cao. This chapter argues that the physical, ecological destruction of the landscape of Vietnam wrought by military activity from munitions, transport, and chemical agents parallels the United States' representations of its war in Vietnam as a quagmire. The human bodies represented in these texts mirror the damaged landscapes of Vietnam, while the traumas suffered by the Vietnamese refugees to the United States parallel the image of the quagmire as a space in which one becomes stuck. Meanwhile, notwithstanding these temporal and physical fixities, both texts also focus, Schlund-Vials contends, on the special slippages of refugee existence, the disjunct experienced by these refugees whose thoughts and memories are of one landscape while they find themselves transported to deeply foreign ones.

Youngsuk Chae's chapter investigates Ruth Ozeki's novel *My Year of Meats,* taking an ecofeminist approach to investigate the conjunction of ecological degradation and race- and class-based marginalization as well as the disproportionate rates by which women are affected by environmental injustice. Moreover, Chae examines the ways that the United States' neoliberal economic influence manifests as an environmental neo-colonialism, spreading agricultural monoculturalism as well as the use of hormones and other toxins in livestock. The willingness, indeed the eagerness, to bend the nonhuman to capitalist wants, Chae contends, grows out of a specifically Euro-American patriarchy steeped in an ideology of white supremacist progressivism. Ozeki's novel, however, offers a demonstration of an ecocritical and environmentalist approach that renounces Eurocentrism, marginalization, and hierarchical power structures in favor of an engagement with the complex communities embodied by ecological connectivity.

Sarah D. Wald focuses attention on Hisaye Yamamoto's poetry, life, and letters, in terms of the influence thereupon of The Catholic Worker movement and its newspaper *The Catholic Worker.* This chapter examines the agrarian impulse within Yamamoto's short stories, not only as a critical literary mode demonstrating Japanese American engagement with agricultural industry prior to internment, but also as part of Yamamoto's journalistic work as a demonstration of the evolution of her relationship to land and agriculture.

Specifically, Wald connects the politics of Yamamoto's post-war fiction to her time spent working on a Catholic Worker communal farm. For Yamamoto, agriculture ultimately fails to address specifically racial inequities that pervade the United States as a whole. While rurality remains for many (especially white) Americans an idealized destination in which to escape the industrialized world, the isolation it allegedly fosters carries with it the very same racial politics of the nation as a whole; ultimately, it represents another incarnation of white flight.

In Chapter 9, Stephen L. Field turns to an examination of *fengshui* in Amy Tan's novelistic oeuvre. This chapter addresses the ways that Chinese American characters in these texts shape their spaces of dwelling (in a Heideggerian sense) according to the metaphysics of fengshui. This philosophy aims to bring into harmony human spaces with their surroundings—an ecological connection that extends to a spiritual connection to the other-than-human. Indeed, Field demonstrates that Tan's use of *fengshui* moves not from the local to the global, as in the classic environmentalist statement, but from the local to the cosmic.

King-Kok Cheung's chapter addresses Ha Jin's *A Free Life* and *The Writer as Migrant*. Jin's protagonist attempts to withdraw from the politics of society, only to realize his implication and interconnectivity. Nonetheless, his refusal to participate in facile nationalism serves a liberatory turn, one which allows him to focus on his art and his family free from the censorship of his birth nation. Cheung asserts the correlation between Jin's protagonist's pastoral conclusions and those of traditional Chinese poets including Tao Qian. Ultimately, the pastoral offers an empowering solitude that provides the poet with an Emersonian confidence he had previously lacked. Thus, Cheung recognizes a transnational pool of ecological and literary connections that shape Jin's work.

As ecocriticism moves beyond its beginnings as an intellectual movement of, by, and for a white middle class, it grows toward an increasing depth, breadth, and relevance. Such a move benefits ecocriticism, of course. But, it also benefits the other fields with which it intersects, offering a canon of texts examining the role of ecological connections that prove immensely valuable. We can see, then, what took so long for a book like this to come to light, but we can find hope in its appearance that ecocriticism and Asian American literary studies will endeavor to maintain their awareness of the interconnections that bind them to one another.

NOTES

1. While ecocriticism has eschewed urban narratives, as Gordon McGranahan et al. note, "the fact that cities have large ecological 'footprints' makes them more, not less, important" to ecologically-minded studies. McGranahan, et al., *The Citizens at Risk: From Urban Sanitation to Sustainable Cities* (London: Earthscan, 2001), 8.

2. This inclusion could itself create a bridge to Asian American literature via Kingston's *Tripmaster Monkey.*
3. Cheryll Glotfelty, introduction to *The Ecocriticism Reader: Landmarks in Literary Ecology,* ed. Cheryll Glotfelty and Harold Fromm (Athens: University of Georgia Press, 1996), xviii.
4. Robert T. Hayashi, "Beyond Walden Pond: Asian American Literature and the Limits of Ecocriticism," in *Coming into Contact: Explorations in Ecocritical Theory and Practice,* ed. Annie Merrill Ingram, Ian Marshall, Daniel J. Philippon, and Adam W. Sweeting (Athens: University of Georgia Press, 2007), 58–75.

BIBLIOGRAPHY

Abbey, Edward. *Desert Solitaire: A Season in the Wilderness.* New York: Ballantine, 1968.

Adamson, Joni. *American Indian Literature, Environmental Justice, and Ecocriticism: The Middle Place.* Tucson: University of Arizona Press, 2001.

Adamson, Joni and Scott Slovic. "The Shoulders We Stand On: An Introduction to Ethnicity and Ecocriticism." *MELUS: Multi-Ethnic Literature of the United States* 34.2 (Summer 2009): 5–24.

Alaimo, Stacy and Susan Hekman. "Introduction: Emerging Models of Materiality in Feminist Theory." In *Material Feminisms,* edited by Stacy Alaimo and Susan Hekman, 1–22. Bloomington: University of Indiana Press, 2008.

Beck, John. *Dirty Wars: Landscape, Power, and Waste in Western American Literature.* Lincoln: University of Nebraska Press, 2009.

Carruth, Allison. *Global Appetites: American Power and the Literature of Food.* Cambridge: Cambridge University Press, 2013.

Commoner, Barry. *The Closing Circle: Nature, Man, and Technology.* New York: Bantam, 1971.

DeLoughrey, Elizabeth and George B. Handley, eds. *Postcolonial Ecologies: Literatures of the Environment.* Oxford: Oxford University Press, 2011.

Deming, Alison H. and Lauret E. Savoy, eds. *The Colors of Nature: Culture, Identity, and the Natural World.* Minneapolis: Milkweed, 2002.

Dillard, Annie. *Pilgrim at Tinker Creek.* New York: Harper, 1974.

Ehrlich, Greta. *The Solace of Open Spaces.* New York: Penguin, 1985.

Finseth, Ian. *Shades of Green: Visions of Nature in the Literature of American Slavery, 1770–1860.* Athens: University of Georgia Press, 2009.

Glotfelty, Cheryll. Introduction to *The Ecocriticism Reader: Landmarks in Literary Ecology,* edited by Cheryll Glotfelty and Harold Fromm, xv–xxxvii. Athens: University of Georgia Press, 1996.

Hayashi, Robert T. "Beyond Walden Pond: Asian American Literature and the Limits of Ecocriticism." In *Coming into Contact: Explorations in Ecocritical Theory and Practice,* edited by Annie Merrill Ingram, Ian Marshall, Daniel J. Philippon, and Adam W. Sweeting, 58–75. Athens: University of Georgia Press, 2007.

Lynch, Tom. *Xerophilia: Ecocritical Explorations in Southwestern Literature.* Lubbock: Texas Tech University Press, 2008.

McGranahan, Gordon, et al. *The Citizens at Risk: From Urban Sanitation to Sustainable Cities.* London: Earthscan, 2001.

Muir, John. *My First Summer in the Sierra.* New York: Houghton Mifflin, 1911.

Myers, Jeffrey. *Converging Stories: Race, Ecology, and Environmental Justice in American Literature.* Athens: University of Georgia Press, 2005.

Outka, Paul. *Race and Nature from Transcendentalism to the Harlem Renaissance.* New York: Palgrave, 2008.

Schweninger, Lee. *Listening to the Land: Native American Literary Responses to the Landscape*. Athens: University of Georgia Press, 2008.

Smith, Lindsey Claire. *Indians, Environment, and Identity on the Borders of American Literature: From Faulkner and Morrison to Walker and Silko*. New York: Palgrave, 2008.

Thoreau, Henry David. *Walden and Other Writings*, edited by Joseph Wood Krutch. New York: Bantam, 1981.

Part I
The Environment and Labor

1 Environmental Narratives of American Identity

Landscape and Belonging in Maxine Hong Kingston's *China Men* and Milton Murayama's *All I Asking for Is My Body*

Andrea Aebersold

Historically, the American landscape has been closely tied to American identity: the freedom to own land, work the land, and explore the land represent the rights of a free American. In particular, the landscape of the American West often plays a defining role in American mythology as a place of rugged individuality and opportunity; it embodies the spirit of adventure and conquest. Historian Donald Worster argues that different groups of people around the globe associate the American West with cowboys, horses, gunfights, and wide open spaces. As a result, "the West has come to symbolize the whole national identity of the United States."[1] However, the role of Asian immigrants in the history of the American West has been downplayed, even ignored at times. The mythology does not imagine them as a part of the American identity that is embedded in the very land itself. Indeed, Hsuan Hsu points out that "[w]hether or not they contain any truth with regard to other groups, frontier stereotypes such as freedom of movement, voluntary self-reinvention, individualism, and westwardness have seldom applied to Asian immigrants and their descendants."[2] The same landscape that promised individual freedom has been used by dominant political and economic powers to prevent Asian immigrants from claiming American identity and citizenship.

The promise of individual freedom and economic opportunity through working the land brought many Chinese and Japanese immigrants to the sugar plantations in Hawaii. Yet once the immigrants arrived there, the plantation owners used low wages, long work hours, and poor living conditions to ensure that the immigrants could not become anything except an anonymous labor force. They were denied profits of the industry and their contributions were almost forgotten.

Maxine Hong Kingston's *China Men* (1980) and Milton Murayama's *All I Asking for Is My Body* (1975) represent and resist this exclusion of Asian immigrants and Asian Americans through their literary portrayals of plantation work in Hawaii. These texts reveal how Chinese immigrants and

Japanese Americans reacted to their work on the Hawaiian sugarcane plantations and how they conceptualized these landscapes in terms of their displacement and loss of self amidst the economic powerhouse of the United States. The landscape believed to represent individual freedom became a site of alienation as the plantation owners controlled the workers' movements, finances, and living conditions.

Yet Kingston and Murayama also demonstrate how Asian immigrants and Asian Americans resisted exclusion by using the landscape to construct and define an American identity of their own. Through acts such as gardening and individual physical training, the characters in *China Men* and *All I Asking for Is My Body* work the land according to their values, rather than for others' economic gain, and resist total erasure by the dominant culture by claiming part of America as their own. Both Kingston and Murayama write against traditional myths of the American West by inserting Asian American agency into history. They ultimately challenge and destabilize the master narrative of American citizenship by writing the land as a flexible concept that cannot be defined unilaterally.

Both Kingston and Murayama write about Asian American relationships with the environment as a means of challenging and redefining the history and meaning of the American West. Reading their works through an ecocritical lens offers an opportunity to advance the field through discussions of landscape and belonging. Asian American literature has not played a conspicuous role in ecocriticism, other than studies of Ruth Ozeki and Karen Tei Yamashita. Robert T. Hayashi argues that "[w]ith their common themes of immigration and acculturation, many Asian American literary works may seem unfit for ecocritical inquiry. Yet even works that stress such typical themes have much to say about how Asian Americans have experienced, described, and shaped their environments."[3] *China Men* and *All I Asking for Is My Body* bring themes of immigration and acculturation into an environmental context and successfully show how the two are not necessarily separate issues requiring different modes of inquiry.

A reassessment of ecocritical practice also helps eradicate stereotypical notions of Asian Americans as having less environmental awareness or concern. Both Kingston and Murayama incorporate the landscape into their works, although these representations have not been recognized as fitting into dominant ecocritical concerns of conserving nature or combating the hazards of poisoned environments. But instead of simply adding Asian American authors to the ecocritical canon, these works force a reconsideration of ecocritical inquiry itself by addressing issues of identity and citizenship and their relationships to the American landscape. This perspective offers benefits to other scholarly fields as well and asks us to reconsider what role the environment has played in the construction of American identity. In order to demonstrate this reconsideration, first I will briefly review ecocritical and historical oversights of Asian American literature as well as Hawaii's place in the American West. Then I will examine a section of Kingston's

China Men and her recasting of both the Hawaiian landscape and Chinese immigrant relationships with the environment as inextricably linked to issues of identity and citizenship. Finally, I will discuss Murayama's portrayal of landscape in *All I Asking for Is My Body* as both denying and creating individual identities for Japanese American plantation workers.

ASIAN AMERICAN ECOCRITICISM AND HAWAII AS THE AMERICAN WEST

The study of Asian Americans and the environment is largely missing from mainstream historical and literary texts. Asian Americans' reactions and relationships with the American landscape have been overlooked and overshadowed by studies of iconic figures such as Henry David Thoreau or John Muir, whose works focus on positive interactions with pristine wilderness and the protection of natural resources. At its onset, ecocriticism was slow to include works by writers of color in its scholarship and maintained a focus on standard definitions of nature and environment as wilderness. The Environmental Justice Movement centered its attention on urban environments and the adverse effects of pollution and other health threats on people of color and the poor. Yet, as scholars such as Hayashi and Julie Sze argue, much of environmental justice activism and literature focuses on contemporary issues without much examination of historical and cultural influences. Although Asian Americans do experience environmental threats, "their literature less directly addresses obvious examples of environmental racism or inequity, and so these texts may be easily overlooked by the ecocritic."[4] Perhaps another way of phrasing this idea is that Asian American literature contains examples of environmental racism and inequity that ecocriticism and environmental justice have yet to consider obvious. If "nature" and "environment" are reframed to include sites such as plantations, coal mines, and agricultural fields, more works of Asian American literature can be examined ecocritically. Examples of environmental racism become more prominent when definitions of the environment are expanded, as do examples of environmental connection through activities of resistance and redefinition.

Historian Patricia Nelson Limerick argues that the history of the western landscape comes from privileged sources, specifically, white people with power, education, and resources at their disposal, at the expense of other histories. In Limerick's words, "Without a margin of assured subsistence, without the opportunity for contemplation and introspection, without a way to enter one's memories into a permanent, written source, a group's response to a new geography can be close to impossible for posterity to hear."[5] When studying accounts of the American West, Limerick points out that fewer records of Asian American environmental experiences do not mean that Asian Americans did not have a response to landscape. What it does mean is that they did not have access to the accepted means of record-ing their responses. Therefore, she argues, we have to look to other sources such as literature, poetry, and graffiti. She claims that it is "a failure of records and not a failure of response" on behalf of Asian Americans that is respon-sible for so few studies.[6]

Like Asian immigrants and Asian Americans, Hawaii has been largely absent from historical and literary discussions of the American West. Its exclusion is due to a number of factors such as its lack of proximity to the mainland, its late recognition by the United States as a territory and then state, and its complex colonial and imperial background. John Whitehead argues that historians have excluded Hawaii from the American West because they believe that it does not share experiences or landscape with the mainland. But Whitehead shows how Hawaii has had major ties and con-nections to the West because "[t]he same forces of commercial expansion and Manifest Destiny that led to the acquisition of the Pacific Coast also flowed to Hawai'i."[7] Commercial expansion in Hawaii began in 1850 when foreigners were allowed to purchase land that had formerly belonged to the Hawaiian monarchy. White entrepreneurs were quick to buy up large tracts of land in order to create a new branch of the sugar industry. Like many other indigenous populations in the American West, native Hawaiians saw their land turned into a "commodity and thus began the subsequent loss of Hawaiians' *aina*, or 'land,' that gave them their identity and attachment to the earth."[8]

The sugar industry played a major role in the American economic pres-ence in Hawaii, yet, as Ronald Takaki points out, it was immigrant labor that "enabled the planters to transform sugar production into Hawaii's leading industry."[9] Immigrant labor became necessary because "[t]he native Hawaiian population was not large enough to furnish all of the needed laborers. In April 1850, during the California Gold Rush, the Royal Hawai-ian Agricultural Society was formed for the purpose of finding enough addi-tional workers to fulfill the demand for the developing sugar industry."[10] In 1852, the first group of Chinese laborers arrived in Hawaii, and, as more followed from Japan, the Philippines, and other countries, white plantation owners grew anxious about their own positions of power. As a result, work-ers were treated oppressively and "[a]ny disturbance was seen as a threat to the whites, who considered themselves the chosen, the only ones who should have power."[11]

When the U.S. Congress discussed making Hawaii a territory, the grow-ing Asian immigrant population was one reason, as Whitehead points out, that the annexation of Hawaii stalled, because Americans balked at view-ing the Hawaiian population as similar to their own: "The Asian migration that transformed Hawai'i's population after 1875 clearly gave the islands a commonly shared social experience with many parts of the American West. But the mainland racism against the Chinese tended to exclude Hawai'i from the consciousness of the western region to which it was increasingly bound."[12] So, despite the presence of Asian immigrants in California, Oregon, and other western states, Hawaii was still kept at arm's length, presumably because the immigrant population was so large.[13] Differences were created between Hawaii and the western United States in order to maintain white definitions of American identity. After annexation in 1898, Whitehead notes, "Hawai'i, the last far western acquisition, became a part of the United States. A banner proclaiming 'Westward the Course of Empire Takes . . .' adorned the balcony during a flag raising ceremony."[14] Here, the same spirit and rhetoric of U.S. expansionism that drove Americans to take and claim land from Mexico also motivated U.S. dominance of Hawaii. Yet, both Asian immigrants' and Hawaii's place in the myth of the American West remains contested.

In his work on Asian American history, Takaki discusses how Asian Americans search for their history by "decipher[ing] the signs of the Asian presence here and there across the landscape of America—the railroad tracks over high mountains, fields of cane virtually carpeting entire islands, and verdant agricultural lands."[15] He demonstrates how the landscape can tell stories and histories, and how identities can be formed and found within it. By examining two literary works that focus on Hawaii and Asian immigrants, my aim in this chapter is to bring them more fully into ecocritical discussions of history and identity associated with the landscape of the American West. The result will be a more complex understanding of how Asian American environmental experiences are connected to and complicit with constructions of American identity. Kingston's and Murayama's writings force a renegotiation of dominant literary and historical depictions of the American West through their representations of Asian Americans' acts of resistance and redefinition.

"TELLING THE EARTH THEIR SECRETS" IN *CHINA MEN*

Published in 1980, *China Men* is a collection of narratives concerning Chinese experiences in the United States. Kingston mixes her own family background with traditional stories and reconstructions of history by multiple characters, such as her grandfather, who describes his work on the railroads, and her brother fighting in Vietnam. I will focus on the chapter entitled "Great Grandfather of the Sandalwood Mountains," which tells the story of Kingston's great grandfather, Bak Goong, and his experiences working on a sugarcane plantation in Hawaii in the nineteenth century.

The narrator of *China Men* begins the chapter with a brief story of visiting modern-day Hawaii in search of connections with ancestors. At first, she is troubled because she cannot see the landscape as anything but a source of pain and racism. She mentions how the wind carries no clear message and "the rows and fields, organized like conveyor belts, hide murdered and raped bodies; this is a dumping ground."[16] The island's nickname,

"Chinaman's Hat," also disrupts her ancestral search as it invokes negative connotations of Chinese immigrants.[17] Still, she resolves to spend the day on the island and by evening, she hears the land. Her thoughts and feelings shift from pain to solace, and she claims, "It's a tribute to the pioneers to have a living island named after their work hat. I have heard the land sing. I have seen the bright blue streaks of spirit whisking through the air. I again search for my American ancestors by listening in the cane."[18] The narrator realizes that the land tells much more than the painful past of her ancestors. It also tells stories of their triumphs, their work, and their positive connections with the landscape. By reclaiming the meaning of "Chinaman's Hat," the narrator takes control of history and finds a link to her past. Patricia Linton points out how "retelling provides a way to change received meaning, to force slippage of the signifier."[19] The sugarcane fields thus become a site of ancestral connection, beyond its painful past and the dominant history of the island. This realization provides the context for the story of Bak Goong and his work on the sugarcane plantation. The telling and retelling of his story recalls Hawaii's landscape as both oppressive and liberating for Chinese immigrant workers.

Like so many Chinese and Japanese immigrants, Bak Goong chooses to go to Hawaii based on promises of high wages and opportunities to later move to the mainland. He is also eager to escape the British colonial dominance of his country. When Bak Goong first arrives in Hawaii, he feels uplifted and connected to the landscape. He marvels at new foods but also notes familiar ones: "He ate fruit and nuts he had never seen before. And mangos like in China. He wished he could give his wife some. With a handful of rice a day, he could live here without working."[20] Hawaii is a new place that still reminds him of China. Kingston immediately sets up an arrival that combines the foreign with the familiar, the "American" with the "Chinese," facilitated by the Hawaiian landscape. As Bak Goong follows his white boss up into the mountains, "He sucked in deep breaths of the Sandalwood Mountain air, and let it fly out in a song, which reached up to the rims of volcanoes and down to the edge of the water. His song lifted and fell with the air, which seemed to breathe warmly through his body and through the rocks."[21] Kingston writes Bak Goong into the landscape; Hawaii's landscape promises beauty and luxury as Bak Goong sings his way into his new home.

But once the Chinese workers reach their work site, everything changes. Bak Goong realizes that they are not there to harvest sugarcane. Instead, their job consists of "hack[ing] a farm out of the wilderness, which they were to level from the ocean to the mountain."[22] The sugar plantation defines the use of the land in Hawaii—to produce profitable commodities—and Bak Goong must conform to this definition. Among the tangled and thick trees, Bak Goong finds the work punishing and exhausting. The white boss forbids talking and Bak Goong feels himself being swallowed up by the plantation. At the end of the day, he runs into the ocean to cool off and, with "the water rushing away from him, he held on to his body and mind with effort."[23] Just one day on the plantation has unsettled Bak Goong's identity. He becomes a faceless, anonymous worker who is merely a cog in the wheel of production. His first paycheck is reduced because he talked during work hours. If his body is doing something other than working, then it has no value to the plantation owners, which the reduced paycheck makes clear. Unlike the myth of the American West, which idealizes owning and working land as a source of freedom and individuality, Bak Goong's story shows how the plantation landscape threatens to erase immigrant identities. Rachel Lee points out how the strict rules against speaking and the absence of family all serve the sugar industry, as well as the preservation of white American identity. She writes,

> The Chinese laborers can neither create families nor speak (both activities which would imprint a Chinese American trace upon an American cultural terrain). Furthermore, both restrictions serve capitalism, the code of silence preventing organized uprisings, while sexual prohibitions not only increase work efficiency but also prevent the possibility of American-born progeny who might claim their "native" rights.[24]

Economic forces seem to control and define people who work in Hawaii's cane fields, preventing immigrants such as Bak Goong from taking root in the land and acquiring an American identity.

Bak Goong's sense of individuality slips further away as the deforestation continues. The workers try to accelerate the job by burning the trees. This does not help, though, and when they cut through the burned trees "the men became sooted black."[25] The land is taking over, marking their bodies as workers, while the "real" Americans watch from the edges of the plantation. The outcome of the work has not measured up to expectations associated with the American myth, and Kingston conceptualizes the workers and the land as an inseparable entity. Both are "owned" and exploited for economic gain. Here Kingston demonstrates how landscape can exclude, which forces a reconsideration of early ecocritical assumptions about relationships to the land being generally positive. The racialized nature of Bak Goong's work marks him as "other" while simultaneously denying him any opportunity to define himself or his environmental views. Kingston points to the exploitive use of landscape and its role in denying identities and relationships for Chinese immigrants, revealing a more complex understanding of how landscape functions in social constructions of identity and belonging.

The plantation work takes its toll on both the Chinese workers and the land they are clearing for planting. Bak Goong develops a violent cough that contains blood. When the men rip stumps from the land, the rain causes the mud to run "like blood."[26] Kingston links the damage to his body with that to the landscape and shows how both are sacrificed for economic gain. Lee reads the destruction of the land as a moment of conflict for Kingston:

"She portrays . . . [Chinese workers] striving against oppression, as well as their own conspiracy in the destruction of the land to serve economic purposes."[27] However, there is much more to this conflict in Kingston's text, beyond revising the myth of the American West. Her more profound insight is that simply working the land does not give everyone rights to it, nor does it provide the worker with individual freedom. She also complicates notions of human roles in environmental destruction by having immigrant workers carry out the damaging work under the orders of powerful white bosses. This suggests a complex understanding of the relationship between race and the environment akin to Hayashi's argument: "The reliance on this binary of good and bad land use practices causes scholars to overlook the issues of power and choice that have played out on the American landscape."[28] He contends that the role of Chinese immigrant workers cannot be viewed through dominant views of positive environmental practices because "unlike other shapers of the American landscape, these individuals often had little say in what their 'contribution' would be."[29] Kingston is reinserting her Chinese ancestors into a history that has erased their presence and contributions to the building of an American empire, and while those contributions did involve environmental destruction, Kingston uses the text to show a dominant environmental attitude with which immigrants were forced to comply in order to make a living. This is where the real problem lies: a global economic force that transforms landscapes and workers into instruments of production under the pretense of achieving individual freedom. Landscapes, workers, and environmental destruction cannot be categorized according to binary terms, thereby deconstructing previous ecocritical approaches while creating new avenues for understanding correlations between race and nature. For Bak Goong, coded language and gardening represent these new avenues, and they allow him to resist dominant forces by forging a relationship with the Hawaiian landscape.

Bak Goong begins his resistance to dominant forces by using his cough in unexpected ways. Since talking is not allowed, Bak Goong realizes "his cough did come in handy. When the demons howled to work faster, faster, he coughed in reply. . . . He let out scolds disguised as coughs."[30] Bak Goong finds his voice again and uses it in a way that his bosses cannot understand. Next he turns to planting a garden. This individual act reasserts his identity, connects him with his Chinese heritage, and offers a more positive interaction with the landscape. Bak Goong's garden is not based on economic gain. Instead, it provides him with food and aesthetic enjoyment. In addition, he is able to plant seeds he brought from China, and this allows him to connect to his heritage in a way that not even the hard work on the plantation can sever. His ability to choose what to grow allows Bak Goong to define his relationship with the land. Furthermore, it allows him to mark the landscape with elements of China, which further reinforces the diversity of the American West.

Gardening also breaks up the monotony of Bak Goong's work on the plantation: "To see how his plants had grown and changed overnight gave him eagerness, a reason, and curiosity for getting out of bed in the morning."[31] Here, Kingston moves from the initial oppressiveness of the landscape to a redefinition of it that leads to resilience and a new identity. Bak Goong realizes that he cannot claim an American identity in the way that the myth of the West has promised. But he also learns through his gardening that the landscape cannot be strictly defined. There is nothing inherently natural about the relationship between land and citizenship, as Ursula K. Heise argues: "local citizenship, far from coming naturally, is painstakingly established and safeguarded through a multiplicity of political, social, and cultural practices and procedures."[32] In other words, the relationship is constructed. With this realization, Bak Goong can begin to construct his own identity based in nature. American identity is therefore possible after all, and it is not as static as the dominant forces would like immigrants to think. By rejecting the plantation view of the land as a commodity that bolsters white American identity, Bak Goong can engage with the landscape on his own terms.

His new approach to the plantation encourages Bak Goong to assert himself more fully. After being ill, he tells the other workers that their enforced silence causes their diseases. Pledging to make his voice heard more, he and some other men go out into a field and dig a large hole. Shouting into the hole, "they buried their words, planted them."[33] The men talk to their families, voice their fears, and loudly announce their regrets, inserting them like seeds in the soil. In this way, they leave their mark and make their presence known in a landscape that has threatened to erase them. By planting their words, they use the landscape as a way to express themselves, to break the enforced silence: "They had dug an ear into the world, and were telling the earth their secrets. 'I want home,' Bak Goong yelled, pressed against the soil, and smelling the earth."[34] The landscape becomes a metaphorical garden filled with expressions of how the men feel. The plantation's design attempts to exclude the Chinese immigrants from any claim to American landscape and identity, but Bak Goong and his fellow workers reclaim the land by disrupting dominant definitions of the landscape. Linton points out how "[o]nce the men have planted their secrets and their longings in the Hawaiian soil, they have made it theirs; eventually it will tell their own stories. They have become American forefathers."[35] Chinese immigrant workers are able to escape total erasure by yelling into the earth. Bak Goong tells them, "That wasn't a custom. . . . We made it up. We can make up customs because we're the founding ancestors of this place."[36] Hawaii now has their stories and their lives embedded in its landscape, and the workers feel a sense of connection outside the sugar plantation. As Lee argues, "this unsanctioned proclaiming represents an alternative means of claiming America, one which has not been co-opted by American economic interests."[37] By referring to themselves as "founding ancestors," they create a sense of belonging and self-definition. Future generations, like the story's narrator, will have a history tied to Hawaii that proclaims American roots.

Although Bak Goong must continue working for the plantation bosses, his sense of self and belonging lead to some improvements in his work. After the men yell into the hole, their actions seem to have confused, even frightened, the white bosses, which allows Bak Goong to sing and talk while he works. He no longer fears punishment. And his work now produces more than just cane for the sugar industry. As he plants, he knows that "[s]oon the new green shoots would rise, and when in two years the cane grew gold tassels, what stories the wind would tell."[38] His story is imprinted in the plants, and years later, the narrator hears her great grandfather's story by listening to the cane. So, the landscape is capable of telling more than one story. This makes the land a part of Chinese American history, as Linton points out: "The account of Bak Goong culminates in a complex and powerful metaphor that demonstrates how people appropriate the land, making it so completely their own that the land itself tells their story."[39] *China Men* crosses generations to tell forgotten stories and to reclaim a place for Chinese Americans in history. The story of Bak Goong challenges dominant beliefs of the American West as a place of freedom and opportunity for all, while also recasting the landscape as a means of claiming an American identity. Kingston's narrative writes back to those who have excluded immigrants by writing the landscape as a fluid concept that generates multiple definitions.

"FREEDOM FROM OTHER PEOPLE'S SHIT" IN *ALL I ASKING FOR IS MY BODY*

Milton Murayama writes a similar story of Japanese plantation workers in *All I Asking for Is My Body*. Published in 1975, Murayama's novel is set later in time, the early 1900s, as Japanese immigrants become the dominant Hawaii plantation workers. The narrator, Kiyoshi, is a young boy who lives with his family in the Japanese section of the plantation camp. His parents and his older brother, Tosh, work on the plantation, and it appears that this will be Kiyoshi's fate as well. While Kingston focuses her story on an immigrant worker, Murayama has the sons of immigrants tell this story. Kiyoshi and Tosh view the plantation as an obstacle to living as Americans. While their work alienates them from the landscape in a fashion similar to that represented in *China Men*, unlike Bak Goong, Kiyoshi and Tosh have no home outside the plantation and do not look for ways to combine Japanese and American culture in the landscape. Instead, they look for ways to escape the plantation and form identities of their own. But their parents are deep in debt and expect their children to work alongside them to help pay off the six thousand dollars they still owe as a result of their grandfather's failed business in Tokyo and unpaid bills to the plantation stores and doctors. Tosh is especially angry about having to work on the plantation and feels that he has no future and little control over his own life.

Kiyoshi begins his story as a young naïve boy who is learning about what it means to be a Japanese American living in Hawaii. His father tries to support the family by working in the fishing industry, but after the birth of another daughter, he quits and moves his family to a sugar plantation in Kahana. Kiyoshi is upset by the move since the family has to live in a rundown plantation house that is further from the ocean than their previous home. Now they are surrounded by sugarcane and Kiyoshi feels like his childhood was "chopped off clean."[40] Kahana is also controlled by the sugar companies and the plantation camp is "set up like a pyramid."[41] The boss, Mr. Nelson, lives in the largest home at the top of the "pyramid" with the Japanese and Filipino camps below it. Kiyoshi notes how the camp's dirt roads were "so red it stained your clothes and feet. The guys in Pepelau used to joke about how they could spot a guy from Kahana by his red feet."[42] Like the workers in *China Men* who become covered in soot from burning down the trees, workers and their families in Kahana are covered with red dirt from the plantation. Their identities become inseparable from the plantation and the red landscape marks them as workers whose lives are defined by the sugar industry. Murayama represents the landscape here as something that is consuming Kiyoshi's family instead of setting them free.

The oldest son, Tosh, is forced to quit school and work in the fields to help pay off the family debt. The hours are long and often Tosh comes home late and falls asleep in his work clothes. Kiyoshi notices how "[t]he work clothes got so red and dirty, mother had to boil them for several hours on Saturdays. She'd done the same thing back in 1915 when she arrived from Japan."[43] This is a significant observation for two reasons. First, the red dirt does not just cover Tosh—it permeates his clothing to the point that it is almost impossible to remove. Tosh longs to make his own way in a country that promises and promotes individual freedom, but the landscape threatens to permanently mark him as a plantation worker, trapping him in a position defined by sugar, not by the myth of the American West. Second, Tosh's fears of never leaving the plantation are justified by Kiyoshi's comment about the laundry. Their mother has been boiling the red dirt out of clothes since she first arrived from Japan. Little has changed and the family is still working to pay off the debts that have been passed down by each generation. Working the land has not freed them.

Kiyoshi slowly learns how the plantation power-holders organize workers in terms of their economic value and mass identity. His teacher Mr. Snook encourages him to see how Mr. Nelson pits different races against each other, maintaining a hierarchy with the plantation on top. He tells the children that freedom means "not being a part of a pecking order. Freedom means being your own boss." Kiyoshi quickly adds, "Freedom means being a plantation boss."[44] Kiyoshi's response shows how the plantation system has defined his sense of freedom in America. He recognizes that Mr. Nelson has more power and accepts the hierarchy without question. Later, Tosh argues with his father about how they need to cut ties with Japan and start identifying themselves as Americans.[45] The plantation system does not allow for dual identities and relies on identity politics to exclude immigrants and their families from American citizenship and to "divide and conquer" in the work force.

In 1921, sugar official Royal D. Mead testified to the U.S. Congress on labor problems in Hawaii. He stated, "The Territory of Hawaii is now and is going to be American; it is going to remain American under any condition and we are going to control the situation out there. . . . The white race, the white people, the Americans in Hawaii, are going to dominate and will continue to dominate."[46] Mead's statement clearly demonstrates how the sugar industry viewed nonwhite workers in Hawaii. His words leave no room for workers to view themselves as Americans. By defining Hawaii as an American landscape that must be dominated by white Americans, he implies that unruly nonwhite workers pose a threat to the "Americanness" of Hawaii. In this way, Tosh and his family are prevented from identifying as citizens of Hawaii and the United States.

Kyoshi later realizes that the plantation really is designed to match the social hierarchy that he had casually noted earlier in the novel. The environs of his home are set up hierarchically, organized around the sewage system. Everybody's waste runs down the hill, with those workers at the bottom literally having to live with more of it. Kyoshi notes the system where "Mr. Nelson was top shit on the highest slope, then there were the Portuguese, Spanish, and nisei lunas . . . then Japanese Camp, and Filipino Camp."[47] Asian workers are confined to the lower end, at the bottom of the hierarchy. White plantation bosses live on cleaner land than nonwhite plantation workers. Murayama demonstrates how environmental racism is not limited to sugarcane fields; it follows the workers back to their homes as well. While much of Bak Goong's story focuses on poor working conditions and alienation from the landscape, Kyoshi's story adds the element of poor living conditions in a polluted landscape, which furthers the alienation and threatens the health of Kyoshi's family. The multiple sites of hazard in the novel require a nuanced ecocritical reading that considers various environments and environmental threats. The power structure of the plantation forces Kyoshi to question what freedom really means, and he decides that "[f]reedom was freedom from other people's shit, and shit was shit no matter how lovingly it was dished, how high or low it came from."[48] Although he needs to try and make it on his own someday, the landscape has shown him how the plantation system will continue to restrict his movement and ability to define himself as an American.

The lack of environmental connection extends to a lack of corporeal connection for the workers as well. Tosh is angry about having to leave school and work in the cane fields. He fights his parents and proclaims, "all I asking for is my body. I doan wanna die on the plantation like these other dumb dodos."[49] Tosh's eponymous statement sums up the plight of the plantation worker. Just as Bak Goong runs into the ocean and tries not to let his body or mind slip away from him, Tosh fights the loss of freedom over his own body. His body performs the work that profits the industry and is physically too exhausted to do anything else. He is unable to create any connection with the landscape here because it is controlled and defined by economic forces, and those same forces control and define Tosh's body as well.

In order to reclaim himself, Tosh chooses to take up boxing. His parents do not support his dream, and Tosh later tells Kyoshi, "You know . . . if it wasn't for boxing, I think I kill the old futts by now. I get so angry sometimes. All I asking for is my body."[50] Boxing gives Tosh a feeling of agency: he is in charge of what his body is doing, and his body is now working for him. His physical strength becomes his way of rejecting plantation life as he attempts to reclaim his body from the back-breaking labor in the cane fields. And although Tosh is successful on the boxing circuit and offered a chance to fight professionally, he turns it down. He hates the plantation, but his family is still in debt and he feels pressure as the oldest son to stay and help work off the debt. The cane fields hold him back as his parents have now made it a symbol of proper filial work. Tosh is trapped in the cane.

Kyoshi comes to the realization that Tosh worked hard to try and escape the plantation. He understands that there are few jobs for Japanese Americans, even with a college degree. Out of anger and hope for escape, Kyoshi begins physical training to be a boxer as well. He runs for miles in the cane fields after work, still angry that he had to "put in ten times the work to get back one part of the result."[51] He turns the cane field into a training space where he can strengthen his body to do something other than work. This reformulation of the plantation landscape offers him the possibility of self-definition and escape. Kyoshi takes a different approach than Bak Goong, who tries to redefine his work in order to feel attachment to and understanding of the American landscape. Kyoshi chooses to redefine the use of the landscape in order to find some connection that is not dictated by the sugar industry. He looks at it as a site that strengthens rather than depletes him.

Unfortunately, however, the Japanese bombing of Pearl Harbor in 1941 changes everything for Kyoshi and his family. In this year, the United States enters World War II, rendering the Japanese an official enemy, and Kyoshi's family is left anxious and confused about what they should do. Kyoshi tries to make sense of the war but cannot find any answers that make him feel better. Walking home at night, he notices how "the proud ground [he had] been standing on had turned into soft shit, and [he] became a zombie."[52] As a Japanese American, Kyoshi now struggles even more with his sense of belonging. He hates the Japanese bombing of Pearl Harbor and that the U.S.

has labeled him an enemy. Unfortunately, the war has exacerbated identity politics that already denied Asian immigrants "the perquisites of American identity because of their inherent unfitness for inclusion, their 'natural' inferiority and foreignness that would allegedly contaminate its purity."[53] The cane fields which had become his ally in escape have now become his prison. Hawaii is put under martial law, and the "shit" that Kyoshi and Tosh worked to escape has suddenly drawn them back in, perhaps even deeper than before. Concluding that the sense of freedom and individuality promised by the American West will never come to him by working the land, Kyoshi joins the army as a *Nisei* volunteer. Before the war, the cane fields became part of his identity as he trained to become a boxer. He learned how to make his body his own, and he holds on to this physical independence.

While serving in the military, Kyoshi's sense of self takes another form when he discovers gambling. He soon wins enough money to pay off the family debt and sends it to Tosh with a note to "[t]ake care the body."[54] Rejecting myths of freedom through working the land has allowed Kyoshi to define freedom in his own way. Instead of creating a personal attachment to the landscape, like Bak Goong, Kyoshi turns the land into a site of physical training which, enabling him to reclaim his body from the control of the sugar plantation, allows him to use it to pursue the individual freedom that the American myth of the West had promised him.

Ultimately, Murayama's novel is "a rejection of the oppressive aspects of the Japanese family system and the plantation system that nurtured it, in favor of the freedom of the individual."[55] Murayama's writing places the Japanese American into the story of American sugar. While American history celebrates the booming industry and America's victory over claiming Hawaii, Murayama restructures that same history by giving face to the Japanese American plantation workers on whose backs the industry grew. He also acknowledges the way the industry included the Hawaiian landscape in its attempt to keep the workers from becoming Americans, but workers were able to redefine and reclaim the land as part of their attempts to mark their place in American history.

Kingston's and Murayama's representations of Asian immigrants and Asian Americans reclaiming and redefining the landscape alter the master narrative of individual freedom through owning and working the land. They show how the American landscape has been defined by dominant (white) forces in order to limit Asian immigrants' citizenship. While their works portray the environmental hardships their characters faced, both authors assert Asian American agency through alternate means of environmental definition achieved through self-expression, gardening, and individual understandings and uses of the landscape. These reformulated definitions work both to dispel notions of Asian Americans as powerless victims of their environments and to destabilize white narratives of freedom by portraying landscapes as flexible concepts that defy static definition. It is this flexibility that allows for alternate narratives of identity to be constructed through the landscape of the American West.

NOTES

1. Donald Worster, *Under Western Skies: Nature and History in the American West* (New York: Oxford University Press, 1992), 34.
2. Hsuan L. Hsu, "Chronotopes of the Asian American West," in *A Companion to the Literature and Culture of the American West*, ed. Nicolas S. Witschi (Malden, MA: Blackwell Publishing, 2011), 145.
3. Robert T. Hayashi, "Beyond Walden Pond: Asian American Literature and the Limits of Ecocriticism," in *Coming into Contact: Explorations in Ecocritical Theory and Practice*, eds. Annie M. Ingram, Ian Marshall, Daniel J. Philippon, and Adam W. Sweeting (Athens: University of Georgia Press, 2007), 61.
4. Ibid.
5. Patricia Nelson Limerick, "Disorientation and Reorientation: The American Landscape Discovered from the West," *The Journal of American History* 79 (1992): 1029.
6. Ibid., 1030.
7. John Whitehead, "Hawai'i: The First and Last Far West?" in *The History and Immigration of Asian Americans*, ed. Franklin Ng (New York: Garland Publishing, 1998), 51.
8. Ah Quon McElrath, "From Old to New Plantations: Labor's Growing Pains," in *New Visions in Asian American Studies: Diversity, Community, Power*, eds. Franklin Ng et al. (Pullman: Washington State University Press, 1994), 6.
9. Ronald Takaki, *Strangers from a Different Shore: A History of Asian Americans* (Boston: Back Bay Books, 1998), 132.
10. McElrath, "From Old to New Plantations," 6.
11. Ibid., 7.
12. Whitehead, "Hawai'i," 53.
13. "By the late 1930s, sugar and pineapple planters had imported over 400,000 men, women, and children." McElrath, "From Old to New Plantations," 7.
14. Ibid., 58.
15. Takaki, *Strangers*, 487.
16. Maxine Hong Kingston, *China Men* (New York: Alfred A. Knopf, 1977), 88.
17. "Chinaman" has been used historically in the U.S. as a pejorative term referring to people of Chinese descent as well as people from other East Asian countries. The derogatory nature of "Chinaman's Hat" also comes from the use of "coolie hat" (the conical hat often worn by field workers in many Asian countries). "Coolie" became a racial slur describing laborers of Asian descent.
18. Kingston, *China Men*, 90.
19. Patricia Linton, "'What Stories the Wind Would Tell': Representation and Appropriation in Maxine Hong Kingston's *China Men*," *MELUS: Multi-Ethnic Literature of the United States* 19.4 (1994): 44.
20. Kingston, *China Men*, 97.
21. Ibid.
22. Ibid., 98.
23. Ibid.

24. Rachel Lee, "Claiming Land, Claiming Voice, Claiming Canon: Institutionalized Challenges in Kingston's *China Men* and *The Woman Warrior*," in *ReViewing Asian America: Locating Diversity*, eds. Wendy L. Ng, Soo-Young Chin, James S. Moy, and Gary Y. Okihiro (Pullman: Washington State University Press, 1995), 149–50.
25. Kingston, *China Men*, 101.
26. Ibid., 103.
27. Lee, "Claiming Land," 149.
28. Hayashi, "Beyond Walden," 65.
29. Ibid.
30. Kingston, *China Men*, 104.
31. Ibid., 105.
32. Ursula K. Heise, *Sense of Place and Sense of Planet: The Environmental Imagination of the Global* (New York: Oxford University Press, 2008), 46.
33. Ibid., 118.
34. Ibid., 117.
35. Linton, "What Stories," 45.
36. Kingston, *China Men*, 118.
37. Lee, "Claiming Land," 152.
38. Kingston, *China Men*, 118.
39. Linton, "What Stories," 45.
40. Milton Murayama, *All I Asking for Is My Body* (Honolulu: University of Hawaii Press, 1988), 28.
41. Ibid.
42. Ibid., 29.
43. Ibid.
44. Ibid., 34.
45. Ibid., 37.
46. Quoted in McElrath, "From Old to New Plantations," 7.
47. Murayama, *All I Asking*, 96.
48. Ibid.
49. Ibid., 48.
50. Ibid., 71.
51. Ibid.
52. Ibid., 83
53. Hayashi, "Beyond Walden," 67–8.
54. Murayama, *All I Asking*, 103.
55. Elaine H. Kim, *Asian American Literature: An Introduction to the Writings and Their Social Context* (Philadelphia: Temple University Press, 1982), 146.

BIBLIOGRAPHY

Hayashi, Robert T. "Beyond Walden Pond: Asian American Literature and the Limits of Ecocriticism." In *Coming into Contact: Explorations in Ecocritical Theory and Practice*, edited by Annie M. Ingram, Ian Marshall, Daniel J. Philippon, and Adam W. Sweeting, 58–75. Athens: University of Georgia Press, 2007.
Heise, Ursula K. *Sense of Place and Sense of Planet: The Environmental Imagination of the Global*. New York: Oxford University Press, 2008.
Hsu, Hsuan L. "Chronotopes of the Asian American West." In *A Companion to the Literature and Culture of the American West*, edited by Nicolas S. Witschi, 145–58. Malden, MA: Blackwell Publishing, 2011.

Kim, Elaine H. *Asian American Literature: An Introduction to the Writings and Their Social Context*. Philadelphia: Temple University Press, 1982.

Kingston, Maxine Hong. *China Men*. New York: Alfred A. Knopf, 1977.

Lee, Rachel. "Claiming Land, Claiming Voice, Claiming Canon: Institutionalized Challenges in Kingston's *China Men* and *The Woman Warrior*." In *ReViewing Asian America: Locating Diversity*, edited by Wendy L. Ng, Soo-Young Chin, James S. Moy, and Gary Y. Okihiro, 147–60. Pullman: Washington State University Press, 1995.

Limerick, Patricia Nelson. "Disorientation and Reorientation: The American Landscape Discovered from the West." *The Journal of American History* 79 (1992): 1021–49.

Linton, Patricia. "'What Stories the Wind Would Tell': Representation and Appropriation in Maxine Hong Kingston's *China Men*." *MELUS: Multi-Ethnic Literature of the United States* 19.4 (1994): 37–48.

McElrath, Ah Quon. "From Old to New Plantations: Labor's Growing Pains." In *New Visions in Asian American Studies: Diversity, Community, Power*, edited by Franklin Ng, Judy Yung, and Elaine H. Kim, 5–13. Pullman: Washington State University Press, 1994.

Murayama, Milton. *All I Asking for Is My Body*. Honolulu: University of Hawaii Press, 1988.

Takaki, Ronald. *Strangers from a Different Shore: A History of Asian Americans*. Boston: Back Bay Books, 1998.

Whitehead, John. "Hawai'i: The First and Last Far West?" In *The History and Immigration of Asian Americans*, edited by Franklin Ng, 39–64. New York: Garland Publishing, 1998.

Worster, Donald. *Under Western Skies: Nature and History in the American West*. New York: Oxford University Press, 1992.

2 Fae Myenne Ng's San Francisco Chinatown as a Social Space of Legal Discrimination

Wenying Xu

Fae Myenne Ng's novels, *Bone* (1993) and *Steer toward Rock* (2008), center on characters and events in Chinatown, San Francisco. Ng's meticulous description represents the environment as a space that shapes and records the history of Chinese American experience. The material realities of this space narrate the full impact of discriminatory legislation on the Chinese American family. In other words, Chinatown in Ng's novels is a repository of material and psychic sediments of legislative racism against Chinese immigrants. Ng achieves historical realism in both novels largely through the representation of San Francisco Chinatown as a social space produced and reproduced by discriminatory immigration laws and their subversion by Chinese and Chinese Americans.

Ng's first novel *Bone* tells a Chinatown story centering on the Leong family's tribulation. Opening with the suicide of the middle daughter Ona, the novel relates the first daughter Leila's narrative, which attempts to identify the cause of Ona's death. Ng depicts Chinatown from Leila's perspective as one who experiences this social space very differently than do visitors. Leila temporarily assumes the view of a tourist and ponders,

> So this is what Chinatown looks like from inside those dark Greyhound buses; this slow view, these strange color combinations, these narrow streets, this is what tourists come to see. I felt a small lightening up inside, because I knew, no matter what people saw, no matter how close they looked, our inside story is something entirely different.[1]

Ng's second novel *Steer toward Rock* is also set in San Francisco Chinatown. Following the life of its protagonist Jack Szeto, the novel spans three decades, depicting racial discrimination and the subsequent economic hardships. Like *Bone, Steer toward Rock* employs the perspective of an insider to express the painful disparity between Chinatown's reality and a tourist's perception. Jack Szeto's daughter Veda remarks,

> I just felt bad that an outsider saw such a cartoon of my home: fake pagoda roofs, a Chinatown gate, rows and rows of souvenir shops, which

I thought were worse than the topless bars just a few blocks away. Now, I was mad at a tourist again and I knew why. Home was a dump. Our street level was all commerce, beautified for tourists. True home was the second level, barred windows, laundry and potted plants on the fire escapes.[2]

The gaudy façade of Chinatowns has been the official representation in mainstream media, whereas Ng's novels succeed in taking the reader into Chinatown's interior to experience complex human dramas more intimately. Chinatown in both novels serves as more than a setting or a geographical space; it is portrayed as a social environment structured both by objects and human relations. It is an emotionally charged space that reverberates with its residents' livelihood, interactions, family histories, and memories, producing a social environment that manifests the legacy of discriminatory legislation, among other things.

LEGAL DISCRIMINATION AGAINST CHINESE IMMIGRANTS AND PAPER SONS

Tracing Chinatown's history to the exclusion era between 1882 and 1943, Ng's novels are organized by the leitmotif of "paper son," a fictional identity Chinese immigrants assumed to overcome unjust immigration laws, such as the 1882 Chinese Exclusion Act and its various extensions until its repeal in 1943. *Bone*, set in the late 1970s and *Steer toward Rock*, in the early 1950s to the late 1970s, describe the unfolding of events that are rooted in this era. Ng's second novel presents a Chinatown beginning the process of its regeneration through family formation, whereas her first portrays what family life has become in Chinatown due to the legacy of legal racism. Thomas W. Kim is accurate in pointing out that *Bone* "reveals how contemporary Chinatown politics and culture have developed from the historical specificity of location, economics, and legislation."[3] Moving back in time, Ng's novels implicate a narrative deeper and broader than that of the family. By doing so, the author suggests that family narratives are integral to political and historical narratives.

Preceding the timeframe of *Bone*, *Steer toward Rock* centers on the impossibility of the family after almost a century of anti-Asian and anti-Chinese legislation. Its protagonist Jack Szeto's attempts at family life are frustrated because of his paper son identity and the complications it has engendered. In *Bone*, the Leong family experiences economic hardships and the tragedy of Ona's suicide, signifying greater and deeper problems beyond the familial. Juliana Chang remarks,

Ng's inscription of the Leong/Fu family as "failed" . . . and incomplete does not represent the dysfunction of a single family unit; rather this failed domesticity encrypts the failures of the nation and symptomatizes the continued exclusion of the Chinese American subject from the time and space of US nation-statehood. *Bone*'s melancholic domesticity subverts the interpretation of Chinese American family formation as signifying racial and national progress. Instead, this melancholia alerts us to what lives on in the transition from bachelor to family sociality: the exploitation of racial labor.[4]

Ng's storylines in both novels burrow deep into a national history as well as loop wide to implicate a national anxiety about race and immigration. Like other significant fiction that gestures, through the personal, toward underlying social, economic, and political conflicts, Ng's novels afford the reader a view of major national and societal conflicts through the individual and the family.

Centering on the unfolding of the Leong's family narrative, *Bone* is a backward glance across family history, insinuating cultural memory, in seeking causality. Many Asian American scholars have noted the reverse chronology in the novel, which reports at the start that Ona has committed suicide by jumping off the "M" floor (the 13th floor) of the Nam Ping Yuen, a housing project in Chinatown. Chang comments, "in this reverse chronology where effects precede cause, the reader expects the eventual, climatic revelation of the cause of Ona's suicide. What we find instead is not a singular cause, but rather the diffuse unfolding of hardship, sorrow, and endurance."[5] Subverting the discourse of historical progress, *Bone* resists closure by enacting a parallel between the structure of the narrative and the lingering motion of sorrow, which "moves through the heart the way a ship moves through the ocean. . . . One mile forward and eight miles back."[6] This reverse chronology tracing the cause of Ona's suicide does not reach its destination; however, it conveys the message that her suicide implodes the family narrative and implicates a socio-political one. *Bone*'s tragedy bleeds into *Steer toward Rock* and finally addresses the cause by depicting the sorrows of Jack Szeto. (Interestingly, both Leon and Jack have arrived in the United States by the same ship: the S.S. *President Coolidge*.) Thus, chronologically speaking, Ng's second novel leads her first, constructing a genealogy of the paper son, detailing his fate in San Francisco Chinatown.

The background of the paper son first began in 1879 when the first federal law affecting Chinese immigration, the Fifteen Passenger Bill, was passed in the U.S. House of Representatives; it prohibited any vessel from bringing more than fifteen Chinese passengers into the United States on any one voyage. Violators could be fined $100 for each passenger and imprisoned for six months. Although President Rutherford B. Hayes vetoed the bill because of its violation of the Burlingame Treaty,[7] this legislation effectively opened the door to one of the most draconian immigration bills in U.S. history—the 1882 Chinese Exclusion Act, the first piece of federal legislation that singled out a group based on nationality and class to be barred from immigration.

This act specifically prohibited Chinese laborers from entering the United States for ten years, with certain classes exempted, such as merchants, teachers, diplomats, students, clergyman, and travelers. It unmistakably targeted working-class Chinese. The consequence was a rapid decline of the Chinese population in America. Angelo Ancheta comments, "The decline in Chinese immigration was precipitous: in 1882, over 39,000 Chinese entered the United States; in 1884, only 279 entered the country; and in 1888, only 10 were admitted."[8] The Chinese Exclusion Act allowed reentry of those who left the United States temporarily with return certificates. However, the Scott Act of 1888 revised the earlier act by prohibiting the entry of all Chinese, including those with return certificates. Erika Lee reports, "The Scott Act of the same year nullified 20,000 return certificates already granted and immediately denied entrance to returning Chinese laborers."[9] Many of those barred from returning had families and property in the United States. What is new in the Scott Act is the removal of "laborers"; the new provisions excluded *all* Chinese except "teachers, students, merchants, or travelers for pleasure or curiosity."[10] Four years later, U.S. Congress passed the Geary Act, which extended Chinese exclusion another ten years. In 1902 Congress renewed Chinese exclusion, and in 1904, Chinese exclusion was extended indefinitely. The Chinese exclusion laws were not repealed until 1943 when China became a U.S. ally during World War II.

Defiant of the exclusionary laws, thousands of Chinese resorted to fabrication in order to enter the country "legally." Some falsely claimed to be a member of the exempt classes, such as merchants, teachers, and students. They obtained the necessary documentation or witness testimony to verify that claim. Lee explains, "Identification papers for children or spouses of exempt class immigrants were especially useful because the U.S. government often lacked reliable documentary evidence verifying births and marriages that had taken place either in the United States or in China."[11] A transnational network emerged through family connections in China, Hong Kong, Macau, and the U.S. to produce and exchange such identification papers. It was common among Chinese immigrants to claim more children than they had and to report fictional births of children during their visits home in order to sponsor relatives or to sell the slots. One of the most referenced identities is the paper son. The young man who purchased the fake identity must memorize the family history of the "paper father" to pass immigration officers' interrogation, and if successful he would bear the "paper father's" name for the rest of his life. Lee observes, "The paper son system, thus instituted a chain migration pattern that allowed multiple generations of Chinese to enter the country, using fraudulent papers, and it facilitated the reunification of family members (mostly male) within the United States."[12] The high success rate is also due to the fact that "[p]rofessional immigration agents provided expertise and connections—often with corrupt immigration officials."[13] The business of illegal immigration flourished. Commenting on paper identities, including the paper son, K. Scott Wong writes, "Many

Chinese constructed and reconstructed their citizenship status, names, and personal pasts, depending on the trail of paper that created their immigration identities and shaped their quest for official recognition as American citizens."[14]

It is against this historical background that Ng's *Steer toward Rock* portrays San Francisco Chinatown as an environment where legal/illegal identities structure residents' lives. The novel begins in the early 1960s when the Federal Confession Program promised that Chinese who had taken fraudulent oaths before July 15, 1957 would not be prosecuted for perjury and called upon them to confess and readjust their immigration statuses. The majority of the chapters in this novel are titled "Tan Bai"—Chinese for "confession." Jack begins his tale in a confessional tone: "The woman I loved wasn't in love with me; the woman I married wasn't a wife to me. Ilin Cheung was my wife on paper. Indeed, she belonged to Yi-Tung Szeto. In debt, I also belong to him. He was my father, paper, too."[15] Jack's confession exposes his father, his wife, and himself. "Paper" is the key word in this opening statement, substituting for flesh and blood. Jack has been purchased as a child to be the son of Yi-Tung Szeto, also known as Gold Szeto, who himself has "bought the Szeto name and entered California as the legal son of a gold miner."[16] The twice-purchased family name sets off the novel's action. Both father and son are paper sons who must live the lives of lies because of the discriminatory socio-political environment. Human relations thus delineated are engendered chiefly by the demand of legality.

Similarly, one of the major themes in *Bone* is the power of paper in the eyes of the law, which fetishizes passports, visas, identity cards, return certificates, and other documentations. Paper renders blood and bone powerless in the eyes of bureaucracy, whereas blood and bone rule the lives of human beings, legal or illegal. Leon, the father figure, often remarks, "In this country, paper is more precious than blood."[17] The incommensurability between paper and blood results in family tragedies. *Bone* tells the story of the Leong family tormented by secrets kept in order to evade the law and conflicts caused by these secrets. Opening the novel with the information of Ona's suicide, Ng propels the reader into the snarl of family secrets centering on Leon's legal/illegal immigration status and his paper and blood relations.

Both Leon and Jack are paper sons bound to their environment and indebted to Chinatown bachelors; dead or alive, both paper fathers continue dictating the lives of their paper sons. Leon is fifteen when he arrives at the port of San Francisco, with a purchased identity, as a son of Grandpa Leong. In addition to $5,000, Leon has to promise Grandpa Leong that he will send the old man's bones back to China after his death. Successfully passing the interrogation at Angel Island, Leon is permitted into the country as a legal immigrant. However, his American life is riddled with confusion and uncertainties. Leon's stepdaughter Leila states, "Leon was always getting his real and paper birthdays mixed up; he's never given the same birthday twice. Old-timer logic: If you don't tell the truth, you'll never get caught in a lie. What Leon didn't know, he made up. Forty years of making it up had to backfire sometime."[18] Leon's debt is the unfulfilled promise to Grandpa Leong about returning his bones to China for burial, and to this broken promise Leon attributes the suicide of his daughter.

Like Leon, Jack owes Gold Szeto for his paper and passage to the amount of $4,000 with a seven percent interest rate, which he can never pay off, no matter how long he works for the old man. Because of this debt, Jack becomes a paper husband to Ilin Cheung, whom the old man has made his wife in secret to evade the law. Gold Szeto commits polygamy, because his first wife in China has been barred from entering the United States by the Chinese Exclusion Act. By the time Chinese women were allowed to join their husbands in the United States, Mrs. Szeto is too old to bear children. Thus, he makes use of his paper son Jack in acquiring his "Replacement Wife."[19]

It is in Chinatown that Leon, Jack, Ilin, and Gold Szeto lead their fictitious and secret lives—secretive, however, only to immigration and naturalization officers, for paper identities were abundantly known in Chinatowns during the exclusionary era and decades afterwards. Paper identities thus acquire a unique ethos in Chinatown; as Leon tells his stepdaughter Leila, "it's time that makes a family, not just blood."[20] Leon and Jack have certainly given their time in memorizing another man's family history, in knowing by heart another man's properties, and in carrying another man's name. One may say that most Chinatowns in the United States were artificial communities for over a century due to discriminatory legislative and social practices that necessitated paper identities. The Chinatowns that emerged during the early decades of the twentieth century were not so much the products of natural social and demographic forces than the distorted outgrowths of immigration and naturalization policies that discriminated against the Chinese in general and against specific classes among them in particular. In other words, the forces of racial prejudice, economic immobility, and cultural marginalization made it extremely difficult for Chinese immigrants to live outside Chinatowns. The Leong family drama in *Bone* and Jack's convoluted relationships in *Steer toward Rock* trace their origins to this particular history of legalized racism against the Chinese.

San Francisco Chinatown was established in the 1850s when some thirty thousand Chinese arrived at California for the Gold Rush.[21] It "centered initially on a one-block portion of Sacramento Street . . . that ran in a straight line from the wharf to Nob Hill."[22] Anthony Lee records, "By the mid-1850s, Chinatown had spread in either direction along Sacramento Street and more vigorously, north along Dupont Street [today's Grant Avenue]. It was this second, perpendicular, line of growth, along Dupont, that to most early observers visually declared Chinatown's existence."[23] Bordering Dupont or Grant Avenue is Portsmouth Square, which has been called the heart of Chinatown and the birthplace of San Francisco. In the 1850s, the Square became the center around which Chinese built businesses to serve the growing population in San Francisco. The Chinese immigrants chose to live in this ethnic enclave not simply because it provided them with mutual support and security but also because "racial discrimination and hostilities in the 1870s prevented them from finding better jobs and housing outside Chinatown."[24]

Reflecting Portsmouth Square's historical significance and centrality in Chinatown, Ng's novels describe the Square as a prominent landmark that renders vivid remnants of the bachelor society. Ng in *Bone* describes the old men with whom Leon associates at Portsmouth Square as "time wasters" with "tattered collars, missing buttons, safety-pinned seams, patch pockets full of fists."[25] These old-timers were once young men, whose labor contributed to the nation-building of this country and made California one of the strongest economies. The law prevented such men from bringing wives into this country. As aging bachelors, they live at the "old-man hotel on Clay Street, the San Fran."[26] Leila informs the reader, "Our Grandpa Leong lived his last days at the San Fran,"[27] and Leon himself has a room there in order to escape the troubles at home. In *Steer toward Rock*, Portsmouth Square is the place where "the fired and retired . . . congregated."[28] Tracing the historical root of aging bachelors, Leila observes that "[i]n this country, the San Fran is our family's oldest place, our beginning place, our new China."[29] As the beginning place, the Square also provides a playground for children. There are "swings on the lower level of the Square,"[30] and it is here that a family friend remembers "pushing Ona on the swings."[31] Ng presents the Square as the heart of the community where people meet to play chess, babysit, trade gossip, and assist each other. More significantly, the Square has been a witness to Chinese American history, bearing its traumatic memories and demonstrating its tenacious will to survive and prosper. Ng's choice of identifying the Square as the "home" of dying bachelors points our attention to this aberrant phenomenon attributable to legislative actions.

The motif of bones in Ng's first novel encapsulates Chinatown's history, both political and personal. As unerasable remains of the dying bachelor society, bones evoke the pathos of the exiled as in scattered bones that will never reach home. Chang, writing about *Bone*, remarks,

> Mixed together and unmarked by proper name, these bones remain homeless and anonymous. The unassailability of these bones into the national symbolic marks their status as the demetaphorized remains that accompany the encryption of a secret. This national secret is the recruitment and exploitation of racial labor, which is necessary to the national economy but must be disavowed by nationalist ideology.[32]

We can see from the haunting quality of Grandpa Leong's bones that the novel's figures of bones are metonyms for the old bachelors: no longer productive, their aging bodies are what remain from lives of underpaid and exploited labor. The bones imagery not only represents the history of the old bachelors but also the doomed present because of the limitations of the discriminatory past. Ona's broken body joining the history of Chinatown's dead bachelors throws into question the future of Chinatown and of the Chinese American family. The fundamental question raised is whether Chinatowns can successfully raise a new generation after over one hundred years of bachelor existence. Ng's stories illustrate the painful passage from aging bachelors to that of dysfunctional familial societies. It is as if the bachelor society being family-less for three generations had forgotten how to raise the young.

BACHELOR SOCIETIES IN CHINATOWNS

To construct the genealogy of the aging bachelor, embodied in Grandpa Leong, Gold Szeto, and Jack Moon Szeto, it is necessary to historicize Chinese women's encounter with U.S. immigration laws. Chinese women became a target for discriminatory legislation as early as 1866, when California passed the "Act for the Suppression of Chinese Houses of Ill-Fame." During the Gold Rush and for several decades thereafter, prostitutes of many nationalities lived in San Francisco. The city government, however, singled out Chinese women for punishment from the very beginning. Sucheng Chan explains that the 1866 Act "declared Chinese prostitution a public nuisance, made leases of real property to brothel operators invalid, provided for the retaking of such premises, and charged landlords who allowed their properties to be so used with a misdemeanor that carried a maximum penalty of $500 or six months in jail."[33] This state law paved the way for the Page Law of 1875, which was the first federal immigration legislation that excluded a group based on its race and gender. It was intended to stop the immigration of Asian women for the purpose of prostitution, and the immigration officers effectively barred the entry of nearly all Chinese women by classifying them as prostitutes. Furthermore, Section 3 of the Expatriation Act of 1907 determined that "any American woman who marries a foreigner should take the nationality of her husband."[34] Until 1931, when expatriation of women married to Asian immigrants was rescinded, an American-born Chinese woman would lose her U.S. citizenship if she married a Chinese immigrant ineligible for naturalization.

These legislative actions created a severely imbalanced sex ratio in the Chinese American population. Because of the traditional gender ideology, few Chinese women attempted migration to the United States even before the Page Law was enacted. According to Erika Lee, 4.4 percent of the Chinese admitted into the United States were women in 1873, 1.8 percent in 1874, and 2.3 percent in 1875, the year the Page Law was passed. This bill effectively sharpened the decline in the number of Chinese women entering the country. Lee reports that in 1876 Chinese women entering the country were 1.1 percent and 0.7 percent in 1877.[35] Roger Daniels points out,

As late as 1920, seventy years after the migration began, women numbered fewer than ten percent of the Chinese American population. During the late nineteenth century, women were even less numerous. In 1880, for example, California listed more than 70,000 Chinese men and fewer than 4,000 women. In the rest of the United States, the imbalance was even greater; almost 30,000 men and fewer than 1000 women.[36]

The impact of this severe imbalance between the sexes made it very difficult for the Chinese American community to regenerate itself; it also created a very conservative and patriarchal culture in the aging bachelor societies of Chinatowns.[37] Furthermore, anti-miscegenation laws lessened Chinese men's chance for attaining family lives even more, as interracial marriage or cohabitation was illegal between whites and people of other races. Some Chinese men, however, married Native American, African American, or Mexican women. It was not until 1967 that the U.S. Supreme Court unanimously ruled in *Loving v. Virginia* that anti-miscegenation laws were unconstitutional, and with this ruling, the enforcement of these laws was ended in all states.

These are the historical forces that produced bachelor societies in Chinatowns. Ng's novels pay tribute to the last remaining generation of bachelors. In the world of her novels, the aging bachelors gather in the same places: Portsmouth Square, Uncle's Café, where "every single table is an old-man table,"[38] and the Underground, a bathhouse that serves old men who live in tenement houses like the San Fran.[39] Ng's second novel takes the reader to a time when these lonely old men were young paper sons. Jack enters the novel in his early twenties, as a butcher working in Universal Market, owned by his paper father Gold Szeto, in order to pay his interminable debt. He spends long hours butchering, cleaning, and selling meat. Feeling like a prisoner, Jack compares himself to the chickens he kills—"I lived as if in a chicken cage. From the Universal, my world extended only a few blocks in each direction."[40] Nevertheless, Jack attracts the attention of young women whose husbands are gone for long periods working "the farmlands in the Central Valley or construction in the Southland."[41] As he puts it, "I was the Lord of the Peach Blossoms, lucky in the garden."[42] When he meets Joice Qwan, an American-born Chinese woman, Jack loses his interest in married women; he falls in love with Joice, but she does not reciprocate in feeling and becomes his "ghost of love, better chased than caught."[43] Joice has no wish to marry Jack, partly because he is the paper husband to Ilin Cheung.

Attempting to free himself from the tangle of lies in order to experience love, Jack goes to the Immigration and Naturalization Services to confess his true identity, knowing the consequence may very well be deportation. In making the following statement, he transforms his status of U.S. citizen to that of alien: "I am willing to concede alienage and wish to apply for Suspension of Deportation. I voluntarily surrender Certificate of Identity No. 387046, which shows that I was admitted to the United States as a citizen, and passport No. 362891, issued by the Department of State, Washington, D.C. I have this day voluntarily registered as an alien."[44] The immigration officer who interviews Jack documents, "In a sworn statement at San Francisco on February 2, 1965, attached as Exhibit A, SUBJECT confessed that his true name is Yuo Seen Leong and made no claim to United States citizenship. His immigration father is not related to him. SUBJECT has no true brothers or sisters."[45] As a result of Jack's confession, his paper father Gold Szeto is arrested and charged with being unlawfully in the United States. The immigration officer states to Gold Szeto, "you entered without inspection under the immigration laws Section 20, and in that you entered in violation of another ('any') law of the United States, to wit, the Chinese Exclusion Laws, Section 21 of the Act of February 20, 1907."[46] Gold Szeto is deported after having resided in the United States for nearly sixty years. As retribution, Gold Szeto's people in Chinatown cut off Jack's right hand, effectively ending his livelihood as a butcher.

In painting the lives of Jack and Leon, Ng employs two contradictory sets of lexicon—that of the heart versus that of bureaucracy—to reveal the contradiction that is Jack's life and to portray the absurdity of the U.S. legal system, which aimed at excluding and dehumanizing the racial other. It is through the convoluted relationships made necessary to evade the law that Ng also succeeds in restoring humanity to her characters. Leon finds himself ineligible for Social Security because of his paper identity despite fifty years as a "legal" immigrant. The white man who interviews Leon asks Leila why he has so many aliases and different dates of birth—"Did he have a passport? A birth certificate? A driver's license?"[47] Ironically, the paper son is penalized for not having the right papers: "the laws that excluded him now held him captive."[48] Grandpa Leong died when Leon was away. Leon blames himself for breaking his promise and believes that his "family's bad luck started when he broke his promise to Grandpa Leong. Leon worried about the reckless bones, and for years, whenever something went wrong—losing a job, losing the bid for the takeout joint, losing the Ong and Leong Laundry—Leon blamed the bones."[49] Losing his second daughter Ona sets Leon off to find the bones. At the cemetery, the guard refuses to let him in, telling him, "you've got to have a piece of paper saying you got people buried here,"[50] which Leon does not. Ng conveys the message that in a world obsessed with paper, rigid classification confines people to binary categories according to a bureaucratic rationality, marking human beings as legal or illegal, insider or outsider, and citizen or alien. Ng's novel portrays the Leong family as a casualty of this rationality.

Chinatown, as a social space, structures the lives of its residents according to a different logic, one that accommodates contradiction, ambiguity, and unpredictability. In defiance of laws and designs, Ng portrays the human drama in Chinatown as full of surprises. It turns out that Jack's confession to the immigration officer neither secures Joice's love nor breaks the tie with his paper wife, Ilin. Joice leaves San Francisco after giving birth to their daughter, Veda, trusting the baby to her mother. Jack and Ilin find themselves in a love affair, and the fake yet legal marriage becomes lifelong friendship. Jack reflects about his paper wife, "I thought about how we had earned each other's comfort and company. Ours was better than a real marriage."[51] After Veda's grandmother dies, Ilin assumes the mother's role, providing maternal guidance to the child. Lacking a real family, Jack, Ilin, and Veda form one outside of the law and despite the law. Ironically, Jack's paper marriage has engendered a real family.

Both paper sons have suffered painful losses—Leon, his daughter Ona, and Jack, his right hand. Donald C. Goellnicht interprets Ona's suicide as a trope gesturing toward the erasure of their original identities as paper sons. He writes, "At a psychological level, these men can be seen as committing symbolic acts of suicide by putting in abeyance their 'original' identities in order to take on the 'paper histories' . . . made necessary by restrictive immigration laws."[52] Leon never recovers from this symbolic death, and recriminates himself for not returning Grandpa Leong's bones to China, for having one's scattered bones sent home symbolically restores one's identity as a member of the imagined community of the ancestral space. Goellnicht goes on to note, "In a strange twist of logic, Leon seems to believe that paper has not simply replaced blood in America; in addition, paper identity must be repaid with blood, so that Ona, who was once the repository of all Leon's dreams in America, becomes his means of restitution, his blood money to his dead 'father' in a morbid system of exchange whereby identity substitution is played out to its pathological extreme."[53] Leon's loss of Ona serves also as a symbol of the loss of the American Dream, the dispelling of the promise of the Chinese American family after the end of the bachelor society and thus the renewal of Chinese American communities in Chinatowns. Juliana Chang insightfully observes, "we can see in *Bone* . . . how the contemporary formation of an almost-normative nuclear family in fact embodies traces of earlier 'bachelor histories.'"[54] Leon, though married, has never acted as a family man. Either he works on a ship for months away from home or he works at odd jobs in Chinatown and lives in the San Fran with other aging bachelors. Leila's mother, abandoned by her first husband Fu, has married Leon for a residency green card. While it is not exactly a loveless marriage, their relationship is fraught with frustration and disappointment, which is partly due to Leon's constant absence from home and partly due to economic hardships.

With its symbolic reach, Ona's suicide on the surface seems to be without a clear reason. Yoonmee Chang describes *Bone* as "a narrativization of narrative failure."[55] Clearly, the causality for the Leong's family tragedy cannot be found in the confines of family narratives; rather it lies elsewhere, implicating a social and political narrative. Leon points his finger at America for "making big promises and breaking . . . every one." He questions, "Where was the successful business? He'd kept his end of the bargain: he'd worked hard. Two jobs, three. Day and night. Overtime. . . . 'America,' he ranted, 'this lie of a country!'"[56]

Chinese labor played an essential role in America's nation-building, solicited for California's economic development and transcontinental railroad construction, with the latter becoming the main artery of the U.S. economy. Ng's evocation of the bachelor society through depicting Leon's and Jack's lives in Chinatown harks back to the oppressive chapter of Chinese American history. Of this history Daniels notes, "During the construction of the transcontinental Central Pacific Railroad, up to 10,000 Chinese were employed in construction gangs; almost all were laid off when the road was completed in May 1869."[57] Anti-Chinese violence ensued when competition in the labor market intensified. During "the earliest urban anti-Chinese riots . . . in 1871 in . . . Los Angeles, twenty-one Chinese were shot, hanged, or burned to death by white mobs . . . Over one hundred Chinese were killed in Idaho in 1866–1867."[58] Similar riots against the Chinese also occurred in the Northwest and Mountain states, such as Denver and Wyoming. In Wyoming the violence occurred in 1885. "The official toll was 28 Chinese dead and 15 wounded; property damage was officially assessed at $147,000."[59]

Although never free from police harassment, San Francisco Chinatown was a relatively safe haven for Chinese immigrants. Despite the mounting anti-Chinese sentiment in California and other Western states, no organized violence against the residents in San Francisco Chinatown was documented. Its bachelor society was in decline at the time during which *Steer toward Rock* is set. In this novel, Ng reincarnates Leon in Jack Moon Szeto, who enters the story in the 1950s. Although *Steer toward Rock* centers on a family narrative as *Bone* does, it reaches more confidently into the social and political history of U.S. legal racism as the cause of private suffering in Chinatown. One can argue that much like Ona's suicide, Jack's loss of a hand also operates as a trope, symbolic of the erasure of identity and of castration. Early in *Steer toward Rock*, Ng makes it known that Jack's hands are vital to his personal identity. He declares, "I was a butcher. What a man did with his hands spoke his worth. . . . I read meat. I moved my fingers through marbled flesh like a vulture's beak. . . . I was a Master."[60] Clearly, the mastery of his hands offers him a sense of sovereignty, and in addition, the imagery of his fingers as "a vulture's beak" connotes aggression that implies displaced hostility toward the oppressive dominant culture. Jack's hands are a key to his self-perception and his relationship to others: "I was a man who sold my sweat. I relied on my own abilities and I did what I could with my own hands."[61] It is his abilities with his hands that attract women to him. It is no surprise that Gold Szeto's punishment of Jack for his confession to the immigration officers is to amputate Jack's right hand. Ng presents the incident sparingly:

> He felt the many arms of a struggling Buddha. He felt the metal chewing through cartilage, slicing through bone.
> The emptying, Noooooooo. . . .
> How far to fly? Which land, which shore? Where was safety?

...

Jack only remembered the last impression of a handshake. In the stillness, he was confused between what was new and what was old.
Which hand did they shake?
Which hand did they take?[62]

Ng's sparse description of this moment of violence effectively magnifies its horror and Jack's anguish. To continue the vulture imagery, Jack imagines his escape by flying to another place, but one of his wings has been amputated. The resultant "emptying" and confusion powerfully suggest his loss of self. After the event, Jack can no longer work as a butcher. He reflects, "My livelihood was lost and butchering was no longer an option."[63] The job options he is now reduced to further undermine his self-identity, for they "felt like boy's work . . . like women's work."[64] The self-analogy migrating from "vulture" to "boy" and "women" directs the reader's attention to Jack's feeling of emasculation. Jack, not knowing who he is and what his purpose is in this world, cannot be a father to his little girl Veda. Jack's loss and anguish are vividly staged in a moment of frustration with his daughter. "*Do you want my blood? Do you want my last breath? I paid everyone back. I lost everything. Where is my fair share?*"[65]

Jack's cry echoes Leon's ranting, "'America,' . . . 'this lie of a country!'"[66] At the beginning of *Steer toward Rock*, Jack is a character who possesses youth, hope, and confidence, but midway Jack ends up in the same place as Leon: old, poor, and heart-broken. Ng seems to suggest that the fate of the paper son in Chinatown is loneliness and misery, because family and community in Chinese culture are supremely important for the individual's identity and happiness. The *Tongs* (family name associations) in Chinatowns provided support and service to Chinese immigrants. However, the paper son belonged neither to the Tong of his true name nor to the Tong of his paper name.

Erasure of identities and emasculation were experiences common to paper sons, and Chinatown was a social environment produced and reproduced by paper relations that propagate equally perilous blood relations. Paper sons—bachelors or married men—as portrayed by Ng endure lifelong guilt, shame, emasculation, and loss of identity. Jack's story is Leon's: brought to America by the same ship, passing interrogations at Angel Island, owing interminable debts to their paper fathers, and keeping unspeakable secrets that impair their parenthood. Neither can experience normative family life. Through their stories, Ng invites her reader to remember the lost generations of Chinese Americans during the exclusion era and afterwards. Jack's and Leon's lives in Chinatown, from youth and hope to disappointment, struggle, and loss, typify the fate of the paper son and the aging bachelor. Even after they father children, they continue the lifestyle of bachelors. Interestingly, Ng gives neither male character a male heir, but it is their daughters who eventually come to their fathers' rescue.

Leila and Veda, American-born daughters to Leon and Jack, inherit their fathers' stories, and what these daughters do with their inheritances becomes part of the genealogy of their paper-son fathers. In *Bone*, Leila discovers Leon's stories in his suitcase holding every piece of paper he has regarded important. The story told by his collection of letters and documents is the life-long rejections Leon has endured—"We Don't Want You."[67] She remarks,

> Leon kept things because he believed time mattered. . . . All the letters addressed to Leon should prove to the people at the social security office that this country was his place, too. Leon had paid; Leon had earned his rights. American dollars. American time. These letters marked his time and they marked his endurance. Leon was a paper son.[68]

Here Leila underscores Leon's entitlement to the imagined community of America through his labor. Leon's stories, however, are transformative of Leila, who comes to embrace Leon's history despite her frustration with him. She tells herself, "I'm the stepdaughter of a paper son and I've inherited this whole suitcase of lies. All of it is mine. All I have is those memories, and I want to remember them all."[69] "Remembering the past gives power to the present."[70] At the end, it is Leila who prepares Leon's document and takes him to the Social Security Office for an interview. Similarly, in *Steer toward Rock*, Veda learns about Jack's stories—he was sold by his mother at age five for $500 and immigrated to the United States under another man's name for $4000. She comments on his father's coaching book: "This book is my father's story. He memorized every lie in it and became another man's son. Now these lies have become his truth and his only truth is his love."[71] Veda learns that her father's coaching book is a map for survival in a hostile environment. The novel ends with Veda, now a grown woman, convincing her father to become legal through naturalization, to stake claim to the land and nation to which he has given everything he has. When compelled by the immigration officer to choose a name for his legal identity, Jack wants both. He cannot choose between his true identity and his paper identity, which has now become his true identity. Veda chooses for him. She declares, "I chose Jack Moon Szeto. I chose his fake name, the name he lived half his life with, the name he made with his own sweat, the name he surrendered for love, the name that made him true."[72] In embracing their fathers' stories, Leila and Veda claim their inheritances and join their stories with their fathers'. In doing so, they critically expose the rigidity and singularity of legal identity and advocate the relational identity that is rendered meaningful and enduring by shared history.

Ng's Chinatown is a social environment that bears the history of racial antagonism in this country, a history that is symptomized in familial conflicts and results in private tragedies. By the rendering of the paper son's genealogy through the Chinatown stories of Leon Leong and Jack Szeto, Ng creates a social and material milieu that refuses to suppress the history of racist legislation and rejects the dominant narrative of historical progress. Articulating Chinatown and its social life against both the image of a tourist site and that of an ethnic ghetto, *Bone* and *Steer toward Rock* present "an archaeology of the richly sedimented, dialectical space of urban Chinatown community"[73] in San Francisco. It is in this environment that Ng portrays the hauntingly entangled lives of three generations.

NOTES

1. Fae Myenne Ng, *Bone* (New York: Hyperion, 1993), 145.
2. Fae Myenne Ng, *Steer toward Rock* (New York: Hyperion, 2008), 224.
3. Thomas W. Kim, "'For a paper son, paper is blood': Subjectivation and Authenticity in Fae Myenne Ng's *Bone*," *MELUS: Multi-Ethnic Literature of the United States* 24.4 (1999): 42.
4. Juliana Chang, "Melancholic Remains: Domestic and National Secrets in Fae Myenne Ng's *Bone*," *Modern Fiction Studies* 51.1 (2005): 114.
5. Ibid.
6. Ng, *Bone*, 145.
7. Named after the American Minister to China, Anson Burlingame, this treaty was signed in 1869 by the Emperor of China and the United States.
8. Angelo N. Ancheta, *Race, Rights, and the Asian American Experience* (New Brunswick: Rutgers University Press, 1998), 25.
9. Erika Lee, *At America's Gates* (Chapel Hill: University of North Carolina Press, 2003), 45.
10. Ibid.
11. Ibid., 190. Kitty Calavita points out the difficulties of enforcing the Chinese Exclusion Law because of the self-contradictory logic underlying "a number of the most stubborn difficulties that the Chinese inspectors and their superiors in the enforcement bureaucracy faced. For it was their task not only to define specifically what constituted an exempt class but to apply that definition to individual, concrete cases. In the process, not only did they confront the usual categorization difficulties, but also operational definitions that were inevitably no more than arbitrary occupational distinctions." Calavita, "The Paradoxes of Race, Class, Identity, and 'Passing': Enforcing the Chinese Exclusion Acts, 1882–1910," *Law and Social Inquiry* 25.1 (2000): 34.
12. Erika Lee, *At America's Gates*, 204.
13. Ibid., 195.
14. K. Scott Wong, introduction to *Paper Son, One Man's Story*, by Tung Pok Chin with Winifred Chin (Philadelphia: Temple University Press, 2000), xi.
15. Ng, *Steer toward Rock*, 3.
16. Ibid.
17. Ng, *Bone*, 9.
18. Ibid., 55.
19. Ng, *Steer toward Rock*, 4.
20. Ng, *Bone*, 3.
21. Judy Yung, *San Francisco's Chinatown* (Charleston, SC: Arcadia Publishing, 2006), 7.
22. Anthony W. Lee, *Picturing Chinatown: Art and Orientalism in San Francisco* (Berkeley: University of California Press, 2001), 9.

23. Ibid.
24. Yung, *San Francisco's Chinatown*, 7.
25. Ng, *Bone*, 7–8.
26. Ibid., 4.
27. Ibid.
28. Ng, *Steer toward Rock*, 73.
29. Ng, *Bone*, 4.
30. Ng, *Steer toward Rock*, 144.
31. Ng, *Bone*, 113.
32. Juliana Chang, "Melancholic Remains," 118.
33. Sucheng Chan, "The Exclusion of Chinese Women, 1870–1943," in *Entry Denied: Exclusion and the Chinese Community in America, 1882–1943*, ed. Sucheng Chan (Philadelphia: Temple University Press, 1991), 97.
34. Expatriation Act 1907, in *The Statutes at Large and Proclamations of the United States of America from December 1869 to March 1871*, ed. George P. Sanders, vol. 34, 1228 (Boston: Little, Brown, and Company, 1871).
35. Erika Lee, *At America's Gates*, 117.
36. Roger Daniels, *Asian America: Chinese and Japanese in the United States since 1850* (Seattle: University of Washington Press, 1988), 16.
37. Maxine Hong Kingston vividly describes the patriarchal values in Chinatown in *The Woman Warrior: Memoirs of a Girlhood among Ghosts* (New York: Vintage, 1975).
38. Ng, *Bone*, 7.
39. Ng, *Steer toward Rock*, 19.
40. Ibid., 8.
41. Ibid., 11.
42. Ibid., 19. In Chinese literary tradition Peach Blossom connotes sexual romance.
43. Ibid., 17.
44. Ibid., 57.
45. Ibid., 63.
46. Ibid., 104.
47. Ng, *Bone*, 56.
48. Ibid., 57.
49. Ibid., 50.
50. Ibid., 73.
51. Ng, *Steer toward Rock*, 176.
52. Donald C. Goellnicht, "Of Bones and Suicide: Sky Lee's *Disappearing Moon Café* and Fae Myenne Ng's *Bone*," *Modern Fiction Studies* 46.2 (2000): 304.
53. Ibid., 308.
54. Juliana Chang, "Melancholic Remains," 113.
55. Yoonmee Chang, "Chinese Suicide: Political Desire and Queer Exogamy in Fae Myenne Ng's *Bone*," *Modern Fiction Studies* 56.1 (2010): 93.
56. Ng, *Bone*, 103.
57. Daniels, *Asian America*, 19.
58. Ibid., 56.
59. Ibid., 62.
60. Ng, *Steer toward Rock*, 6.
61. Ibid., 8.
62. Ibid., 112–13.
63. Ibid., 119.
64. Ibid.
65. Ibid., 148.
66. Ng, *Bone*, 103.

67. Ibid., 57.
68. Ibid., 58.
69. Ibid., 61.
70. Ibid., 89.
71. Ng, *Steer toward Rock*, 220.
72. Ibid., 225.
73. Lisa Lowe, *Immigrant Acts: On Asian American Cultural Politics* (Durham: Duke University Press, 1996), 120.

BIBLIOGRAPHY

Ancheta, Angelo N. *Race, Rights, and the Asian American Experience*. New Brunswick: Rutgers University Press, 1998.
Calavita, Kitty. "The Paradoxes of Race, Class, Identity, and 'Passing': Enforcing the Chinese Exclusion Acts, 1882–1910." *Law and Social Inquiry* 25.1 (2000): 1–40.
Chan, Sucheng. "The Exclusion of Chinese Women, 1870–1943." In *Entry Denied: Exclusion and the Chinese Community in America, 1882–1943*, edited by Sucheng Chan, 94–146. Philadelphia: Temple University Press, 1991.
Chang, Juliana. "Melancholic Remains: Domestic and National Secrets in Fae Myenne Ng's *Bone*." *Modern Fiction Studies* 51.1 (2005): 110–33.
Chang, Yoonmee. "Chinese Suicide: Political Desire and Queer Exogamy in Fae Myenne Ng's *Bone*." *Modern Fiction Studies* 56.1 (2010): 90–112.
Daniels, Roger. *Asian America: Chinese and Japanese in the United States since 1850*. Seattle: University of Washington Press, 1988.
Expatriation Act 1907. In *The Statutes at Large and Proclamations of the United States of America from December 1869 to March 1871*, edited by George P. Sanders, vol. 34, 1228. Boston: Little, Brown, and Company, 1871.
Goellnicht, Donald C. "Of Bones and Suicide: Sky Lee's *Disappearing Moon Café* and Fae Myenne Ng's *Bone*." *Modern Fiction Studies* 46.2 (2000): 300–30.
Kim, Thomas W. "'For a paper son, paper is blood': Subjectivation and Authenticity in Fae Myenne Ng's *Bone*." *MELUS: Multi-Ethnic Literature of the United States* 24.4 (1999): 41–56.
Kingston, Maxine Hong. *The Woman Warrior: Memoirs of a Girlhood among Ghosts*. New York: Vintage, 1975.
Lee, Anthony W. *Picturing Chinatown: Art and Orientalism in San Francisco*. Berkeley: University of California Press, 2001.
Lee, Erika. *At America's Gates*. Chapel Hill: University of North Carolina Press, 2003.
Lowe, Lisa. *Immigrant Acts: On Asian American Cultural Politics*. Durham: Duke University Press, 1996.
Ng, Fae Myenne. *Bone*. New York: Hyperion, 1993.
———. *Steer toward Rock*. New York: Hyperion, 2008.
Wong, K. Scott. Introduction to *Paper Son, One Man's Story*, by Tung Pok Chin with Winifred Chin, xi–xx. Philadelphia: Temple University Press, 2000.
Yung, Judy. *San Francisco's Chinatown*. Charleston, SC: Arcadia Publishing, 2006.

3 "Delving and Carving Rude Nature"
An Ecocritical Reading of Don Lee's *Wrack and Ruin*

Bella Adams

Staple genres of American environmental literature such as nature-writing and the pastoral have tended to be by, for, and about privileged whites, typically Thoreauvian types whose relationships with nature apparently enable their self-recovery by seemingly offering a simpler, more rewarding life divorced from degraded urban environments. Rather than approaching nature as a privileged white refuge, race scholars, including environmental justice critics, postcolonial ecocritics, and a growing number of Asian Americanists, historicize the category of nature in order to understand how nonhuman environments and affiliated discourses are constructed. Through a process of historicization, so-called natural landscapes, for example, Thoreau's New England pond, John Muir's Californian mountains, and Aldo Leopold's Wisconsin sand counties, become national landscapes. The American ideology of geopolitical mobility may encourage the belief that all citizens are equally entitled to frequent or inhabit these national-natural landscapes, but, crucially, not all are afforded equal recognition in mainstream discourses as having been there, much less of belonging there, because these landscapes are racialized. As T. V. Reed observes in a slightly different context, "white folks go to play with wilderness, while others are locked into urban 'jungles.'"[1]

Geopolitically confined thus, nonwhite others are assumed to contribute little to the historical formation of national-natural landscapes. Just as a New England pond is most readily associated with a white man, rather than Chinese itinerant workers,[2] the nineteenth-century American West where Asian immigrants worked in large numbers is generally assumed to be white: "Just who built California?" asks a working-class white man. "Certainly not the Chinese, Japanese, and Hindus."[3] This impoverished view of American history provides Leopold with a pertinent environmental analogy when he observes that "a dead Chinaman" and "the erasure of Silphium" are "largely painless—to us" because "we grieve only for what we know."[4] Such limited perspectives have effectively whitened labor and environmental histories, if not national-natural landscapes per se, thus leaving unacknowledged the parts played by nonwhites in their construction.

Necessary for historical revision are more creative analyses of the racial-ized nature/culture dynamic beyond the Eurocentrism that powerfully determines both conventional and cultural nationalist discourses, albeit for different reasons. Indeed, Asian American cultural nationalism and Asian American Studies have traditionally defined themselves as human-centered or anthropocentric discourses critical of domestic social injustices which are so forcefully felt that references to nature seem, at best, anachronistic or irrelevant and, at worst, politically dangerous. Such references potentially contribute to what Sau-ling Cynthia Wong terms "denationalization" or "the easing of cultural nationalist concerns"[5] that began in the 1980s at a time of white racial backlash against antiracist policies. Although Wong's critical foci are recent linguistic and transnational turns, an ecocritical turn towards the nonhuman environment could also be understood as contribut-ing to this so-called denationalizing trajectory. In light of continuing racial inequalities, Wong demands that Asian Americanists focus antiracist cri-tique on domestic social issues, rather than turn away from them to indulge in what are for her privileged discourses about language/theory, transna-tionalism, and, by extension, ecocriticism.

Wong's is a powerful argument, not least because her binary oppositions between theory and politics, domestic and diasporic, nature and culture cir-culate institutionally, although it is important to note that they do so *against* Asian American history and literature. In this latter regard, Tomo Hattori, for one, insists on recognizing the "extravagance" of Asian American writ-ing so as to "liberate . . . both textual and historical moments in Asian American culture that would otherwise be repressed by the need to conform to the ideological and canonical proprieties of a conventional national lit-erature."[6] In ecocritical terms, the chief propriety is the racialized nature/culture binary opposition that both conventional and cultural nationalists endorse. In so doing, these discourses repress the fact that the nonhuman environment is important to Asian American culture—although not neces-sarily as a pastoral retreat.

In Asian American history and literature, the nonhuman environment often represents a site of hard labor or, worse, entrapment and death.[7] More-over, rhetorical appeals to nature have helped legitimate anti-Asian racism via assumed connections between Asianness, germs, plants, and animals: from "eroticized . . . exotic playthings" like Madame Butterfly and Lotus Blossom,[8] to altogether more "ugly," "degraded," and "beastly"[9] things such as "poisonous weeds,"[10] scavenging "blackbirds,"[11] and "the almond-eyed Mongoloid . . . waiting to assassinate you and your children with one of his many maladies."[12] This anti-Asian history emerged most powerfully in the American West, chiefly in California where the labor market was vio-lently divided between whites and Asians (and Mexicans), with nonwhites working as "voiceless 'hands,'" especially in agriculture.[13] Clearly, nature is always already in Asian American culture, typically as a blind spot that it is a task of Asian American ecocriticism to articulate in ways that can serve both social and environmental justice agendas through consideration of how nature is shaped by class-race politics, and how art (about nature) can generate understanding of more ethical interpersonal and interspecies relationships.

The Korean American writer Don Lee contributes to this debate between cultural nationalism and so-called denationalizing perspectives. Mainstream reviews of his work praise the complexity of his representation of Asian America. Of his short-story collection, *Yellow* (2001), one reviewer asserts that Lee's "Asian American characters represent the new California, no longer boxed in by exoticized definitions,"[14] while his first novel, *Country of Origin* (2004), has been admired for its depiction of characters who do not "stay . . . put in one nation or one race and nobody's identity remains fixed."[15] Although it is set in one location, Lee's 2008 novel *Wrack and Ruin* resists static racialized definitions principally in terms of characterization.

Familiar to readers of *Yellow*, the fictional small Californian town of Rosarita Bay provides *Wrack and Ruin* with the pastoralized setting for Lee's two Asian American protagonists, Lyndon and Woody Song, to pursue identities economically and culturally tied to nature, principally through their respective roles as farmer/artist and developer/aesthete. This setting and these roles raise questions about Asian American identity vis-à-vis the American pastoral tradition and by extension mainstream environmental and aesthetic discourses. Lee's protagonists may consider Rosarita Bay a refuge, but their respective returns to an environment with a history so powerfully shaped by Eurocentric attitudes to nature and nonwhites serve to complicate the American pastoralist tradition. This tradition is further problematized by nature insofar as it resists anthropocentric appropriation in a range of environmental discourses from development to its apparent opposite mainstream conservation. Both of these discourses are satirized in Lee's novel in order to expose their ideological limitations, a critical approach also adopted towards cultural nationalism. Of Lee's human characters, it is his eco-artist who most strongly feels the limitations of a racialized aesthetic when his peers criticize him for "trying to deny his cultural heritage and whitewashing himself."[16] It seems that nature is off limits to him for a reason that is only too clear to another of Lee's artists who announces that such charges of race betrayal emerge from "the white hegemony."[17]

This ecocritical reading of *Wrack and Ruin* responds to such debate about Asian American eco-art in three interrelated ways: first, by highlighting the limitations of traditional identity politics for Asian American self-understanding; second, by historicizing nature in terms of class-race politics made possible by an ecocritical reading of the novel's California Labor Day setting; and third, by demonstrating how eco-art can generate understanding of more ethical interpersonal and interspecies relationships beyond mainstream environmental and cultural nationalist discourses. By calling into question often binary political, aesthetic, and environmental debates, *Wrack and Ruin* helps to liberate not only Asian American identity and art but also American ecocriticism from ideological and canonical norms, crucially *without* abandoning a commitment to social and environmental justice agendas.

NATURE AND ASIAN AMERICAN IDENTITY

Lee's Asian American characters in *Yellow, Country of Origin,* and *Wrack and Ruin* tend not to adhere to a singular racialized identity. His prose transgresses traditional racial categories in ways that help to demonstrate the limitations of a question fundamental to both conventional and cultural nationalisms: "What are you?"[18] Although vital to civil rights and antiracist critique, this question can lead to a politics that bypasses the complexity of Asian Americanness, with the unintended consequence of bolstering racism. In Lee's bildungsroman short story, "Yellow," for example, the Korean American protagonist Danny Kim repeatedly grapples with this question, although its racist underpinnings are only made explicit to him in the early 1980s at a time of white racial backlash against increasingly competitive Asian "tiger" economies. "Yellow" references the racist murder in 1982 of Chinese American Vincent Chin by two unemployed white autoworkers who declare, "'It's because of little Jap[s] . . . like you that the car industry's going down the tubes,' and then got off on probation."[19] For Danny, this state-sanctioned, racist murder highlights the main limitation of the identitarian question, which turns out not to be a question about "you" at all, only an assertion about "us" as Americans against a singular Asianness regarded as foreign.

Questioning traditional identity politics further by shifting from "what you are" to "what you do," *Wrack and Ruin* represents two Korean-Chinese American brothers whose self-understanding develops through work aligned to nature. Lyndon is an eco-artist and organic Brussels sprouts farmer, while his brother Woody is a corrupt investment banker turned first-time film producer and would-be developer (by association). Only recently reunited after a sixteen-year estrangement following Woody's indictment for embezzlement, to the financial cost of the family, the brothers nevertheless remain opposed in their appearances, behaviors, and attitudes to the environment. Their differences are reinforced when Woody betrays Lyndon to his archrival, the developer Ed Kitchell of The Centurion Group. With support from Rosarita Bay business folk, Ed wants to transform Lyndon's organic farm into a toxic golf course for an oceanfront residential/tourist complex, complete with "Romanesque . . . McMansions."[20] Further reinforcing these links with European and American imperialisms in the form of the "Mc" prefix that signifies cultural homogeneity, or McDonaldization, is Ed's super-white masculine identity, represented by his strong jaw, blonde hair, and heroic triumphalism. This cultural homogeneity reaches a global scale by virtue of a multinational corporation with financial interests in both

The Centurion Group and the European distributor of Woody's film; on their discovery of the Songs' relationship, the investors ask Woody to persuade Lyndon to accept The Group's multi-million dollar land deal.

Lyndon disputes The Group's development plans, typically via "monkey wrenching"[21] techniques against Ed that resemble children's pranks rather than anything more insidious. Although Lyndon does not self-identify as an environmentalist as such, other characters in the novel do, including ecofeminist lesbian couple, Trudy Nguyen and Margot Schrempp, and the Planet Liberation Front (PLF). Trudy and Margot articulate eco-populist or New Age theories that are part Buddhist, part deep ecology, and part lobbyist in their promotion of all-too familiar ecological principles—"everything is related. . . . There's a dynamic balance between every organism"[22]—against Western philosophical and religious dualisms, specifically, for Trudy, patriarchal philosophical aesthetics. The two women also volunteer on seabird restoration projects and are currently relocating a western snowy plover family displaced by The Group's development. Conservation seems not to concern the PLF, however, whose monkey wrenching or ecotage proves altogether more destructive. Although intended for The Group's water supply, one such act of ecotage pollutes Lyndon's irrigation pond instead. With his Brussels sprout crop poisoned, Lyndon is finally forced to sell his farm—to a non-profit conservationist land trust, rather than to The Centurion Group.

In this land dispute, Lee's characters articulate a range of environmental and aesthetic ideologies, the most politicized of which protest against the instrumental whiteness of The Group and Ed, to which Woody also subscribes for financial reasons considered crucial to his sense of identity. In contrast, Lyndon and Trudy define themselves against neo-imperial capitalist development and aestheticized visions of nature. With its characters and ideologies so clearly split along binary and hierarchical lines, *Wrack and Ruin* makes obvious its critique of instrumental views of nature, but crucially not without complicating and interrogating this politics. Not even pastoral retreat can resolve the natural and cultural crises in the novel since it comes with its own class, race, and environmental politics. While Trudy's ecopolitics and, for that matter, a multinational corporation demonstrate how everything is related, *Wrack and Ruin* offers a more radical understanding of interrelatedness that helps to reveal a long history of Asian American experiences of nonhuman environments, contrary to the norms of American ecocriticism and Asian American Studies.

ECOCRITICISM AND ASIAN AMERICAN HISTORY

Rather than simply adding Asian Americans to rural environments, *Wrack and Ruin* adopts a more radical approach that in part emerges from an ecocritical reading of setting. According to Lawrence Buell, a key "ingredient . . . [of] an environmentally oriented work" is close attention to setting, or "*the nonhuman environment,*" which is "*present not merely as a framing device but as a presence.*"[23] Importantly, he continues, this presence is in "*process,*" and "*begins to suggest that human history is implicated in natural history.*"[24] *Wrack and Ruin* is closely tied to a familiar (for Lee's readers) and specific setting of small-town California over the Labor Day holiday weekend, these geographical and historical details in particular helping to promote an understanding of the novel's setting in terms of its significance for human/nonhuman relationships. The social and environmental implications of these relationships are made especially clear in *Wrack and Ruin*'s explanation of Labor Day. Quoting from a speech made in 1882 by labor leader Peter J. McGuire, one of Lee's minor characters explains that this end-of-summer public holiday celebrates the American workers "who from rude nature have delved and carved all the grandeur we behold."[25]

Before its un/official celebration in 1882 and 1894 respectively, American labor, particularly that performed by the husbandman[26] and the artisan,[27] was considered crucial to nation-building. From the 1780s, right through to the Civil War, these celebrated figures represented Americanness increasingly against a mass of exploited and often unskilled or semi-skilled workers. Under industrial capitalism, exploitation increased, but so did labor organization in the form of union-backed strikes and demonstrations determined to dignify even the lowliest of workers with better conditions and higher wages—at least if they were white.

In a "creative use of language, performance, and ritual," write Michael Kazin and Stephen J. Ross, the first unofficial Labor Day parade combined different public events, including the strike demonstration, the medieval artisan festival, the patriotic pageant or election rally, and the community picnic where workers were treated to entertainment and oratory, all for the purpose of promoting class-national consciousness in a political and economic environment increasingly hostile to organized labor for disrupting production.[28] "Time is money," although, as Leigh Eric Schmidt observes of this "old Yankee maxim, . . . the commercialization of the calendar would give [it] new meaning" because disruption to production opened up possibilities for consumption at official Labor Day events, with Labor Day floats, stalls, and sales providing excellent advertising and purchasing opportunities that ultimately proved more appealing than class-conscious oratory.[29] According to Kazin and Ross, the development of a consumer society contributed to Labor Day's "'politically anesthetized' status,"[30] so much so that today it seems to represent little more than seasonal holiday when, as Ellen Litwicki describes, "Americans make one last pilgrimage to the beach or the mountains, do some last-minute school shopping, or gather for a final summer barbecue."[31]

Lee's Rosarita Bay offers its visitors and inhabitants alike a Labor Day festival that seems similarly anesthetized by economic or commercial concerns. The festivities are sponsored by The Centurion Group, although its McDonaldizing approach has developed into a folksy multiculturalism promulgating local and exotic arts and crafts. Although this festival seems to promote diversity, Lyndon observes that it is marked by homogeneity mass-produced for such "manufactured occasion[s]."[32] His obvious disdain for the festival's commercialism aside, Lyndon does gain a sense of belonging from attending it: "He was part of this town, and . . . it was part of him. Not a single person . . . mentioned The Centurion Group's bid to buy out his farm."[33]

This rhetorical strategy whereby the land dispute is mentioned by not being mentioned, together with an ecocritical reading of the novel's California Labor Day setting, helps to ensure that *Wrack and Ruin* works against mainstream tendencies to politically anesthetize this public holiday. Labor Day may honor American workers, but importantly the social inclusiveness of this category is undermined by the assumption of white privilege as it is reinforced by dominant ideologies, including nativism, racism, and pastoralism. This assumption helps to obscure a nonwhite history of hard labor in hazardous natural and social environments, particularly in nineteenth-century California.

In mainstream American history, California is accorded a special place on environmental and social grounds. "From 1870 to 1940," Kazin observes, "California left its glorious isolation on the fringe of European settlement and became both an economic giant and a significant political region."[34] Commenting on its history up until the 1890s, Frederick Jackson Turner noted that California was "distinctive" among the frontiers because of a wealth of natural resources.[35] In his view, the adventurous frontiersman was most capable of resource exploitation, and was rewarded financially for it, although, as Turner makes clear, even greater rewards could be had from an instrumental view of nature, specifically building the nation (and empire) up from "savagery" towards agriculture and industry in ways he decreed both inevitable and natural: "Thus civilization in America has followed the arteries made by geology, pouring an ever richer tide through them," comprising "individualism, democracy, and nationalism [that] powerfully affected the East and the Old World."[36] Whether materially or ideologically conceived, this rich tide as it was exploited by whites (using nonwhite "hands") helped make California distinctive economically, politically, and environmentally. In this latter regard, California and other western states were a focus of early American political and literary environmentalisms, most notably the world's first national parks and nature writing.

California also holds a special place in Asian American history, which stretches back to the sixteenth century, although it was not until the 1849 Gold Rush that Asian workers arrived in significant numbers to work in the extraction industries and, later, in construction, manufacturing, and agriculture.[37] For white Californians, however, Chinese "coolie" labor was too pervasive: "Every branch of industry in the State of California swarms with Chinese . . . a barbarous race, devoid of energy and careless of the State's weal," whose "debasement" threatens to "ruin . . . the capitalist and poor man together."[38] In a battle of "American Manhood against Asiatic Coolieism," or as two influential labor leaders put it, "Meat vs. Rice,"[39] whites in California and later the nation put class and other differences aside by uniting against a common enemy in exclusion leagues and labor organizations—to momentous effect in 1882. This year saw not only the first unofficial Labor Day parade, but also the first Asian Exclusion Act against the Chinese. Subsequent Labor Days provided further opportunity to demand Asian exclusion for reasons of white self-defense consistent with biopolitics. For example, the 1907 Labor Day in Bellingham, Washington, saw whites riot against "cheap" labor performed by Hindu workers who, as one local newspaper reported, "contribute nothing to the growth and upbuilding of the city as a result of their labors," and so should depart to make room for more desirable and supportive white workers.[40] Some newspapers criticized mob violence, but not its aims or ends: "When men who require meat to eat and real beds to sleep in are ousted from their employment to make room for [Asians] . . . it is rather difficult to say at what limit indignation ceases to be righteous."[41]

While American racist and nativist ideologies help to maintain white privilege in mainstream national and labor histories, American pastoralism bolsters this politics by depicting nature as a refuge for dominant white masculinity, rather than a site of hard labor. As such, pastoralism reinforces at least two marginalizations—of nonwhites and nonhumans. For Robert T. Hayashi, this division between nature and hard labor obscures the fact that Asian American and other nonwhite workers were "often the very engine of environmental change, . . . the land's miners, railroad workers, farm hands, and fisherman: its workers,"[42] in favor of an idealized form of white labor performed by husbandman and artisan. This hierarchy of labor effectively ensures that the changed nonhuman environment also functions as a site of white self-recovery, even if it is only during weekends and holidays. The acts of "delving and carving" so celebrated on Labor Day thus apply as much to the material and ideological formation of the nation and the people therein, as they do to "rude nature," if only ever partially since the realization of the national-natural landscape as a privileged white refuge occurs not in spite of but because of violent exploitation of nonwhites and nonhumans alike.

In Asian American literature, California also resonates powerfully, with early canonical texts from Carlos Bulosan's *America Is in the Heart* (1946) to Louis Chu's *Eat a Bowl of Tea* (1961) typically identifying Californian landscapes as "the center" and "the heart" of Asian America.[43] These texts represent California as originary for Asian American masculinity, and, in so doing, rework the American pastoral political ideal of nature as a privileged white refuge. Despite his experiences of racism, Bulosan's narrator observes towards the end of his personal history as an itinerant worker that California is where he belongs, "here in the color of green, the bitter taste of lemon peels, the yellow of ripe peas; in the pleasure, the beauty, the fragrance."[44] California also appeals to Chu's impotent and cuckolded protagonist who moves from New York to San Francisco to start a new life. Soon after his arrival, he eats a bowl of herbal tea that cures more than his impotence: "New frontiers, new people, new times, new ideas unfolded. He had come to a new golden mountain."[45] Their respective returns to California make possible self-recovery, the sexual politics of these experiences most clearly portrayed in Chu's novel when the protagonist regains his manhood by becoming a husband and a father.

Lee follows this literary tradition when in *Wrack and Ruin*'s opening pages "California"[46] is given a sentence of its own. In relation to its Labor Day setting, this one-word sentence serves to highlight the state's importance to Asian American masculinity, specifically the history of hard labor in hostile natural and social environments powerfully determined by Eurocentrism. Unlike Bulosan's working-class narrator, however, Lee's middle-class Asian American protagonists are not economically compelled to return to California to work as "hands" in conditions akin to slavery. At worst, the Song brothers' education and employment histories are a little checkered, their class position ultimately providing them with levels of security and mobility not available to their predecessors. With this said, however, Lyndon and Woody still feel a compulsion to return to California for ideological reasons linked to racist stereotyping, specifically the model minority that accords some white, middle-class advantages to certain Asian Americans in order to sustain the national myth of racial democracy.

Lyndon and Woody have different experiences of the model minority stereotype and different levels of insight about it. Lyndon's ecocritical turn apparently away from culture to nature seems to make him "the Uncle Tong of the art world," whereas Woody is so desperate to succeed educationally and economically that he cheats on his exams and embezzles at a bank, all so that he can rank himself among "the Future Leaders of the Ruling Privileged Wasp Elite."[47] Occurring in New York, Cambridge, and Boston, these negative experiences damage the brothers psychologically, almost to the point of suicide, so they independently decide to return west hoping for self-recovery. Lyndon's return to Rosarita Bay is meant to restore his sense of integrity, the so-called simple life of a farmer (and possible father) proving preferable to New York, which he perceives as increasingly hostile, socially and environmentally.

Woody's return to California, specifically Los Angeles, allows him to begin again as a film producer, although his seemingly more profound reinvention from capitalist destroyer to ecophilic savior occurs on Lyndon's farm. While the Song brothers regard the farm as a refuge, *Wrack and Ruin* does not lose sight of the class-race reasons underpinning their desire for pastoral retreat from a stereotype that although not obviously as life-threatening as those confronting their predecessors can still reap damage.

Although Rosarita Bay is regarded as a refuge by Lyndon and Woody, if not a good many of Lee's characters, because it seems so close to nature, *Wrack and Ruin* problematizes American pastoralism, as this ideology also informs mainstream environmentalism. An older generation of Rosarita Bay townsfolk opposes industrial and commercial expansion, although their commitment to environmentalism is satirized as NIMBY-ism (Not In My Back Yard) and other eco-populist practices that are mainly pursued for personal and demographic reasons. To this generation's dismay, new people do move to the town, with their gated community, trendy art gallery, and New Age health center suggesting that they are also in search of pastoral retreat. Even Ed the developer believes that Rosarita Bay offers him the possibility of a simpler and more meaningful life. Despite their different attitudes to the environment, the town's inhabitants are typically motivated by anthropocentric concerns that belie their retreat into a supposedly more natural environment. Moreover, the green areas they hold so dear, including chemically-maintained farmland and golf course, turn out to be toxic environments.

Whether Lee's characters want to escape from industry, commerce, people, or the class-race pressures of the model minority, *Wrack and Ruin* suggests that the nonhuman environment ultimately resists these (and other) ideological or anthropocentric appropriations. Indeed, Rosarita Bay is generally inhospitable to humans: its isolated geography and rainy weather are more suited to Brussels sprouts (and other plants like artichokes, pumpkins, and marijuana) than tourists whose visits are further disrupted by inadequate road links prone to landslides. Most disruptive to Rosarita Bay becoming a tourist destination, at least from the perspective of The Centurion Group, is a decomposing humpback whale calf that mysteriously comes and goes. This dead animal is described as Ed's "personal Moby-Dick,"[48] a literary allusion that serves to highlight how Lee's whale also exposes human limitations vis-à-vis irrepressible nature. Ed cannot accommodate the putrid carcass in his pastoral touristic vision of Rosarita Bay, with even the marine agencies denying responsibility for this sea animal. Lacking a place in human and nonhuman environments, the humpback whale is, not surprisingly, an endangered species. Equally, there seems to be no place for the novel's other endangered species, the western snowy plover family whose chicks are at risk from The Group's toxic development. Even Lyndon's pet dog Bob is at risk from poisoning by industrial and everyday domestic chemicals. Lee's use of infantilized animals that are vulnerable even in their home environments seems to make plain the novel's politics for environmentalism against neo-imperial capitalist development.

Importantly, however, *Wrack and Ruin* upsets this politics, not for the purpose of undermining environmental justice, but for complicating more mainstream or eco-populist versions of it that typically view environmental struggle in binary terms which pit ecocentric saviors against anthropocentric destroyers. Despite Trudy and Margot's best conservation efforts, the plover chicks die towards the end of the novel. The two women are nearly killed at Rosarita Bay's Labor Day festival by the Asian elephant Esther after she is freed by the Planet Liberation Front. Ironically, perhaps, it is capitalist developer Woody who rescues Trudy and Margot. Woody also rescues Bob following his near-fatal poisoning in the PLF's act of ecotage that forces Lyndon to sell his farm to the land trust, despite Ed and Woody's best efforts to persuade him otherwise. Regardless of Lee's characters' intentions towards nature, it remains indifferent to human intentionality in ways that serve to decenter anthropocentrism in a range of environmental ideologies, from development to its apparent opposite, mainstream conservation. Importantly, however, *Wrack and Ruin* does not simply abandon environmental justice, since the recognition of nonhuman indifference and human-centeredness in fact makes possible more ethical human/nonhuman relationships.

ECOCRITICISM AND ASIAN AMERICAN ART

Wrack and Ruin explores the possibility of developing these more ethical human/nonhuman relationships via art. While an ecocritical reading of the novel's setting serves to decenter Eurocentrism and anthropocentrism in social and environmental histories, an analysis of its thematic emphasis on aesthetics reinforces this critique of white privilege as it operates in and beyond the novel. Many of Lee's characters work in the culture industries, and their experiences as artists inform a metafictional debate about aesthetic and political freedoms. Lee's Asian American film director, Dalton Lee, articulates this debate in typically forthright terms that arguably echo the views of critics who affirm Asian American heterogeneity against oppressive norms: "Look," says Dalton, "I'm not naïve. Nothing happens in this country without the involutions of race. But if we let it dictate what we can and cannot do and start limiting ourselves as artists, then we're no longer free. We're oppressed. We're slaves."[49]

Lee's thematic emphasis on aesthetics is reinforced by his representation of a debate about modern philosophical aesthetics that powerfully determines responses to nature and art. The "dead white male chauvinist" philosopher Edmund Burke is a main target of critique for ecofeminist Trudy, who proclaims that his aesthetic judgments are ethically and epistemologically problematic since they reduce nature to a source of white male "self-propagation" and "self-preservation."[50] For her, nature is best approached from a position of humility, informed by Buddhist and deep ecology principles that question the human/nonhuman hierarchy and recognize nature's intrinsic value without recourse to dominant white men. From this more ecocentric position, Trudy perceives the value of even the smallest pebble, the marks of change on its surface helping to ensure that it exceeds Burke's aesthetic ideology, if not patriarchal philosophical aesthetics per se.

Trudy's ecofeminist critique of Burke's aesthetic ideology seems to have a profound effect on Woody by informing his transformation from chemically-maintained "germaphobe"[51] to ecophilic savior. The impact of his eco-education is intensified by experiences related to (near) death and sex, or self-preservation and self-propagation, when he gets caught in quicksand and is rescued by Trudy and Margot, who then take him to a hot spring where they indulge themselves. Later, Woody ventures into the woods where he defecates and uses leaves to clean himself. This is a transformative experience for such a germaphobic character, and one apparently worthy of Burkean aesthetic judgment: "Beauty has nurtured me, and I know what terror is now, I've seen the sublime in it. I've encountered the other, and conquered it. I've never been so alive."[52] However, Woody's self-propagation is limited when the leaves turn out to be poison oak, which causes genital itching so uncomfortable that his masculinist conquering of nature is satirically undermined.

Like Woody, Lyndon describes his experiences of nature utilizing a sexual politics, although, importantly, his love is less anthropocentrically conceived since it emerges from a more humble position akin to Trudy's ecopolitics. As an organic farmer vulnerable to unpredictable nature, Lyndon is made to feel "insignificant, and paradoxically that feeling was useful, freeing."[53] This feeling not only seems to free him from the megalomaniac self and judgmental others, but it also informs many of the novel's natural descriptions. Although they are idealized, these descriptions tend towards simplicity rather than hyperbole. For example:

> Lyndon . . . heard the call of a red-winged blackbird, *check, deeek,* and turned toward a stand of red alders. He stared at the lichen and moss mottling the bark, a swaying branch, the bobbing yellow catkins, and there, spreading its wings, was the bird, glossy black, with startling red patches on its shoulders.
>
> Out here, Lyndon's senses always felt heightened, everything—light, shadows, contours, textures, colors—more vivid. The quiet mornings alone in the fields, next to the sea, they were what he loved most about farming. The purity of the natural world, and the sweet gestation and growth, the blooming of his labors.[54]

There is a sense here that the nonhuman environment exists in its own right, with even a "voice" of its own in the form of the blackbird's "*check, deeek,*" which is onomatopoeically rendered without being forced to signify in exclusively ideological or anthropocentric terms. The italicized script further suggests the "purity" of "*check, deeek*" from human thought and behaviors, as does Lee's tendency to use simple sentences in which Lyndon's sensory experiences are minimally described. Lyndon hears and stares but does not presume to conquer nature through Burkean aesthetic judgments. Indeed, Lyndon's is a more ecocentric human/nonhuman relationship (almost) based on reciprocity. This reciprocity is suggested by tropes that blur or deconstruct the human/nonhuman hierarchy so fundamental to patriarchal philosophical aesthetics: Lyndon's labors bloom, but, importantly, Brussels sprouts are also described as "fussy, eccentric vegetables"[55] that are paradoxically resistant to anthropocentric appropriation.

Aesthete Woody provides a further point of contrast with Lyndon in their different approaches to art (about nature). Again, Woody expects to conquer or, at the very least, grasp the significance of Lyndon's eco-art, arguably the sort of expectation that forced Lyndon to withdraw from the New York art scene at the height of his fame. Over his short yet lucrative art career, Lyndon develops an aesthetic represented by three sequences of welded sculptures made from bits of recycled metal acquired from junk-yards and construction sites. His is not a Burkean aesthetic designed to nurture and reassure; rather, the key principles informing his art are dynamism and destabilization.

Lyndon's first set of sculptures is untitled, and inspired by a memory of his parents' Korean screen featuring "a continuous landscape of lotus blossoms, fish and birds."[56] The lack of title, alongside this emphasis on continuity in nature, time, and space helps to generate the disorientating effect of Lyndon's aesthetic. His sculptures attract the attention of SoHo gallery owner, Alvin Zukof, whose only proviso for helping Lyndon gain worldwide fame is contextualizing the sculptures. Alvin (re)names them and provides catalogue entries alerting the audience to contemporary theoretical perspectives, such as, for example, Georges Bataille's denunciation of Western industry and technology. In this way, Alvin provides the sculptures with ecocritical and transnational contexts, without mentioning race.

Race, however, is a key point of focus for Lyndon's critics: "Apparently he was not an artist. He was an Asian-American artist,"[57] although even this categorization is debatable since a racialized aesthetic dictates that both sculptor and sculptures are appreciated for their Asianness. Not only do the critics presume Lyndon's foreignness but they also claim to see in the metal scraps "ethnicity and identity," "assimilation and diaspora . . . racism and post-colonialism."[58] To them, barbed wire signifies the demilitarized zone between North and South Korea, while spaghetti-thin metal strips reference Marco Polo's appropriation of Chinese noodles. More outrageously still, Lyndon's critics interpret metal rods and wires in terms of a Korean aphrodisiac and they discuss Orientalist stereotypes demeaning Asian masculinity. Satirized thus, critical views of Lyndon's sculptures seem all the more inappropriate because emphasis is repeatedly given to their materiality; if the sculptures resemble anything at all, it is the nonhuman environment, not stereotypes of Asianness.

With Lyndon's second set of Chinese-ideogram sculptures, critical opinion divides along racial lines. While white critics praise his work, again, in terms of Orientalism, Asian American critics condemn the sculptures as fake because the Chinese characters are meaningless fabrications. For Asian American cultural nationalists in particular, authenticity is such an important issue because mainstream national discourses have historically promoted fake images of Asianness.[59] Any Asian American text that appears to fake the real, in Lyndon's case, blatantly so, risks the charge of race betrayal for personal gain from a reactionary form of multiculturalism that offers rich financial rewards to nonwhite artists who uncritically reproduce dominant ideologies. For faking Asianness apparently consistent with white standards, Lyndon is swiftly proclaimed the art world's Uncle Tong. From whomever they emerge, these standards serve to restrict Asian American creativity, an irony that *Wrack and Ruin* highlights most forcefully when Dalton asserts that whiteness underpins Asian American cultural nationalism. In Lyndon's case, this irony means that he is not Asian American enough, even when he seems at his most Asian American: "somewhat contradictorily, they condemned him for not challenging the media's narrow categorization of . . . 'Asian American,' for willingly ghettoizing himself."[60]

With Lyndon's third set of sculptures of birds, fish, and other sea animals that he saw on a trip to Belize, condemnation is universal. Alvin's title, "Certain Epistemological Issues of Bestial Perversion,"[61] highlights an ecocritical dimension, as do his references to Michel Foucault's concept of biopower and Jorge Luis Borges' Chinese animal taxonomy. Yet, the critics remain unconvinced by the Belizean animal sculptures: white critics proclaim them "unmitigated trash" and taxidermy, better suited to the American Museum of Natural History, whereas Asian American critics criticize Lyndon "for *not* including any discernible Asian references . . . regardless of what the catalogue was trying to appropriate."[62] Before, Lyndon's Asian American peers criticized his transnational perspective, or his (fake) Asian references, but now it seems that certain forms of transnationalism are permitted by them.

Generating further problems for the critics is Lyndon's emphasis on process over (a metaphysics of) of presence when he claims that his work tends towards banality rather than profundity. Significant in itself, the process of sculpting resists interpretation, even his, because it involves sensations rather than ideas. As he explains, but "not believing the words coming were coming from his mouth [,] 'I'd start a piece, and I'd just see it flowing in front of me, but it wasn't solid matter anymore, but viscous, with a life of its own.'"[63] Lyndon remains unconvinced by all attempts at profundity, particularly those that endow recycled bits of metal with Asian meanings and references against the sculptures' disorientating effects. Too disorientating—as is the case with the Belizean animal sculptures that seem to be neither art nor Asian—Lyndon is dismissed from the New York art scene, his work reduced to an object of ridicule and mere ornament. Alvin dismisses the critics as stupid, although his playful postmodern interpretation of Lyndon's eco-art also risks reducing it to a joke, thus missing Lyndon's, if not the novel's, point that Asian American eco-art has serious antiracist and other radical possibilities.

Seventeen years after leaving New York and arriving in Rosarita Bay, Lyndon still finds time after farming (and his casual jobs as a welder and barman) to do eco-art, albeit secretly in his barn. Here, he is free to work in a way that privileges process over (a metaphysics of) presence, or the banal practicalities of welding and sculpting, guided by sensations that are further enhanced by music and marijuana. The narrative moves towards disclosing Lyndon's secret and unfinished sculpture to its main characters in the form of a drug bust partly engineered by Woody, who confirms Ed's suspicions regarding Lyndon's cultivation of marijuana when a crop intended for personal use proves so successful that it attracts the attention of a drug dealer and the police. In a bitter act of fraternal betrayal, Woody (mis)informs Ed about Lyndon's so-called marijuana farm, thus making possible a resolution to the novel's land dispute—or so Ed hopes, until a Drug Enforcement Administration agent opens the barn doors:

> A cramped rain forest of gnarled alloys and steel . . . extending upward towards the roof . . . and spreading over the walls . . . populated by copper and aluminum birds of paradise, hawks, bats, butterflies, and cockatoos, . . . lotus blossoms, orchids, . . . and wild mushrooms, . . . geckoes and snails, and snakes, turtles and frogs and fish.[64]

This very large, interlinked, unfinished, and immobile structure seems useless in the traditional sense. Not deterred by the fact it cannot be displayed in a gallery or museum, Alvin gives it an eco-title that supports his comparison with a banyan tree and Lyndon's Belizean animal sculptures. But still the banyan tree sculpture defies meaning to those gathered at the barn. To them, it signifies artistic insanity, rather than, as Lyndon sees it, "a product of working without design or scheme or foreseeable end . . . unchecked by any aesthetic and commercial concerns; a product of an imagination allowed to run amok."[65] This sculpture disrupts all attempts at profundity, the banal processes involved in its production serving to reinforce a dynamic and disorienting aesthetic that is resistant to ideological and canonical norms. By defying these norms or an instrumentalist view of art (about nature), the banyan tree sculpture suggests the possibility of more ethical human/nonhuman relationships.

From the Korean-screen and Chinese-ideogram sculptures to the Belizean-animal and banyan-tree sculptures, Lyndon's unfinished body of work serves a metafictional function charting a so-called denationalizing trajectory that involves various turns towards transnational, linguistic, and, more recently, ecocritical perspectives. While it is possible to understand this trajectory in terms of race betrayal, *Wrack and Ruin* interrogates this argument by demonstrating that nature is important to Asian American history and art, contrary to a racialized aesthetic that operates in and beyond the novel. Indeed, Lyndon's aesthetic features plants and animals from start to (un)finish, and, in so doing, suggests a history of Asian American eco-art not traditionally acknowledged by cultural nationalists committed to a domestic social justice agenda. Somewhat paradoxically, social justice is compromised by this agenda, as Dalton makes clear when he criticizes the way in which a racialized aesthetic stifles Asian American artistic and political freedoms. Whether Asian American artists betray or observe a social justice agenda, their choice seems to be determined by the white hegemony, if only up to the point when Dalton asserts that even art *not* about race and identity *is* about race and identity, at least in such a thoroughly racialized nation as the United States. Just as nature is shaped by class-race politics, so is art, although, importantly, eco-art can generate understanding of more ethical human/nonhuman relationships.

Such relationships emerge via a decentering of anthropocentrism in art about nature. When directly asked about the meaning of the unfinished banyan-tree sculpture by Woody, Lyndon informs his brother that such a question misses the point. Instead, he argues, the point is "the process. Just doing the work"[66] in a creative and spontaneous way, beyond traditional aesthetic and political concerns. He explains that this way of working generates a sense of oneness with both art and nature, but, as Lyndon anticipates, Woody still misses the point. An ecocritical reading of their dialogue privileges ecocentrism over the artist's apparent egocentrism, and it also highlights the social and environmental benefits of acknowledging human limitations—even Woody's. Not understanding or conquering art and nature arguably makes possible a future for more ethical human/nonhuman relationships and, as it turns out, a fraternal relationship, too.

At the novel's end, the Song brothers form an uneasy alliance as they share a meal of meat, rice, and the few Brussels sprouts not poisoned by the Planet Liberation Front. Such an ending works on a number of levels relevant to both environmental and social discourses. It may be described as "a simple meal, not much of it, just the basic elements, but filling,"[67] but the ingredients and the fact that it is a shared meal serve to highlight how the production and consumption of food influences both interspecies and interpersonal relationships. Compared to traditional farming methods, an organic approach is shown to contribute to a more diverse ecosystem that benefits Lyndon, his Brussels sprouts, and other flora and fauna. The Song brothers also reap another benefit from food in the sense that the act of sharing a meal provides them with opportunities for improved self-understanding through a stronger fraternal relationship.

In keeping with the American pastoralist tradition, this positive ending highlights how simple, honest "food can be a source of material and cultural empowerment," although crucially not without forgetting that food and this tradition can simultaneously "reflect, and even create, social and economic hierarchies."[68] Apart from a fresh, local organic vegetable, the brothers' meal comprises meat and rice, a combination of ingredients that resonated so powerfully for influential labor leaders that they referenced them in their campaign leaflet, "Meat vs. Rice," supporting the extension of the 1882 Chinese Exclusion Act indefinitely. These labor leaders politicized what were for them incompatible foods and by extension incompatible masculinities and races. From an Asian American ecocritical perspective, the appearance of these foods on the Song brothers' plates serves as *Wrack and Ruin's* final reminder of a history of Asian American labor which, far from being incompatible with American national-natural landscapes, actually contributed to their formation.

An ecocritical reading of *Wrack and Ruin's* setting helps to establish Asian American masculinity in national-natural landscapes, particularly Californian landscapes so prized by influential figures in national, labor, and environmental histories, all of whom in their own ways vigorously affirm dominant white masculinity. Whether frontiersman, Thoreauvian, white worker, or, in Lee's novel, conquering aesthete and developer, such men are generally recognized for "delving and carving all the grandeur we behold" with little or no reference to nonwhite contributions to nation-building. At its worst, the removal of Asian immigrants and Asian Americans from national-natural landscapes and their affiliated discourses is justified according to a biopolitical rhetoric of white self-defense, reinforced through associations of Asianness with germs, plants, and animals. Asian American cultural nationalism seeks to resolve this historical marginalization, principally in terms of identity politics. As Lee's prose highlights, however, this politics can inadvertently bolster racism by homogenizing Asian Americanness against more diverse, multiracial and multicultural experiences, among them a long history of labor aligned to nature—from extraction and construction industries to, in *Wrack and Ruin,* farming, conservation, development, and eco-art.

The novel's land dispute provides occasion for the representation of different environmental ideologies, most of which are satirized in order to expose their Eurocentric and anthropocentric underpinnings vis-à-vis "rude nature," or Ed's personal Moby-Dick, Woody's case of poison ivy, Lyndon's eccentric Brussels sprouts, and Trudy's near-fatal encounter with an elephant. In satirizing these characters, *Wrack and Ruin* generates understanding of human limitations that is elaborated further in terms of the debates about art and aesthetics, specifically a racialized aesthetic. While Dalton angrily denounces this aesthetic as a form of slavery, Lyndon responds to increasingly hostile critical responses regarding his so-called denationalizing trajectory towards eco-art by withdrawing to rural California. So determined by the racialized nature/culture binary opposition, these responses miss the fact that the nonhuman environment is represented in Lyndon's series of sculptures from start to (un)finish. Although it is on a much smaller scale, Lyndon's artistic trajectory alludes to a history of Asian American cultures of nature reinforced by an ecocritical reading of the California Labor Day setting. The fact that Lyndon's final yet unfinished eco-sculpture cannot be displayed, exchanged, or judged, at least not in ideologically definitive terms, suggests more ethical, perhaps even ecocentric ways of doing Asian American ecocriticism consistent with both social and environmental justice agendas.

NOTES

I would like to thank my coeditors for their valuable suggestions, and Liverpool John Moores University for funding my research for this chapter. Special thanks also go to Professor Graham Huggan for feedback on early chapter drafts.

1. T. V. Reed, "Toward an Environmental Justice Ecocriticism," in *The Environmental Justice Reader: Politics, Poetics, and Pedagogy*, ed. Joni Adamson, Mei Mei Evans, and Rachel Stein (Tucson: University of Arizona Press, 2002), 157.
2. Robert T. Hayashi, "Beyond Walden Pond: Asian American Literature and the Limits of Ecocriticism," in *Coming into Contact: Explorations in Ecocritical Theory and Practice*, ed. Annie Merrill Ingram, Ian Marshall, Daniel J. Philippon, and Adam W. Sweeting (Athens: University of Georgia Press, 2007), 63.
3. "Okie" laborer, quoted in David R. Roediger, *Towards the Abolition of Whiteness: Essays on Race, Politics, and Working Class History* (London: Verso, 1994), 190.
4. Aldo Leopold, *A Sand County Almanac and Sketches Here and There* (Oxford: Oxford University Press, 1949), 46, 48.
5. Sau-ling Cynthia Wong, "Denationalization Reconsidered: Asian American Cultural Criticism at a Theoretical Crossroads," *Amerasia Journal* 2.1/2 (1995): 1.
6. Tomo Hattori, "China Man Autoeroticism and the Remains of Asian America," *Novel* 31.2 (1998): 233.
7. See, for example, Hayashi, "Beyond Walden Pond," 63–72.
8. Jessica Hagedorn, introduction to *Charlie Chan Is Dead: An Anthology of Contemporary Asian American Fiction*, ed. Jessica Hagedorn (New York: Penguin Books, 1993), xxii.
9. Samuel Colville, quoted in Alexander Saxton, *The Indispensable Enemy: Labor and the Anti-Chinese Movement in California* (Berkeley: University of California Press, 1971), 18.
10. *Truth*, quoted in Saxton, *Indispensable Enemy*, 275.
11. Hinton R. Helper, quoted in Saxton, *Indispensable Enemy*, 19.
12. *Organized Labor*, quoted in Saxton, *Indispensable Enemy*, 244.
13. Michael Kazin, "The Great Exception Revisited: Organized Labor and Politics in San Francisco and Los Angeles, 1870–1940," *Pacific Historical Review* 55. 3 (1986): 379–80.
14. *Asian Week*, quoted in Don Lee, *Yellow: Stories* (New York: Norton, 2001), 2.
15. Danzy Senna, quoted in Don Lee, *Country of Origin: A Novel* (New York: Norton, 2004), 2.
16. Don Lee, *Wrack and Ruin* (New York: Norton, 2008), 222.
17. Ibid., 267.
18. Lee, *Yellow*, 198, 238.
19. Ibid., 238.
20. Lee, *Wrack and Ruin*, 91.
21. Ibid., 92–93, 233.
22. Ibid., 188–89.

23. Lawrence Buell, *The Environmental Imagination: Thoreau, Nature Writing, and the Formation of American Culture* (Cambridge: Harvard University Press, 1995), 7; original emphasis.
24. Ibid.
25. Peter J. McGuire, quoted in Lee, *Wrack and Ruin*, 40.
26. Leo Marx, "Pastoralism in America," in *Ideology and Classic American Literature*, ed. Sacvan Bercovitch and Myran Jehlen (Cambridge: Cambridge University Press, 1986), 50–51.
27. Ellen M. Litwicki, "'Agitate, Educate, Organize': Labor Day in America," in *Encyclopedia of American Holidays and National Days*, ed. Len Travers (Westport: Greenwood Press, 2006), 336.
28. Michael Kazin and Steven J. Ross, "America's Labor Day: The Dilemma of a Workers' Celebration," *The Journal of American History* 78.4 (1992): 1299, 1301.
29. Leigh Eric Schmidt, "The Commercialization of the Calendar: American Holidays and the Culture of Consumption, 1870–1930," *The Journal of American History* 78.3 (1991): 890, 893.
30. Kazin and Ross, "America's Labor Day," 1321.
31. Litwicki, "Agitate," 362.
32. Lee, *Wrack and Ruin*, 286.
33. Ibid.
34. Kazin, "The Great Exception," 373.
35. Frederick Jackson Turner, "The Significance of the Frontier in American History," http://xroads.virginia/edu/~HYPER/TURNER (accessed January 11, 2012).
36. Ibid.
37. See, for example, Sucheng Chan, *Asian Americans: An Interpretative History* (New York: Twayne Publishers, 1991).
38. 1869 miners' union address, quoted in Saxton, *Indispensable Enemy*, 59.
39. Samuel Gompers and Herman Gutstadt, "Meat vs. Rice, American Manhood against Asiatic Coolieism: Which Shall Survive?" http://archive.org/stream/cu31924074468350#page/n33/mode/2up (accessed September 18, 2012).
40. *The Reveille*, quoted in Gerald N. Hallberg, "Bellingham, Washington's Anti-Hindu Riots," *Journal of the West* 12.1 (1973): 173.
41. *Seattle Morning Times*, quoted in Hallberg, "Bellingham," 173.
42. Hayashi, "Beyond Walden Pond," 65.
43. Elaine Kim, preface to *Charlie Chan Is Dead*, ix-x.
44. Carlos Bulosan, *America Is in the Heart* (Seattle: University of Washington Press, 1973), 270.
45. Louis Chu, *Eat a Bowl of Tea* (New York: Lyle Stuart Books, 2002), 246.
46. Lee, *Wrack and Ruin*, 14.
47. Ibid., 221, 177.
48. Ibid., 66. For a discussion of pastoralism in *Moby-Dick* see Marx, "Pastoralism in America," 53–54.
49. Lee, *Wrack and Ruin*, 268.
50. Ibid., 191.
51. Ibid., 47.
52. Ibid., 236.
53. Ibid., 164–65.
54. Ibid., 163–64.
55. Ibid., 50.
56. Ibid., 217.
57. Ibid., 219.
58. Ibid.

59. See Frank Chin, "Come All Ye Asian American Writers of the Real and the Fake," in *The Big Aiiieeeee! An Anthology of Chinese American and Japanese American Literature*, ed. Jeffery Paul Chan, Frank Chin, Lawson Fusao Inada, and Shawn Wong (New York: Meridian, 1991), 1–92.
60. Lee, *Wrack and Ruin*, 220–21.
61. Ibid., 221.
62. Ibid., 221–22.
63. Ibid., 226.
64. Ibid., 314.
65. Ibid., 315.
66. Ibid., 331.
67. Ibid., 333.
68. Alison Hope Alkon and Julian Agyeman, introduction to *Cultivating Food Justice: Race, Class, and Sustainability*, ed. Alison Hope Alkon and Julian Agyeman (Cambridge: MIT Press, 2011), 11.

BIBLIOGRAPHY

Alkon, Alison Hope, and Julian Agyeman. Introduction to *Cultivating Food Justice: Race, Class, and Sustainability*, edited by Alison Hope Alkon and Julian Agyeman, 1–20. Cambridge: MIT Press, 2011.

Buell, Lawrence. *The Environmental Imagination: Thoreau, Nature Writing, and the Formation of American Culture*. Cambridge: Harvard University Press, 1995.

Bulosan, Carlos. *America Is in the Heart*. Seattle: University of Washington Press, 1973.

Chan, Sucheng. *Asian Americans: An Interpretative History*. New York: Twayne Publishers, 1991.

Chin, Frank. "Come All Ye Asian American Writers of the Real and the Fake." In *The Big Aiiieeeee! An Anthology of Chinese American and Japanese American Literature*, edited by Jeffery Paul Chan, Frank Chin, Lawson Fusao Inada, and Shawn Wong, 1–92. New York: Meridian, 1991.

Chu, Louis. *Eat a Bowl of Tea*. New York: Lyle Stuart Books, 2002.

Gompers, Samuel and Herman Gutstadt. "Meat vs. Rice, American Manhood against Asiatic Coolieism: Which Shall Survive?" http://archive.org/stream/cu31924074468350#page/n33/mode/2up (accessed September 18, 2012).

Hagedorn, Jessica. Introduction to *Charlie Chan Is Dead: An Anthology of Contemporary Asian American Fiction*, edited by Jessica Hagedorn, xxi-xxx. New York: Penguin Books, 1993.

Hallberg, Gerald N. "Bellingham, Washington's Anti-Hindu Riots." *Journal of the West* 12.1 (1973): 163–75.

Hattori, Tomo. "China Man Autoeroticism and the Remains of Asian America." *Novel* 31.2 (1998): 215–36.

Hayashi, Robert T. "Beyond Walden Pond: Asian American Literature and the Limits of Ecocriticism." In *Coming into Contact: Explorations in Ecocritical Theory and Practice*, edited by Annie Merrill Ingram, Ian Marshall, Daniel J. Philippon, and Adam W. Sweeting, 58–75. Athens: University of Georgia Press, 2007.

Kazin, Michael. "The Great Exception Revisited: Organized Labor and Politics in San Francisco and Los Angeles, 1870–1940." *Pacific Historical Review* 55.3 (1986): 371–402.

—— and Steven J. Ross. "America's Labor Day: The Dilemma of a Workers' Celebration." *The Journal of American History* 78.4 (1992): 1294–323.

Kim, Elaine. Preface to *Charlie Chan is Dead: An Anthology of Contemporary Asian American Fiction*, edited by Jessica Hagedorn, vii-xiv. New York: Penguin Books, 1993.

Lee, Don. *Country of Origin: A Novel*. New York: Norton, 2004.

———. *Wrack and Ruin*. New York: Norton, 2008.

———. *Yellow: Stories*. New York: Norton, 2001.

Leopold, Aldo. *A Sand County Almanac and Sketches Here and There*. Oxford: Oxford University Press, 1949.

Litwicki, Ellen M. "'Agitate, Educate, Organize': Labor Day in America." In *Encyclopedia of American Holidays and National Days*, edited by Len Travers, 333–63. Westport, CT: Greenwood Press, 2006.

Marx, Leo. "Pastoralism in America." In *Ideology and Classic American Literature*, edited by Sacvan Bercovitch and Myran Jehlen, 36–69. Cambridge: Cambridge University Press, 1986.

Reed, T. V. "Toward an Environmental Justice Ecocriticism." In *The Environmental Justice Reader: Politics, Poetics, and Pedagogy*, edited by Joni Adamson, Mei Mei Evans, and Rachel Stein, 145–62. Tucson: University of Arizona Press, 2002.

Roediger, David. *Towards the Abolition of Whiteness: Essays on Race, Politics, and Working Class History*. London: Verso, 1994.

Saxton, Alexander. *The Indispensable Enemy: Labor and the Anti-Chinese Movement in California*. Berkeley: University of California Press, 1971.

Schmidt, Leigh Eric. "The Commercialization of the Calendar: American Holidays and the Culture of Consumption, 1870–1930." *The Journal of American History* 78.3 (1991): 887–916.

Turner, Frederick Jackson. "The Significance of the Frontier in American History." http://xroads.virginia/edu/~HYPER/TURNER (accessed January 11, 2012).

Wong, Sau-ling Cynthia. "Denationalization Reconsidered: Asian American Cultural Criticism at a Theoretical Crossroads." *Amerasia Journal* 21.1/2 (1995): 1–27.

Part II
The Environment and Violence

4 Contested "Frontier" and "Pioneers" in Writings about Japanese American Concentration Camps

Zhou Xiaojing

> The intertwinings of social and ecological projects in daily practices as well as in the realms of ideology, representation, esthetics, and the like are such as to make every social (including literary or artistic) project a project about nature, environment and ecosystem, and vice versa.
>
> —David Harvey[1]

> Be prepared for the Relocation Center, which is a pioneer community. So bring clothes suited to pioneer life and in keeping with the climate or climate likely to be involved. . . .
>
> —War Relocation Authority Pamphlet, 1942[2]

David Harvey's argument about the "intertwinings of social and ecological projects in daily practices as well as in the realms of ideology, representation, and esthetics" relates to wartime government definitions for the mass incarceration of 120,000 Japanese Americans in ten concentration camps located in remote areas and deserts of the United States.[3] Those barbed-wire-enclosed spaces, each holding 7,000 to 18,000 persons of Japanese ancestry in a square mile guarded by armed military, were defined by the camp administration, The War Relocation Authority (WRA), as "pioneer communities," and those incarcerated there were called "colonists." In fact, the first Director of the WRA, Milton Eisenhower, mandated the definitions of "pioneer communities" and "relocation centers" for the camps.[4] The Japanese Americans sent to the camps were supposed to believe in and reinforce the official definitions of the camps, which were a social and political project about race and nation, as well as nature and the environment. The World War II U.S. concentration camps for people of Japanese ancestry are contested sites, as demonstrated by competing narratives of official history and counter-memory.

The official discourse on the camps coerced some Japanese Americans into accepting its terms and underlying ideology. For example, a 1942 report from the Minidoka Camp by *Nisei* journalist Larry S. Tajiri, entitled, "Minidoka: Preliminary Report in a New Frontier Community," claims that this community of 10,000 "evacuee colonists" located on "68,000 areas of virgin desert sageland" represents "a modern American city—frontier style."[5] Tajiri's report echoes the terms of the official discourse which normalize the mass incarceration of Japanese Americans during World War II through "Americanizing" projects that re-enact the American frontier myth. Such euphemistic terms not only elide the racial injustice embedded in the mass expulsion, displacement, and confinement of Japanese Americans, but also entail environmental transformation coached in the American frontier ideology underlying the camp administration's multi-layered public service projects, including water management for agricultural and domestic use.[6] As Tajiri's report reveals, cultivation of agricultural land on the desert is a major part of the "service projects" the "colonists" are expected to carry out like "pioneers" who are making home on the "virgin desert sageland."[7] While the report's subheading, "Future Lies in the Land," seems to emphasize the promise of the land for this twentieth-century pioneer community, its description of the camp "policy on agricultural production" reveals a careful plan for protecting white farmers in the adjacent agricultural district from produce grown by the "colonists" of Japanese ancestry. Such camp policies evoke government initiatives such as the Alien Land Laws, from 1913 onwards, which prevented Japanese immigrants and their children from owning land as a way of protecting white farmers from Japanese immigrant farmers before World War II, exposing contradictions and omissions of particular historical facts in the discourses and practices regarding the camps.[8]

But, racial injustice underlying these contradictions is suppressed and rendered invisible in the celebratory definitions and representation of the camp as a pioneering project of Americanism. Dillon Myer, who succeeded Milton Eisenhower as Director of the WRA, emphasized the Americanizing mission of the camps in his address to the American Legion.[9] According to John Howard, "A 1943 subcommittee report on the WRA concluded that the camps represented 'an almost unparalleled opportunity to inaugurate a vigorous educational program for positive Americanism.'"[10] Master narratives of the frontier and pioneer myth were not only central to the camp educational program for positive Americanism, but they were also a dominant theme in advocating the camp relocation and agricultural projects. Howard points out the assimilation effect of such official discourse on Japanese Americans: "The pioneer myth was deployed repeatedly in camp discourse, well beyond the classrooms—and not only by camp administrators but also by Japanese American advocates of assimilation."[11]

Imbued with the pioneer rhetoric of the frontier myth, Tajiri's report from Minidoka expressed an enthusiastic confidence in modernity equated with subjugation of the wild land. Such association of conquest of the land with modernity as progress reiterates the dominant ideology and practice of the WRA's management of the camps' agricultural projects, which can be traced to the American westward expansion and subsequent land reclamation and conservation programs.[12] In fact, Minidoka and two other camps, Tule Lake in California and Heart Mountain in Wyoming, were on federal reclamation lands which had formerly been Native American territories.[13] The locations of other camps are also connected to American national policies and regional histories regarding the land and its resources. The two camps in Arkansas, Jerome and Rohwer, "were on lands the Farm Security Administration had purchased for poor southern farm families." Three camps—Manzanar in California, Topaz in Utah, and Granada (Amache), in Colorado—"were on lands obtained from various sources, federal, municipal, and private," and the two Arizona camps, Gila River and Poston, were on Native American reservations.[14]

Embedded in these locations are histories of the dispossession, displacement, and confinement of Native Americans, whose experience is related to environmental transformation and degradation resulting from "the agricultural vision" of Jeffersonian Democracy.[15] As Robert T. Hayashi points out, "The transfer of personnel from the Department of Agriculture to form the WRA signified a transfer of an institutional philosophy, one that had previously defined Nikkei in terms of their potential to realize the traditional plan of an agricultural West."[16] The camp agricultural projects were promoted and implemented in the name of the American frontier myth which erases the presence of Native Americans, along with alternative ways for inhabiting the land other than subjugating "wilderness" into productive farms. Such erasures help re-produce the dominant knowledge about history and a homogeneous perspective on the "American frontier" and the Japanese American relocation centers. Moreover, the master narratives about the frontier and the camps construct nature, the frontier, and the camps as sites of both symbolic meanings and actual enactment of policies, which simultaneously shape the relations between human beings and the environment, between race and nature.

A large body of Japanese American writings, however, shows that incarcerated Japanese Americans resisted the official inculcation of positive Americanism, subverted its frontier myth, and practiced alternative ways of inhabiting the land. While reasserting strategies for resistance, subversion, and intervention, Japanese American literature about the camps re-interprets the meanings of the camp environment, both "natural" and built, re-represents the pioneer communities, and recovers the erased presence of Native Americans from the land. This chapter explores the ways in which Japanese American writings about the camps function as counter-memories that undermine the dominant pioneer myth and offer an alternative relationship between human beings and nature in shaping the environment. My investigation draws on multiple critical perspectives, including ecocriticism and Michel Foucault's concept of the dynamic, mutually constitutive relationship between power and knowledge, particularly the concept of counter-memory as a critical framework for reading Japanese American texts.

Foucault articulates the effects of counter-memory in his discussion of genealogy as a critique of "'monumental history': a history given to reestablishing the high points of historical development and their maintenance in a perpetual presence."[17] Breaking away from this linear construction of history naturalized as objective records of memory, as truth, "given as continuity or representative of a tradition," a genealogical use of history "severs its connection to memory, its metaphysical and anthropological model, and constructs a counter-memory—a transformation of history into a totally different form of time."[18] A counter-memory then challenges the dominant discourse, myth, and history, calling into question the production of knowledge and offering an alternative to master narratives. As such, counter-memories are subversive and interventional, opening up new possibilities for critical inquiry and for recovering excluded or erased experience of marginalized and subjugated peoples.

George Lipsitz' interpretation of counter-memory further reinforces its subversive and recuperative potentials:

> Counter-memory is a way of remembering and forgetting that starts with the local, the immediate, and the personal. Unlike historical narratives that begin with the totality of human existence and then locate specific actions and events within that totality, counter-memory starts with the particular and the specific and then builds outward toward a total story. Counter-memory looks to the past for the hidden histories excluded from dominant narratives. But unlike myths that seek to detach events and actions from the fabric of any larger history, counter-memory forces revision of existing histories by supplying new perspectives about the past. . . . Counter-memory focuses on localized experiences with oppression, using them to reframe and refocus dominant narratives purporting to represent universal experience.[19]

With attention to oppression, to exclusion, and to the local and personal in relation to homogenizing dominant narratives of official history, counter-memory thus gives rise to multiple perspectives and marginalized perspectives, which resist totality and domination, making available what has been silenced and made invisible in master narratives.

By reading Japanese American writings as counter-memories in relation to normative discourses and practices of the camp administration, I seek to foreground the critical possibilities opened up by linking the internment and race to the environment and by investigating the connections between Japanese American relocation centers and Native American reservations. Critical attention to those connections, particularly to the unofficial stories about the camps as counter-memories, I argue, helps further interdisciplinary critical studies by addressing the lack of visibility of Asian American authors in the field of ecocriticism and the marginalization of environmental issues in Asian American criticism.[20] The World War II concentration camps in Japanese American writings such as those by Mitsuye Yamada, Lawson Fusao Inada, and Jeanne Wakatsuki Houston are sites of counter-memories, contested ideologies, and resistance. The ways in which the environments of the camps are represented play a crucial role in producing subversive meanings and identities of both place and inhabitants.

CAMP ENVIRONMENTS AS SITES OF RESISTANCE AND RECUPERATION: YAMADA

Yamada, who was interned in the Minidoka camp, depicts the location from her own and other Japanese Americans' experience in such a way as to disrupt the dominant frontier representation of the desert as virgin land waiting to be conquered. In her poem "Desert Run," for instance, Yamada portrays the desert as a place of exile for "criminals," and the sagebrush land as resistant to subjugation:

> I return to the desert
> where criminals
> were abandoned to wander
> away to their deaths
> where scorpions
> spiders
> snakes
> lizards
> and rats
> live in outcast harmony
> where the sculptors' wreck
> was reclaimed
> by the gentle drifting sands.[21]

The speaker in this poem "spent 547 sulking days here / in [her] own dreams" forty years ago without sharing any of the officially-promoted pioneering spirit or vision about the alleged potentialities of Minidoka. For her, "there was not much to marvel at" except "miles of sagebrush and lifeless sand."[22] The government project to establish a frontier agricultural community failed like "the sculptors' wreck" "reclaimed / by the gentle drifting sands." While creatures such as scorpions, spiders, snakes, lizards, and rats continue to inhabit the desert, the modern-American-city-to-be in a frontier style, as Tajiri's Minidoka report anticipated, was reclaimed by the sands.

Interestingly, however, something else remains for the speaker to claim:

> I am back to claim my body
> My carcass lies
> Between the spiny branches

of two creosote bushes
it looks strangely like a small calf
left to graze and die
half of its bones are gone
after all these years.[23]

Forty years ago, the speaker wrote her "will here / . . . / in the hot sand / . . . / three words: I died here / the winds filed them away."[24] Now she has returned to claim her symbolically dead body so as to give herself "a ritual burial" with a "stick."[25] Paradoxically, to claim and bury this self which died in the desert is to give a new life to what died there. In other words, the speaker returns to claim what is lost in the camp—her individuality, her voice, her dignity, and her agency. Recovering this loss entails transformation of the self that was subjugated by her incarceration in the desert. The ritual burial as recovery means breaking silence about expulsion, imprisonment, exile, loss, and subjugation and asserting what was muted and made invisible in representations of the camp as a new frontier community.

The next section of "Desert Run" enacts the agency of the self, reclaimed from the desert. Addressing "you"—arguably, white America and the War Relocation Authority—directly with irony and defiance, the speaker counters the pioneering rhetoric in the master narrative about the camps. She calls into question the official definition of the camp by evoking the displaced bull snakes:

Like the bull snakes brought
into this desert by the soldiers
we were transported here
to drive away rattlers
in your nightmares
we were part of some one's plan
to spirit away spies
in your peripheral vision.[26]

The speaker adapts to the environment, her skin turning "pink brown / in the bright desert light," her body slithering "in the matching sand" like the bull snakes brought to the camp by the soldiers to evict the dreaded rattlers.[27] But, as one of those incarcerated potential "spies" transported to the desert by the soldiers, the speaker states, "I am that odd creature / the female bull snake / I flick my tongue in your face / an image trapped in your mirror."[28] Identifying herself with this strange, dangerous female bull snake, whose image "trapped in your mirror" is constitutive of "your" own image, the speaker unsettles the construction of American identity vs. alien Japanese Other, a construction underlying the mass incarceration of Japanese Americans as an "enemy race" during World War II. This mutually constitutive logic of the dominant and the subjugated is also embedded in the production of the camp identity by the official discourse, whose definitions of the camps erased the histories, experience, and perspectives of racial minorities from the master narrative. Thus, by reclaiming those elisions and exclusions and by refusing entrapment and subjugation, Yamada's speaker undermines the official discourse on the camps and reclaims her agency of resistance.

Moreover, as the speaker continues to recall her experience of living in the camp, the desert takes on a new dimension, revealing a habitat for desert creatures resistant to agricultural production. The speaker indicates by the end of the poem that neither the Japanese American "aliens," nor any agricultural projects, belong there:

> The desert is the lungs of the world.
> This land of sudden lizards and nappy ants
> Is only useful when not used
> We must leave before we feel we can
> change it.[29]

An ecological perspective, one that places the desert, lizards, ants, and human beings in an interconnected and interdependent ecosystem of the world, underlies the statement, "The desert is the lungs of the world. . . . only useful when not used," which opposes both the exile of Japanese Americans in the desert and the agricultural projects intended to subjugate the sagebrush land by turning it into productive farms behind or beyond barbed-wire fences.

"Desert Run" and Yamada's other poems about the camps illustrate that resistance can be enacted from an alternative perspective on "wilderness" to that constructed by the dominant frontier discourse and official definitions of the camps as pioneer communities. Against the coercive power of the frontier myth and its assertion of human dominion over "nature," Yamada's poem "Lichens" articulates a counter narrative as resistance to the subjugation of both Japanese Americans and nature or the desert by governmental agricultural programs. Rather than being transformed into farmland by the pioneers, the desert retains its vitality and unconquerable, irresistible power of renewal and reproduction of a variety of life, including lichens, whose "new generations . . . spill over / on sandblasted rocks."[30] The resilient, uncontainable lichens inhabit the host culture of the desert, displacing the central, dominant presence of human pioneers:

> Volcanic mass turns to soil
> one grain at a time
> enough for pioneering moss
> and fledgling ferns to
> make our desert lawn.[31]

While evoking the official definitions for the Minidoka camp and Japanese Americans confined there through references to "pioneering moss" and "our desert lawn," Yamada relies on the image of the lichens to convey multi-layered meanings, introducing an anti-anthropocentric view of the desert that resists the cultivation of wilderness into productive land and the subjugation of the incarcerated into obedient subjects.

Yamada's alternative representation of nature in her poems such as "Lichens" takes on more political valence when they are read along with her poems that focus more directly on the built environment and its impact on those confined in the camps. In "Desert Storm," for example, Yamada reveals the uniform, confining, collective way of life in the Minidoka camp, while depicting the living environment in the desert. As the speaker describes how the people are getting ready for a twister, the living conditions of the camp are portrayed in such a way that they counter the master narrative about both the frontier community and the land being conquered by new pioneers:

> Near the mess hall
> along the latrines
> by the laundry
> between the rows of
> black tar papered barracks
> the block captain galloped by.
> Take cover everyone he said
> here comes a twister.
> Hundreds of windows
> slammed shut.
> Five pairs of hands
> In our room
> with mess hall
> butter knives
> stuffed
> newspapers and rags
> between the cracks.
> But the Idaho dust
> persistent and seeping
> found us crouched
> under the covers.
> This was not
> im
> prison
> ment.
> This was
> re
> location.[32]

Instead of acres of cultivated land marking the place as a pioneer community, Yamada directs the reader's gaze to the mess hall, the outhouses, and laundries, and the spatial organization of the camp, which reflect the subjugated racial position of those who are imprisoned there. Both the natural and built environments in the poem serve to mobilize the speaker's personal memory as counter-memory that subverts the camp's official definitions, which reinvent the frontier myth.

By engaging critically with the frontier myth in the official discourse of the camps, Yamada is able to link the wartime incarceration of Japanese Americans to the experience of other racial minorities made invisible in the official history of the American frontier which was central to the inculcation of positive Americanism in the camps. In his provocative study on the Americanization programs in the camps, Howard points out how the frontier myth was promoted in pedagogical proposals in the monthly *Community School Forum* which was "mailed to all educators in the camp school systems."[33] In carefully selected teaching materials about American history, freedom of movement, the pioneering spirit, and challenges were central themes of "American heritage." As a piece in a 1943 issue of *Community School Forum* asserts: "[T]he history of America is one of continuous relocation. The story of the incessant movement of the American people from east to west, from north to south, from farm to city, has always been a thrilling tale of continuous readjustment to new environments."[34] In advocating the camps' Americanizing educational programs, the WRA insisted on emphasizing that "[f]ar greater dangers confronted the pioneers who were always moving westward than confront these people in relocating. The spirit of America is in such pioneering."[35]

Countering the normalizing official discourse, Yamada's writings about the camps as sites of counter-memories entail making visible exclusions and erasures of displaced Native Americans and Chinese "coolie" laborers from the master narrative of "positive Americanism." Her poem "Hole in the Wall" about "our narrowed lives" in the desert uses as its epigraph a quotation from *Daughter of Earth* (1929), an autobiographical novel by the American author and journalist Agnes Smedley about Native American resistance to displacement: "*I understood why Geronimo had fought for so long to hold the land he loved.*"[36] This quotation anticipates the theme of the erasure of Native Americans from the official master narratives of the frontier, thus activating it as a counter-memory that ruptures the unity of monumental history by suggesting a parallel between the expulsions of Native Americans and Japanese Americans from places that used to be their homes. Their forced removals expose racial injustice in the mythologized account of pioneering movement in the frontier.

In a similar way, Yamada brings another aspect of racial injustice into her engagement with the master narrative of the frontier by using a quotation from Mary Austin's *The Land of Little Rain* (1903) as the epigraph of her poem "Desert Mystique." The quotation reveals the exploitation, subjugation, and dehumanization of Chinese immigrant laborers in the "frontier" West: "*There was a line of shallow graves; they used to count on dropping a man or two of every new gang of coolies brought out in the hot sun.*"[37] In contrast to the desecration of the racially marked body and of the conquered land by settlers as depicted in Austin's collection of short stories, the speaker in "Desert Mystique" pays homage to the desert every year, "bearing private gifts / to walk under a million stars / between giant yuccas."[38] Her annual visit to the desert brings about a transformation of both the racialized body and the anthropocentric myth of desert frontier. As the speaker states,

> I am transfused
> by the creosote
> shrubs squatting
> close to the ground
> by their vibrant wax leaves
> not parched
> never wilted
> . . .
> In the haze of night
> I look for my creosotes
> growing in patterned rows
> around a natural boulder
> like a well-combed
> Zen garden.[39]

Rather than attempting to domesticate the wilderness, the speaker venerates the desert, allowing herself to be "transfused" by the vibrant creosote shrubs which spread on the "wide expanse of land" unconquered and unconquerable by pioneers.[40] Moreover, by comparing this desert landscape to a Zen garden, which is a practice of living in harmony with nature, Yamada points to an alternative way of inhabiting the land. At the same time, she asserts with defiance the Japanese culture deemed undesirable by the Americanizing educational programs in the camps.

Yamada's representation of the Zen-garden-like desert landscape becomes even more politically charged when juxtaposed with the Japanese-style garden located at the Minidoka camp entrance behind the Honor Roll board, listing the names of 1,000 Japanese American soldiers from Minidoka. The design of the latter garden highlights patriotism and loyalty to the United States. As Anna Hostricka Tamura notes, "The shapes and configuration of boulders placed on the largest mound" of the garden "resembled an eagle, complementing the eagle atop the Honor Roll board."[41] While this Japanese style loyalty garden may assert a form of resistance to the exclusion of Japanese Americans from U.S. society, it also serves to promote the dominant ideology of patriotism as proof of loyalty to the U.S. in coercing conformity from incarcerated Japanese Americans.[42]

Yamada's desert garden and the Minidoka honor-roll garden demonstrate the multiplicity of meanings and functions embedded in the natural and built environments of the camps. This multiplicity poses challenges to and presents new possibilities for interpreting the politics of gardening in the camps. For example, Kenneth Helphand, a scholar of landscape architecture, offers detailed examples of the ways in which the internees "transformed the camps at all scales, from the interiors of barracks to the landscape itself."[43] Following his examination of the internees' transformation of the bleak landscape into a variety of gardens in the camps, Helphand notes that surrounded by a barbed-wire fence and guarded by armed soldiers, the gardens could be understood as "acts of resistance, directed toward the maintenance of cultural integrity and self-respect. They were tangible symbols of hope that helped people survive their internment . . . and were psychological and also political defiance."[44]

However, the "political defiance" of these gardens is compromised by Helphand's citations and interpretations that echo the official discourse on the frontier and the camps. Helphand quotes extensively and uncritically from the diary of Arthur Kleinkopf, the superintendent of education at Minidoka, who recorded his close observations of agricultural activities, including "victory gardens" in the Minidoka camp.[45] He notes that Kleinkopf "insightfully referred to the internees as 'colonists,' although one significant distinction between colonists and the internees was that the latter had not volunteered to be relocated." "However," he adds, "like colonists," the internees "were engaged in an encounter with a strange territory, and they adapted their culture to these alien conditions and environments."[46] Later in the chapter, Helphand cites again Kleinkopf's observations of the ornamental gardens at Minidoka as further evidence of the internees' transformations of the camp environment, stating that "Kleinkopf admired the internees' abilities as colonists to see a strange environment with new eyes and to recognize the value and usefulness of the new things they encountered."[47]

In a similar vein, Helphand unwittingly reiterates the dominant frontier ideology underlying the official definitions for the camps, as he concludes: "Garden making also allowed internees to identify with the historic western experience. The camps were essentially frontier communities in wild landscapes, which internees 'civilized' with their frontier gardens."[48] Likewise, Helphand's citations from the camp newspapers *Minidoka Irrigator* and *Topaz Times* resonate with the master narrative about the frontier and the camp agricultural projects: "Our great adventure is a repetition of the frontier struggle of pioneers against the land and the elements."[49] In addition to echoing the dominant ideology embedded in the quotation from *Minidoka Irrigator*, the citation from *Topaz Times* links the pioneer spirit to patriotism: "Topaz is born of the great Mother America. We are again the pioneer, blazing the road into the wilderness of our social frontiers."[50]

By representing the camps as characteristically American pioneering projects, the racial injustice of mass incarceration of Japanese Americans is erased. However, Helphand unwittingly concurs: "The task was clear to the internees at all the camps: make this a 'home' in the way the pioneers domesticated the American West in the past century."[51] Interpreted in this light, the concentration camps for Japanese Americans then were "pioneer communities" just as the WRA defined them in terms of a continuity of an American tradition. Thus racial inequality and racial injustice retreat from the normalized environment of the racialized spaces of the camps. Nevertheless, Helphand's interpretation of the camp gardens as "acts of resistance" and gardening as manifestation of the internees' agency in transforming the camp environment helps open up new possibilities for further investigation into the connections between the environment and the camps.

Scholars from different disciplines, such as historian Gary Okihiro, landscape architect Anna Hosticka Tamura, anthropologist Jane Dusselier, and environmental historian Connie Chiang, have examined the politics of gardening as a form of resistance and as a means for survival, healing, and claiming a measure of autonomy and ownership. In his seminal study of resistance in the camps, Okihiro considers the camp gardens one of the cultural expressions of resistance to the WRA's Americanization program.[52] In her provocative study of gardening in the camps, Tamura explores the complex, even apparently contradictory, meanings and functions of the design and form of the camp gardens, which "helped to redefine Japanese traditions and resisted the WRA's Americanization regime." As she observes, "some gardens functioned as political symbols of sedition and non-compliance as well as loyalty and patriotism, and they were often used as staging grounds for political acts."[53] Rather than simply carrying out the WRA's projects of agriculture and settlement, Tamura notes, garden-building provided the inmates with "a point of entry into negotiations with officials over the conditions of incarceration."[54] Moreover, Tamura points out that the Block 22 garden, "the most beautiful garden at Manzanar," was also "a place of covert and overt defiance, vehement protest, and then the organizational center of Manzanar riots."[55] Further exploring the politics of aesthetics in the camp gardens, Dusselier examines the ways in which the internees "re-territorialized the camps," altering the racially marked "spatial order of these physical landscapes by joining aesthetics with politics and engaging with the art forms of gardening and landscaping as strategies for creating survivable places."[56] In doing so, "the internees imagined and enacted portable senses of place," which helped them articulate identities "unmoored from physical boundaries of nationhood."[57]

Expanding further on the existing scholarship on the environment of the camps, Chiang focuses her investigation on "site selection, outdoor recreation, and labor to suggest how an environmental analysis can reshape historical understandings of the Japanese American incarceration" as "another instance of environmental injustice in which one group used the natural world to assert authority over another group."[58] Her study concentrates on four camp sites: Manzanar in California, Topaz in Utah, Minidoka in Idaho, and Gila River. With an emphasis on "the role of the environment in the subjugation and resistance of a racial minority," Chiang explores "how the natural world has helped to structure the dynamics of racial oppression, accommodation, and resistance."[59] While noting that the WRA "employed the pioneer myth . . . to encourage and reinforce the transformation of the camp landscape," Chiang finds evidence of resistance in the detainees' use of the frontier rhetoric. She argues that "for the detainees, the frontier was also a potentially subversive place where they could claim a distinctly American identity at a time when they were shunned by most Americans. If they could make desolate land bloom, like the white pioneers before them, and contribute to the war effort, their confinement might appear all the more undemocratic."[60] Chiang is commenting on the same piece, "Eyes on Tomorrow" that appeared in *Minidoka Irrigator* on September 10, 1942, which Helphand cites in his work. In other words, for the incarcerated Japanese Americans to demonstrate loyalty, patriotism, and pioneering spirit and ability comparable to that of white pioneers serves to challenge the government's incarceration of a racial minority who were excluded from democracy. However, such a strategy for inclusion in mainstream America fails to challenge the frontier myth or its underlying notions of conquest and domination over nature, which resulted in dispossession and displacement of Native Americans, as well as degradation of the environment. Nevertheless, Chiang's study, like the others discussed above, helps expand critical investigations of the connections between environmental injustice and racial exclusion, between environmental transformation and resistance.

POLITICS AND ETHICS FOR INHABITING THE LAND OTHERWISE: INADA

These insights from multidisciplinary approaches into the environment and the internment help situate Japanese American writings about the camps in more specific historical and geographical contexts. They also help highlight the multiple and different modes of resistance and contestation that literary writings as counter-memories enact. In his representation of gardening in the camps, Lawson Fusao Inada articulates an alternative way of inhabiting the land to that embedded in the pioneer rhetoric. Moreover, his depictions of the camp sites confront omissions and exclusions that underlie the frontier myth. Rather than re-articulating normative Americanism promoted in the camp projects, his writings about gardening and environmental transformation behind barbed-wire fences revise and re-imagine what it means to be American. In his prose poem, "The Real Inada," Inada portrays Uncle Yoshitaro Inada as a "remarkable" American who "never had to become 'Americanized,'" because he is as American as "a Navajo."[61] What "truly exemplified his 'American-ness' was his love of the *land* . . . and all that came with it."[62] In fact, Uncle Yoshitaro was "*of* the land," and his love, appreciation, and knowledge of it suggest a sense of oneness: "He lived with the land, on the land, and was *of* the land; he knew it as he knew his hands, and they went together, like harvest and rain, like sunsets and song."[63] Moreover, he brought this oneness with the land to "a concentration camp in Arkansas, hard by the Mississippi."[64] While serving on the camp's "work crew that went out into the swamp each day to chop firewood," he smuggled in his various "found-treasures: plants, more plants, some wild creatures, and special chunks of wood."[65] With these "found treasures," Uncle Yoshitaro created miniature landscapes and improved the everyday living environment for his family and his neighbors in the camp. In fact, he fostered an eco-habitat:

> And while the rest of the camp proceeded in the prescribed concentration-camp manner—grim, grimy, like a grainy black-and-white newsreel— my uncle transformed his barrack-grounds into a technicolor nature documentary. Everything from outside had made its way into the barrens to flourish, including fish and frogs and crawdads in the ponds; the effect was not artsy either, but more like an extension of the swamps; as a result, many birds and insects gathered in the foliage.[66]

It is worth noting that this diverse, interdependent habitat asserts an ecological and ethical principle of inclusivity that runs counter to the exclusionary logic of the concentration camps, where persons of Japanese ancestry were confined and controlled by white administrators and soldiers. Inada emphasizes that Uncle Yoshitaro "didn't necessarily feed those creatures to alter or tame their nature; rather, they fed themselves in his organic environment."[67] Instead of replicating the anthropocentric view typical of the dominant frontier discourse, this eco-habitat and its support of a variety of lives require the responsibility and humility of human beings as partners or stewards in creating and maintaining the habitat as an eco-community. Such an environmental perspective dismantles the dichotomy of domination vs. subjugation embedded in the pioneer rhetoric of the master narrative and the WRA's agricultural projects in the camps.

Inada's prose poem about Uncle Yoshitaro's relationship with the environment, like Yamada's poems discussed above, operates as counter-memory that undermines the normative discourse and practice regarding the camps and the frontier, by resisting dominant ideologies and introducing a counter-perspective. In addition, Inada seeks to make visible omissions that help constitute the master narrative about "positive Americanism." When commenting on Uncle Yoshitaro's transformation of his living environment in the camp, which entailed making "a fura," a wooden Japanese-style bath tub out of scraps, Inada writes: "the warm scent of wet wood served to negate the smell of industrial disinfectant. Eventually, Uncle Y might have invited his fellow laborers on the outside to come in and partake, to ease their aches from plantation cottonfields."[68] While the industrial disinfectant recalls the damage to the laborers' body and the environment by toxins used in industrial agriculture, the reference to plantation cottonfields evokes slavery and links Japanese Americans' experience in the camp to the racial subjugation and exploitation of African Americans outside the camp. Furthermore, when asserting Uncle Yoshitaro's American connection to the land, Inada points to "Navajo" rather than "white pioneers" as quintessentially American, hence displacing whites as the normative embodiment of American identity.

Inada further undermines the pioneer myth and its underlying relationship between humans and nature in his poem "Legends from Camp." He situates the wartime incarceration of Japanese Americans in a broader historical context by linking the camp sites to the displacement and genocide of Native Americans. Section XV, "The Legend of the Full Moon Over Amache," connects the Amache camp in Colorado, where Inada and his family were confined, to the site of the "Sand Creek Massacre" on November 29, 1864, when 700 men in the Colorado Territory militia attacked and destroyed a village of Cheyenne and Arapaho, killing and mutilating an estimated 150 Native Americans, about two-thirds of whom were women and children.[69] Thus, the poem uncovers through Native Americans' experience a part of American history buried by the frontier myth:

> As it turned out,
> Amache is said to have been named
> for an Indian princess—
> . . .
> who perished upstream,
> in the draw,
> of the Sand Creek Massacre.
> Her bones floated down
> to where the camp was now.[70]

The desert location of the Amache camp was not virgin land for white pioneers to conquer and domesticate. By foregrounding Native Americans, normally erased from the frontier myth and the official discourse on the camps, Inada subverts the definitions of the camps as pioneer communities through an implied link between the incarceration of Japanese Americans and the violent subjugation and displacement of Native Americans.

In his Introduction to *Legends from Camp* (1993), Inada draws attention to other convergences and their implications in the experiences of Native Americans and Japanese Americans. While highlighting the fact that Native American reservations were used as the sites for more than one Japanese American incarceration camp, including "Leupp—a 'mini-camp'—right on the Navajo Nation," Inada further foregrounds what is suppressed in the

frontier myth and its normative rhetoric for the camps.[71] Leupp was an isolation center administered by the WRA for imprisoning Japanese American
"trouble makers" transported from the other camps from April to December 1943. It was surrounded by a high barbed-wire fence and patrolled by
150 military police. The building in which the Japanese American "trouble
makers" were confined used to be a boarding school for Native Americans,
established in the early 1900s by the Bureau of Indian Affairs.[72] By making
visible the little known "mini-camp," Leupp, a "penal colony" for Japanese
Americans on the territory of Navajo Nation,[73] Inada produces a counter-
perspective to that of the camps as "pioneer communities." As he comments
on the intersections of Native American and Japanese American histories,
"And, yes, we had major camps on other reservations; so you might say that
it makes sense that the chief camps administrator went on to become chief
of the Bureau of Indian Affairs, where he 're-deployed' his policy of 'relocation.' Which included, yes, 'termination.'"[74]

Deploying his writings as counter-memory by insisting on excavating the
hidden histories of Native Americans and Japanese Americans, Inada revises
the official history about the frontier and the camps and resists Americanizing assimilation of racial minorities. Thus enacted as counter-memory to
official history, Inada's poetic representation of the camps counters the normative frontier rhetoric and practice of subjugating wilderness into productive land, while proposing an ecological and ethical mode of inhabiting the
land otherwise.

CONVERGING HISTORIES OF RACIAL SUBJUGATIONS, DISPLACEMENTS, AND ENVIRONMENTAL DEGRADATION: WAKATSUKI HOUSTON

Japanese American writings about the camps as counter-memories make
visible marginalized and erased histories, including environmental histories
excluded from the dominant narratives about the frontier. In so doing, they
also make available counter and alternative perspectives that put into question dominant discourses and practices. Breaking away from reiterating the
pioneer myth as a normative discourse for Americanizing Japanese Americans, Jeanne Wakatsuki Houston, like Yamada and Inada, uncovers exclusions and omissions that help constitute and sustain the dominant frontier
discourse. Moreover, in conceiving the camp as a site of converging stories
of racial minorities' subjugation and displacement, her writings about the
Manzanar camp also become counter-memory that uncovers the environmental history of the frontier along with histories of subjugation, displacement, and desertification of the land.

In her memoir *Farewell to Manzanar*, written with her husband James
Houston, Jeanne Wakatsuki Houston strategically describes the environmental transformation of the area where the Manzanar camp is located

in such a way as to highlight the intersections of environmental and racial injustice.

> In Spanish, Manzanar means "apple orchard." Great stretches of Owens Valley were once green with orchards and alfalfa fields. It has been a desert ever since its water started flowing south into Los Angeles, sometime during the twenties. . . . In the spring of 1943 we moved to block 28, right up next to one of the old pear orchards.[75]

The desertification of this environment was the consequence of the loss of water resources of the region to Los Angeles. The transformation of the landscape and environment of Owens Valley also entails the displacement of Native Americans. But this earlier history of the place remains unexplored in *Farewell to Manzanar* until Houston revisits the Manzanar camp site decades later in her essay "Crossing Boundaries" (2011). Still, a remnant of Native Americans' presence in the region appears in her memoir when she recalls that one Saturday a Native American turned up in the camp, "billing himself as a Sioux chief, wearing bear claws and head feathers. In the firebreak he sang songs and danced his tribal dances while hundreds of us watched."[76] Ironically, this presence of displaced Native Americans was part of a Saturday entertainment program for displaced Japanese Americans who were trying to live a normal life in the camp. And when water, bought by the WRA from Los Angeles, returned to Manzanar to make life possible and bearable for Japanese Americans, Native Americans remained absent from the place that had been their home.

By linking Japanese American incarceration to the history and environment of Owens Valley shaped by power relations, Houston's description of the gardens at Manzanar breaks away from the dominant pioneer rhetoric of conquest and patriotism. "With water siphoned off from the Los Angeles-bound aqueduct, a large farm was under cultivation just outside the camp, providing the mess hall with lettuce, corn, tomatoes, eggplant, string beans, horseradish, and cucumbers."[77] The availability of water in the desert made it possible for Japanese Americans to transform the camp environment: "Gardens had sprung up everywhere, in the firebreaks, between the rows of barracks—rock gardens, vegetable gardens, cactus and flower gardens."[78] Against the imposed confinement of crowded, uniform collective living space of the camp, Japanese American internees created alternative spaces, including a Japanese-style park which served as a common space of healing and temporary escape from incarceration. As Houston describes, "Sometimes in the evenings we could walk down the raked gravel paths. You could face away from the barracks . . . and for a while not be a prisoner at all."[79] Nevertheless, there is no real escape even in this comforting space, which is part of what Houston calls "our desert ghetto."[80] Her portrayal of Japanese Americans' transformation of the camp environment through gardening refuses to rehearse the pioneer myth of conquering wilderness and turning it into productive land and ownership as a normative "American" tradition. Contrary to earning full American citizenship through the Americanizing pioneer communities, Houston notes, "our years of isolation at Manzanar had widened the already spacious gap between the races, and it is not hard to understand why so many preferred to stay where they were."[81] But without access to water, not even this desert ghetto could remain home for Japanese Americans. As Houston's description of the transformation of the landscape indicates, "At its peak, in the summer of '42, Manzanar was the biggest city between Reno and Los Angeles, a special kind of western boom town that sprang from the sand, flourished, had its day, and now had all but disappeared."[82]

Environmental transformation entangled with racial formation in the frontier of the United States becomes an even more prominent theme in Houston's essay "Crossing Boundaries." As she continues to investigate the histories of Manzanar, Houston finds a

> remarkable pattern of "displacement". . . . For over a thousand years, Native Americans had flourished, living off the earth and the game and fowl teeming about streams and lakes fed by the Sierra Nevada runoff. When prospecting and mining on the eastern slopes began in the early 1850s, it heralded the end of the Native Americans' stewardship.[83]

But this lush environment was drastically altered by Euro-American pioneers. A mining district was opened east of the Sierra in 1861; before long cattlemen and farmers moved in. Within a few years, white settlers violently displaced the Paiutes who had been living there. When violence broke out between white settlers and the Paiutes, nearly 1,000 Native Americans in 1893 "were imprisoned at Camp Independence and force-marched to Fort Tejon, a reservation 175 miles south."[84] Driven out of their homeland and deprived of resources of livelihood, the Paiutes lost their independence and autonomy. Some of them returned to become farm laborers, working "as expert irrigation managers" for white farmers "on this land inhabited for centuries by their ancestors, who had created intricate water systems and lush game reserves."[85]

With land taken from Native Americans, along with abundant water resources and irrigation system, white pioneers' orchards and ranches prospered at Manzanar until 1924 when Los Angeles bought land along with water rights and channeled the water used by the farms and ranches to the sprawling city.[86] Forced to leave the fertile valley, white farmers and ranchers became another "displaced" group, but their social position as whites was fundamentally different from that of both Native Americans and Japanese Americans. Yet, their displacement added to the complexities of environmental history shaped by multiple participants and contesting ideologies and practices. Houston situates the displacement of Japanese Americans confined at Manzanar in the layered histories of environmental degradation and racial subjugation and resistance in the frontier.

As counter-memory, "Crossing Boundaries" also allows the Paiute presence and perspective to emerge where they were banished by white settlers and erased by the dominant frontier discourse. On her return to Manzanar with her family, Houston met with a Paiute named Richard Stewart, who was working as a docent at Manzanar because he became interested in the camp's history after "seeing similarities in the uprooting of his people and Japanese Americans."[87] Stewart's perspective on the place adds a new dimension to the relationship between the history of displacements and the environment of Manzanar:

> He tells of his love for the land, about the Northern Paiutes and their history. Confirming the pattern of "displacement" I had come upon, he relates the "dispersement" of Indians by white settlers, the "water wars" of Owen Valley between Los Angeles and local ranchers, the creation of another "reservation" for Japanese Americans during World War II. This history of exploitation and exile, he says, has left a residue of dark energy that pervades the site.[88]

A Native American environmental ethics is embedded in Stewart's words, which indicate that the land can never be reduced to property, ownership, or commodity. The relationship between human beings and the environment is at once physical and spiritual, as well as ethical and ecological. This means that the destructive force and its "dark energy" cannot prevail in this land inhabited by Native Americans for millennia. As Stewart says to Houston, "'The whole desert is filled with spirit-rocks. The Big One,' he points toward the mountains, 'is our grandfather.'"[89]

The converging histories at Manzanar in Houston's writings are more than stories of violence and destruction against racial minorities and "nature." In countering the dominant discourse on the frontier and its pioneer myth, they offer alternative ways for inhabiting the land as a member of a more diverse and heterogeneous community, and as a steward, dependent on an ecosystem whose wellbeing demands an ethical, spiritual, and ecological relationship with human beings. But this perspective is often excluded from the dominant discourse on the frontier myth, along with the subjugation of Native Americans and "wilderness" in the pioneer myth.

Native American writers such as Simon Ortiz and Leslie Marmon Silko represent the garden as "a powerful symbol not only of nature but of livelihood or the right of humans to derive a living from the earth," as Joni Adamson shows in her ecocritical study of Native American literature and environmental justice. By "incorporating the garden into their work, multicultural writers confront and problematize the dichotomization of people and nature that pervades contemporary environmentalism and much American nature writing."[90] As counter-memories, Japanese American writings about gardens and other environmental aspects of the concentration camps accomplish this task and much more. They challenge environmental studies and ecocriticism to cross disciplinary, as well as racial, cultural, and national, boundaries in order to seek more inclusive ecological, racial, and environmental justice and to develop a more copious and rigorous ecocriticism grounded in multiple histories, geographies, and critical theories. The writings by the three Japanese American authors examined in this chapter demonstrate the necessity for pushing the boundaries of ecocritical theories and methodologies.

NOTES

1. David Harvey, *Justice, Nature and the Geography of Difference* (London: Wiley-Blackwell, 1997), 189.
2. War Relocation Authority pamphlet, "Questions and Answers for Evacuees" (1942), in Records of the War Relocation Authority (Washington, D.C.: National Archives Building). Quoted in *Beyond Words: Images from America's Concentration Camps*, ed. Deborah Gesensway and Mindy Roseman. (Ithaca: Cornell University Press, 1987), 46.
3. The term "concentration camps" here must not be confused with the Nazi death camps. The term "internment" for the mass incarceration of 120,000 in ten confined locations guarded by armed military is a misnomer. Terminologies for historical injustice can serve to help or prevent a better understanding of this particular part of American history. As Karen L. Ishizuka points out, "One effective method with which the reality of the camp experience has been kept from honest scrutiny is the use of official language to describe it." According to Ishizuka, President Franklin D. Roosevelt used "concentration camp" with regard to Japanese immigrants and Japanese Americans in a White House memorandum dated August 10, 1936." Ishizuka also provides examples for the wide use of the term "concentration camps" in scholarly studies such as *America's Concentration Camps* (1967) by Allan R. Bosworth; *Concentration Camps, USA* (1971) by Roger Daniels; *Years of Infamy: The Untold Story of America's Concentration Camps* (1976) by Michi Weglyn; and *Keeper of Concentration Camps* (1987) by Richard Drinnon, among others. Ishizuka, *Lost and Found: Reclaiming the Japanese American Incarceration* (Urbana: University of Illinois Press, 2006), 8.
4. Richard Drinnon, *Keeper of Concentration Camps: Dillon S. Myer and American Racism* (Berkeley: University of California Press, 1987), 63.
5. Larry S. Tajiri, "Minidoka: A Preliminary Report in a New Frontier Community," 1. Densho ID: denshopd-p155–00018, http://www.densho.org/archive/fromthearchive/news_2009–02–002.htm (accessed August 6, 2012).
6. I use the term "Japanese Americans" to refer to all those confined in the camps even though they were not all U.S. citizens, because the first generation immigrants of Japanese ancestry were banned by law from naturalization.
7. Tajiri, "Minidoka," 4.
8. Colleen Lye, *America's Asia: Racial Form and American Literature, 1893–1945* (Princeton: Princeton University Press, 2005), 110.
9. Dillon S. Myer, "The Relocation Program," 7, box I, folder I, Robert A. Leflar Collection, University of Arkansas Libraries Special Collections Division, Fayetteville, Arizona. Quoted in John Howard, *Concentration Camps on the Home Front: Japanese Americans in the House of Jim Crow* (Chicago: University of Chicago Press. 2008), 155.

10. Myer, quoted in Howard, *Concentration Camps*, 155.
11. Howard, *Concentration Camps*, 156.
12. See, for example, Lye, *America's Asia*; Howard, *Concentration Camps*; and Robert T. Hayashi, *Haunted by Waters: A Journey through Race and Place in the American West* (Iowa City: University of Iowa Press, 2007).
13. Richard Drinnon, *Keeper of Concentration Camps: Dillon S. Myer and American Racism* 8.
14. Ibid.
15. See, for example, Hayashi, *Haunted by Waters*.
16. Ibid., 77–78.
17. Michel Foucault, "Nietzsche, Genealogy, History," in *Language, Counter-Memory, Practice: Selected Essays and Interviews*, trans. Donald F. Bouchard and Sherry Simon, ed. Donald F. Bouchard (Ithaca: Cornell University Press, 1977), 161.
18. Ibid., 160.
19. George Lipsitz, *Time Passages: Collective Memory and American Popular Culture* (Minneapolis: University of Minnesota Press, 1990), 213. I am indebted to Meredith Criglington for calling my attention to Lipsitz' definition of "counter-memory" and her excellent use of it as a theoretical framework for reading fiction in "The City as a Site of Counter-Memory in Anne Michaels's *Fugitive Pieces* and Michael Ondaatje's *In the Skin of a Lion*," in *Essays on Canadian Writing* 81 (2004): 129–51.
20. See, for example, Robert T. Hayashi, "Beyond Walden Pond: Asian American Literature and the Limits of Ecocriticism," in *Coming into Contact: Explorations in Ecocritical Theory and Practice*, ed. Annie Merrill Ingram, Ian Marshall, Daniel J. Philippon, and Adam W. Sweeting (Athens: University of Georgia Press, 2007), 58–75. Also see Julie Sze, "From Environmental Justice Literature to the Literature of Environmental Justice," in *The Environmental Justice Reader*, ed. Joni Adamson, Mei Mei Evans, and Rachel Stein (Tucson: University of Arizona Press, 2002), 163–80.
21. Mitsuye Yamada, *Desert Run: Poems and Stories* (Latham, NY: Kitchen Table: Women of Color Press, 1988), 1. Permission granted by Rutgers University Press and Mitsuye Yamada.
22. Ibid., 2.
23. Ibid.
24. Ibid.
25. Ibid.
26. Ibid., 3.
27. Ibid.
28. Ibid.
29. Ibid.
30. Ibid., 7.
31. Ibid.
32. Yamada, *Camp Notes and Other Poems* (Latham, NY: Kitchen Table: Women of Color Press, 1992), 19. Permission granted by Rutgers University Press and Mitsuye Yamada.
33. Howard, *Concentration Camps*, 182.
34. *Community School Forum*, June 1943, Series 3, Folder 4, Virginia Tidball Collection, University of Arkansas Libraries Special Collections Division, Fayetteville, Arizona. Quoted in Howard, *Concentration Camps*, 155.
35. Ibid.
36. Yamada, *Desert Run*, 6.
37. Quoted in Yamada, *Desert Run*, 10.
38. Ibid.

39. Ibid., 11–12.
40. Ibid., 11.
41. Anna Hosticka Tamura, "Gardens Below the Watchtower: Gardens and Meaning in World War II Japanese American Incarceration Camps," *Landscape Journal* 23.1 (2004): 17.
42. Those who objected to being enlisted into the army for various reasons, including protest against the violation of their civil rights, were branded as "disloyal" and transported to the segregated Tule Lake camp in California.
43. Kenneth Helphand, *Defiant Gardens: Making Gardens in Wartime* (San Antonio: Trinity University Press, 2006), 163.
44. Ibid., 189
45. Ibid., 165.
46. Ibid.
47. Ibid., 179.
48. Ibid., 192.
49. "Eyes on Tomorrow," *Minidoka Irrigator*, September 10, 1942, 2 (Japanese American Historical Museum, Los Angeles). Quoted in Helphand, *Defiant Gardens*, 192.
50. *Topaz Times*, September 17, 1942 to December 30, 1943 (Japanese American Historical Museum, Los Angeles). Quoted in Helphand, *Defiant Gardens*, 193.
51. Helphand, *Defiant Gardens*, 193.
52. Gary Okihiro, "Religion and Resistance in America's Concentration Camps," *Phylon* 45.3 (1984): 220–33.
53. Tamura, "Gardens Below," 1.
54. Ibid., 10.
55. Ibid., 17.
56. Jane E. Dusselier, *Artifacts of Loss: Crafting Survival in Japanese American Concentration Camps* (New Brunswick, NJ: Rutgers University Press, 2008), 51.
57. Ibid., 51–52.
58. Connie Y. Chiang, "Imprisoned Nature: Toward an Environmental History of the World War II Japanese American Incarceration," *Environmental History* 15.2 (2010): 239.
59. Ibid.
60. Ibid., 248.
61. Lawson Fusao Inada, *Drawing the Line* (Minneapolis: Coffee House Press, 1997), 31, 32. Permission granted by Coffee House Press.
62. Ibid., 32.
63. Ibid.
64. Ibid.
65. Ibid.
66. Ibid., 33.
67. Ibid., 38.
68. Ibid., 33.
69. See Dee Brown, *Bury My Heart at Wounded Knee* (New York: Macmillan/Holt, 2001), 67–102.
70. Inada, *Legends from Camp* (Minneapolis: Coffee House Press, 1993), 18. Permission granted by Coffee House Press.
71. Ibid., vi.
72. For more information about Leupp, see Drinnon, *Keeper of Concentration Camps*.
73. Ibid., 109.
74. Inada, *Legends from Camp*, vi.

75. Jeanne Wakatsuki Houston and James D. Houston, *Farewell to Manzanar* (New York: Bantam Books, 1973), 69.
76. Ibid., 73.
77. Ibid., 71.
78. Ibid.
79. Ibid., 72.
80. Ibid., 93.
81. Ibid.
82. Ibid., 135.
83. Houston, "Crossing Boundaries," in *The Colors of Nature: Culture, Identity, and the Natural World*, ed. Alison H. Deming and Lauret E. Savory (Minneapolis: Milkweed Editions, 2011), 34.
84. Ibid.
85. Ibid.
86. On the contested histories of Manzanar with regards to the establishment of the Manzanar camp location as a national historic site, see Robert T. Hayashi, "Transfigured Patterns: Contesting Memories at the Manzanar National Historic Site," *The Public Historian: A Journal of Public History* 25.4 (Fall 2003): 51–71.
87. Houston, "Crossing Boundaries," 39.
88. Ibid., 38.
89. Ibid., 39.
90. Joni Adamson, *American Indian Literature, Environmental Justice, and Ecocriticism: The Middle Place* (Tucson: University of Arizona Press, 2001), 181.

BIBLIOGRAPHY

Adamson, Joni. *American Indian Literature, Environmental Justice, and Ecocriticism: The Middle Place*. Tucson: University of Arizona Press, 2001.
Brown, Dee. *Bury My Heart at Wounded Knee*. New York: Macmillan/Holt, 2001.
Chiang, Connie Y. "Imprisoned Nature: Toward an Environmental History of the World War II Japanese American Incarceration." *Environmental History* 15.2 (2010): 236–67.
Criglington, Meredith. "The City as a Site of Counter-Memory in Anne Michaels's *Fugitive Pieces* and Michael Ondaatje's *In the Skin of a Lion*." *Essays on Canadian Writing* 81 (2004): 129–51.
Drinnon, Richard. *Keeper of Concentration Camps: Dillon S. Myer and American Racism*. Berkeley: University of California Press, 1987.
Dusselier, Jane, E. *Artifacts of Loss: Crafting Survival in Japanese American Concentration Camps*. New Brunswick, NJ: Rutgers University Press, 2008.
Foucault, Michel. "Nietzsche, Genealogy, History." In *Language, Counter-Memory, Practice: Selected Essays and Interviews*, translated by Donald F. Bouchard and Sherry Simon, edited by Donald F. Bouchard, 139–64. Ithaca: Cornell University Press, 1977.
Gesensway, Deborah and Mindy Roseman, eds. *Beyond Words: Images from America's Concentration Camps*. Ithaca: Cornell University Press, 1987.
Harvey, David. *Justice, Nature and the Geography of Difference*. London: Wiley-Blackwell, 1997.
Hayashi, Robert T. "Beyond Walden Pond: Asian American Literature and the Limits of Ecocriticism." In *Coming into Contact: Explorations in Ecocritical Theory and Practice*, edited by Annie Merrill Ingram, Ian Marshall, Daniel J. Philippon, and Adam W. Sweeting, 58–75. Athens: University of Georgia Press, 2007.

———. *Haunted by Waters: A Journey through Race and Place in the American West.* Iowa City: University of Iowa Press, 2007.

———. "Transfigured Patterns: Contesting Memories at the Manzanar National Historic Site." *The Public Historian: A Journal of Public History* 25.4 (2003): 51–71.

Helphand, Kenneth I. *Defiant Gardens: Making Gardens in Wartime.* San Antonio: Trinity University Press, 2006.

Houston, Jeanne Wakatsuki. "Crossing Boundaries." In *The Colors of Nature: Culture, Identity, and the Natural World*, edited by Alison H. Deming and Lauret E. Savory, 33–40. Minneapolis: Milkweed Editions, 2011.

——— and James D. Houston. *Farewell to Manzanar.* New York: Bantam Books, 1973.

Howard, John. *Concentration Camps on the Home Front: Japanese Americans in the House of Jim Crow.* Chicago: University of Chicago Press. 2008.

Inada, Lawson Fusao. *Drawing the Line.* Minneapolis: Coffee House Press, 1997.

———. *Legends from Camp.* Minneapolis: Coffee House Press, 1993.

Ishizuka, Karen L. *Lost and Found: Reclaiming the Japanese American Incarceration.* Urbana: University of Illinois Press, 2006.

Lipsitz, George. *Time Passages: Collective Memory and American Popular Culture.* Minneapolis: University of Minnesota Press, 1990.

Lye, Colleen. *America's Asia: Racial Form and American Literature, 1893–1945.* Princeton: Princeton University Press, 2005.

Okihiro, Gary. "Religion and Resistance in America's Concentration Camps." *Phylon* 45.3 (1984): 220–33.

Sze, Julie. "From Environmental Justice Literature to the Literature of Environmental Justice." In *The Environmental Justice Reader*, edited by Joni Adamson, Mei Mei Evans, and Rachel Stein, 163–80. Tucson: University of Arizona Press, 2002.

Tajiri, Larry S. "Minidoka: A Preliminary Report in a New Frontier Community." Densho ID: denshopd-p155–00018. http://www.densho.org/archive/fromthearchive/news_2009–02–002.htm (accessed August 6, 2012).

Tamura, Anna Hosticka. "Gardens Below the Watchtower: Gardens and Meaning in World War II Japanese American Incarceration Camps." *Landscape Journal* 23.1 (2004): 1–21.

War Relocation Authority, War Relocation Authority pamphlet, "Questions and Answers for Evacuees" (1942). In Records of the War Relocation Authority. Washington, D.C.: National Archives Building.

Yamada, Mitsuye. *Camp Notes and Other Poems.* Latham, NY: Kitchen Table: Women of Color Press, 1992.

———. *Desert Run: Poems and Stories.* Latham, NY: Kitchen Table: Women of Color Press, 1988.

5 Tilling the Soil in the Killing Fields
Cambodian American War Memoirs

Helena Grice

> Surviving the Khmer Rouge years was the most important fact of our
> lives, and the very center of our identities. . . . The Cambodian holo-
> caust ripped through our lives, tossing us randomly, leaving none
> of us the way we were. You can blame who you want, the outside
> powers for interfering, or our own internal flaws like corruption and
> *kum*, but when the talking is over we still do not know why it had to
> happen. The country is still in ruins, millions have died and those of
> us who survived are not done with our grieving
>
> —Haing S. Ngor, *Survival in the Killing Fields*

In a landmark speech to Veterans of Foreign Wars on August 22, 2007,
President George W. Bush said, "One unmistakable legacy of Vietnam is
that the price of America's withdrawal was paid by millions of citizens
whose agonies would add to our vocabulary new terms like 'boat people,'
're-education camps,' and 'killing fields.'" Cambodia under the Khmer
Rouge, including the creation of the Khmer Rouge leader Pol Pot's notorious "killing fields," has been named the second holocaust in global memory.
This period of atrocity, although lasting only four years—from 1975, the
year which marked the end of the Vietnam War, until 1979—claimed the
lives of some two million people, one quarter of Cambodia's population,
due to starvation, illness, or the brutal executions carried out by Khmer
Rouge soldiers.[1] In a massive misguided experiment, Pol Pot tried unsuc-
cessfully to turn Cambodia into a self-sufficient agrarian economy.

From an ecocritical perspective, I wish to argue in this chapter that the
Cambodian holocaust offers a tragically new perspective on the intercon-
nection between the production of life-writing and the environment. I also
wish to suggest that Cambodian life-writing offers a different perspective
on the relationship between humanity and nature than is usually discussed
in literary ecocriticism. This story of the Khmer Rouge regime and Cambodia's killing fields is still not well-known outside Asia. Yet, increasingly,
as Bush's comments attest, the United States is turning its attention to this
history, a history which has been told primarily to date in a series of war

memoirs published in the period between the late 1980s and the 2000s. These include Haing S. Ngor's *Survival in the Killing Fields* (1987); Loung Ung's diptych, *First They Killed My Father: A Daughter of Cambodia Remembers* (2000) and *After They Killed Our Father: A Refugee from the Killing Fields Reunites with the Sister She Left Behind* (2007); Chanrithy Him's *When Broken Glass Floats* (2000); Denise Affonço's *To The End of Hell: One Woman's Struggle to Survive Cambodia's Khmer Rouge* (2005); and Chileng Pa's *Escaping the Khmer Rouge* (2008).[2] The shrouded past which forms the subject of these life stories reveals unprecedented hardship and the obliteration of political and personal freedom. The dilemma for the personal memoirists who have sought to tell the story of Cambodia under the *Mahantdori* ("time of destruction") in the latter part of the twentieth century is the compelling yet vexing question of how to relate a story almost too horrific to recall. It is a tale of political persecution, of individual suffering, and, ultimately, of both a land and a country in crisis.

POL POT'S KILLING FIELDS: HUMAN TRAUMA AND ENVIRONMENTAL CATASTROPHE

Pol Pot's failed agrarian experiment illustrates the intimate causal link between human trauma and environmental catastrophe, since it was as a direct consequence of the Khmer Rouge's abuse and misuse of the land later known as the "killing fields" that agricultural mismanagement resulted in mass starvation. This link also erodes the distinction between "natural" and "man-made" as concepts, since the "man-made" catastrophe of the Pol Pot revolution resulted in the "natural" consequences of crop failure and famine. E. A. Méng-Try's study of the population and development effects of the *Angkar* years published in the immediate wake of the Cambodian holocaust confirms this.[3] Méng-Try observes that one of the principal causes of mortality under the Khmer Rouge was the failure of the rice crop in 1974–75 and subsequent years (with a yield reduced from 3.813 million tons in 1969–70 to 493,000 tons four years later), which meant that "production was insufficient to feed the population" and with "no sources of food . . . famine and epidemics were widespread throughout the country."[4] Karl Jackson states that by 1974 rice production in Cambodia had fallen twenty-five percent from the levels of the early 1960s.[5] Floods, drought, and monsoons by turn exacerbated the problem.

Undoubtedly, though, it was partly the Khmer Rouge's ineptitude that led to this plight: revolutionary forces had seized and closed the Mekong river, which was the main route of food supply; the Khmer Rouge also largely depended upon the unskilled "new people" from urban centers to work the land, either raising rice crops or constructing dams, dykes and canals, which resulted in poor or failed rice and vegetable crops as well.[6] These new laborers also received inadequate food rations. Méng-Try quotes a figure of "200–250 grams of rice per day, a small amount of salt, and a small amount of fish for three or four days. . . . This quantity of calorific intake corresponds to the bare minimum requirement for a man engaging in very moderate physical activity."[7] This near-starvation also disproportionately affected future generations: "Malnutrition and undernourishment severely attacked the weakest (children, the elderly, and the ill) and the poorest . . . [The] mortality rate of children ranged from 20 to 25 percent. . . . Children who did not die immediately from lack of food were emaciated from starvation."[8] The stark result of these mortality rates was that whereas the Cambodian population in 1979 should have been in the region of 9.5 million people, it was actually five to six million.[9]

Yet despite these horrific statistics, and even in the face of mounting contemporaneous evidence, at the time Pol Pot continued to insist that his agrarian revolution was proving successful and that crops were adequate to feed the population. In 1977, he announced in a speech that rice production levels met the needs of the population.[10] He also customarily reiterated statements about the need for agrarian reform as the basis of the Khmer Rouge's social transformation of Cambodia:

> We take agriculture as the basic factor and use the fruits of agriculture to systematically build industry in order to advance toward rapidly transforming a Cambodia marked by a backward agriculture into a Cambodia marked by a modernized agriculture. We also intend to rapidly transform the backward agricultural Cambodia into an industrialized Cambodia. [This resulted in] a national society characterized by equality, justice, genuine democracy and the absence of the rich, poor, exploiting and exploited classes and in an independent, united, peaceful, neutral, nonaligned and sovereign Cambodia with full territorial integrity.[11]

Pol Pot's stated agrarian goals provided a foil for the transformation of Cambodia into a country controlled by terror, since the mass creation of forced labor camps in the countryside was "ostensibly to do agricultural work more effectively."[12]

CAMBODIAN LIFE-WRITING

Most of the narratives I discuss here follow a similar schema: framed by both a preface and a politically strident introduction, they plead for human rights and political intervention to achieve justice for the victims; the authors write quite self-consciously about their suffering under the Khmer Rouge with the advantage of historical hindsight and from the comparative comfort and freedom of the United States. Their books are also typically similar in including timelines, photographs, maps, agricultural plans, and family trees. There is a good deal of unevenness and divergence between the texts, though, as well. The majority of Cambodian literature written originally to date in English, as opposed to in translation,[13] comprises refugee memoirs, frequently transcribed by a third party, and oral histories.[14]

SURVIVAL STORIES AND THE HOSTILE ENVIRONMENT

Cambodian life narratives illustrate the direct relationship between the degree of trauma experienced by the individual and the subsequent compulsion to record it. These refugee memoirs not only describe life at the very limits of humanity and offer a hitherto unseen glimpse into this shrouded period of history, but they also reveal a key tension between the ideals and goals of the Khmer Rouge's agrarian revolution and the reality of environmental destruction and the brutality of life in the killing fields. Their stories are rendered all the more poignant when we consider that the majority of Cambodians who were uprooted from their homes and expelled from the capital, Phnom Penh, in 1975, were largely educated city professionals with little or no experience of an agricultural economy. As a Khmer soldier shouts at memoirist Chileng Pa,

> The big city officials with all their fancy education and degrees will never again hold power. You city dwellers who consider yourselves better than the peasants who labored in the rice fields will now be made to understand that there are no diplomas in the countryside, and certificates of achievement are worthless in the eyes of *Angkar.*
>
> You become valuable to *Angkar* when you learn that land is the paper and the hoe is the pen. When you can dig dirt, build canals, and work in the rice fields, you'll earn the only certificate you'll need.[15]

Khmer Rouge ideology was organized against a single common class enemy: the urban city-dweller. Ethnologist Alexander Hinton has explored the manner in which the Khmer Rouge managed to mobilize rural peasant resentment against city-dwellers by figuring such people as enjoying the "cognac and concubine circuit" and by employing such slogans as "trees in the country, fruit in the town."[16] Revenge was meted out in the form of forced relocation to the rural labor camps, a form of class re-education, which saw the urban population reclassified on the lowest rung in the new class structure. In this way, the Khmer Rouge operated a policy of what Michael Vickery has called "poor-peasantism," or "peasant populism," which stemmed from an ideology of faith in the sacredness of soil and those able to till it.[17] The so-called "new people"—those who were expelled from the city and forced to work in the Khmer Rouge's agricultural labor camps—were systematically denied food, medication, and family contact, and were also forced to endure the hardest labor and torture in the killing fields.

In sharp contrast to other Asian American memoirs of war and revolution, most notably China's Cultural Revolution, but also memoirs of both the Korean War and the Vietnam Conflict, Cambodian American life-writing inscribes an unresolved tension between life on the land as peasants and life before the Khmer Rouge period.[18] Although as memoirist Loung Ung observes, "The Khmer Rouge government, or *Angkar*, sought to create a pure utopian agrarian society," life under *Angkar* is figured in these memoirs just about as removed from a rural idyll as it is possible to imagine.[19] In this manner, I wish to suggest, Cambodian life-writing offers a different perspective on the relationship between humanity and nature than is usually discussed in literary ecocriticism. Rather than a more usual pastoral depiction of a rural idyll which provides humanity with a tranquil yet crucial sanctuary from the terrors and traumas of densely populated and war-torn city spaces, and which contrasts sharply with a hostile city/urban environs, Cambodian life-writing records and remembers the city as a safe and nurturing space from which citizens were forcibly expelled, and describes the descent into an increasingly horrific and hostile countryside environment. Thus, in these memoirs there is a markedly unusual distinction between the urban city as a remembered space of pre-revolution tranquility and the rural dystopia which succeeded it. Furthermore, in distinction from environmental writing which celebrates the potential of the land to sustain and nurture life, in Cambodian life-writing we repeatedly encounter the failure of the land itself, as well as its increasing toxicity to the peasants forced to work on it.[20] "Survival" in the killing fields is not just figured in these memoirs as an escape from the torture of the Khmer Rouge, but the ability to endure the hostility of the rural environment.

The disastrous consequences of the Khmer Rouge years are further underscored by the degree of trauma and guilt experienced by the survivors who went on to tell their stories; the recording of individual psychological anguish comprises an integral and unforgettable characteristic of this life-writing. The strategic use of the victim's voice as testimony here underscores the potential of what we might call these "literatures of atrocity" to intervene in a global discourse of human rights. Cambodian life-writing quite uniquely connects human catastrophe with environmental trauma, in a manner which insistently reminds us of President Jimmy Carter's memorable comment in the wake of the Cambodian genocide that human rights extend beyond rights of citizenship and culture to include environmental rights as well:

> There are real and growing dangers to our simple and most precious possessions: the air we breathe; the water we drink; and the land which sustain us. . . . For this generation, ours, life is nuclear survival, liberty is human rights, the pursuit of happiness is a planet whose resources are devoted to the physical and spiritual nourishment of its inhabitants.[21]

THLEK TUK CHET: TRAUMA AND LIFE-WRITING

The outcome of the Cambodian environmental catastrophe is immediately apparent when we turn to consider the literature. A noticeable feature of these Cambodian American memoirs is the expression of what Sucheng Chan has called "the abysmal mental health of Cambodian refugees."[22] As she notes, levels of mental health disturbance and specifically post-traumatic stress disorder (PTSD) were present in unusually high numbers amongst the Cambodian American refugee population in the 1980s and 1990s. Chan writes:

> Most refugees who entered after 1979 were in terrible shape, both physically and mentally, after enduring years of near starvation, sleep deprivation, unremitting hard labor, and constant terror. . . . We know that Cambodians had suffered more trauma than any other group.[23]

Many Cambodians never recovered from the holocaust emotionally or physically. Even Haing S. Ngor, a former doctor, Academy award-winning actor, and accomplished author of the memoir *Survival in the Killing Fields*, and possibly the most successful author amongst this group, failed to make a recovery, as his friend and collaborator Roger Warner recalls: "Haing Ngor never found peace. . . . He was like his country: scarred, and incapable of fully healing."[24] Chan describes the findings of a group of Cambodian-oriented therapists, who have worked extensively with victims of the Pol Pot regime and believe that storytelling is the key to curing their trauma. In the article "Healing the Wounds of the *Mahantdori*," Khmer Health Associates, based in California, assert that their clinical experience and research indicate that storytelling does have the potential to heal the depression which Cambodians describe as *thlek tuk chet* or "the heart and mind are no longer connected," especially when the storytelling represents the ways the storyteller tried to help others, a strategy which can tangibly help to assuage feelings of survivor guilt.[25] This is a belief which is widely echoed in academic work on survivor discourse.

The twin urge to reconcile with yet also forget the past is recurrently expressed in Cambodian American memoirs. It is also a recognized feature of "survivor" narratives, a form of narrative whereby, in Linda Martín Alcoff and Laura Gray-Rosendale's formulation, victims are transformed into survivors via the processes of speaking out and telling their stories.[26] The Khmer Health Associates' belief in the therapeutic potential of storytelling is likewise closely echoed in what trauma theorist Suzette Henke has written about the cathartic possibilities of life narrative, a process of narrative self-healing she has called "scriptotherapy," which in her words is "writing out and writing through traumatic experience in the mode of therapeutic re-enactment."[27] Cambodian American war memoirs bear a striking resemblance to Henke's description of the workings of trauma and testimony in life-writing, as outlined in her seminal study *Shattered Subjects*. Henke describes how the act of inscription itself becomes a mode of therapeutic intervention that short-circuits the cycle of intrusive agonized memories and psychologically debilitative silence that characterizes the experience of the traumatized. Henke's own exploration of scriptotherapy life-writing is generically highly flexible:

> [It] challenge[s] the traditional limits of autobiography through the use of a category that encompasses memoirs, diaries, letters and journals, as well as the bildungsroman and other personally inflected fictional texts. This expanded genre embraces the flux and discontinuity that so frequently characterizes the orts, scraps, and fragments of self/ life-writing found in confessional novels, romans á clef, biomythography, and tantalizing autofictions.[28]

For Henke, these forms characteristically share the features of "an author attempting to fashion an enabling discourse of testimony and self-revelation, to establish a sense of agency," and she writes that "[a]utobiography could . . . effectively mimic the scene of psychoanalysis."[29] Connecting Henke with the example of Pol Pot survivors enables us to see how Cambodian American life narratives recreate the scene of both the intrusion of traumatic memory and the scene of therapy, via the promotion of healing, enablement, and agency, through the outward re/articulation (testimony) of the traumatic past.

The present physical environment of the memoirists writing their life stories in the United States is also figured as supportive, safe, and healing, even though several still remain haunted by trauma-filled nightmares. Life-writing theorists Sidonie Smith and Julia Watson have usefully described the relationship between traumatic memory and life-writing:

> People suffering the agonies of traumatic memory are haunted by memories that obsessively interrupt a present moment and insist on their presence. . . . In life narratives . . . narrators struggle to find ways of telling about suffering that defies language and understanding; they struggle to reassemble memories so dreadful they must be repressed for human beings to survive and function in life.[30]

This observation precisely describes the intrusive cycle of remembering and suffering that is recurrently expressed in Cambodian American memoirs. For instance, Ngor writes,

> Ever since coming to the United States I'd had nightmares. If I thought too much in the daytime about what had happened, I had dreams that night. Huoy [my wife] died in my arms over and over and over. I saw my father tied to the tree and trying to tell me something, but afraid to speak.

It didn't take much to set off my nightmares—the sound of water dripping from the faucet was enough. It put me back in prison, looking up at water dripping from a hole in a bucket.

Almost every night I woke suddenly and sat up to make the dreams fade. Outside the louvered windows the streetlights were shining.[31]

Texts like Ngor's also clearly belong to the category of "survivor narrative," characterized by Smith and Watson as:

narratives by survivors of traumatic, abusive, or genocidal experience. . . . [E]ffective voicing of certain kinds of trauma must go beyond the confessional to acts of witnessing. . . . Victims must be remade as survivors through acts of speaking out, telling their stories in ways that move beyond a concentration on personal feelings to testimony that critiques larger cultural forces.[32]

In fact, most Cambodian American memoirs clearly testify and bear witness to the acts of atrocity committed by the Khmer Rouge, but this act of witnessing is also transformed from a simple statement of survival to another significant act, which is an active intervention in the increasingly global debate over human rights, in the manner described by Smith and Watson above. As Smith and Watson emphasize, the act of witnessing in a politically active manner is a move that addresses another, and requires— indeed expects—a response, and engenders a quite active, alert relationship between witness/survivor/writer–text–reader. Certainly it has been my experience while researching this literature that the effects of reading *about* such extreme acts of atrocity and experiences of deprivation uniquely engenders something of a trauma-by-proxy, a reading process which cannot but mobilize a political impetus as well.[33] Many of these life stories carry an epigraphic dedication to those who died, often in Khmer as well as in English, but at the same time express a strong desire for their stories to be both cautionary and educational.[34]

But a reluctance to speak and to remember is also a problem for these life writers. Partly this is due to a specific aspect of the Khmer Rouge control of the Cambodian people, whereby *telling*, either in the form of the forced confessions of individuals, or by informants (*chhops*), often led to torture or execution. The prohibition against telling is a recurrent feature in these narratives. There is also a sense of a deliberate amnesia on the part of many of the survivors, which is a kind of survival tactic in its own right, as well as a suspicion on the part of victims as to the reasons for telling. In their discussion of survivor discourse, Alcoff and Gray-Rosendale warn of one of the major pitfalls of telling:

Survivor discourse . . . is fraught with dangers. . . . [O]ne of the dangers of the confessional discourse is that the survivor speech becomes a media commodity that has a use value based upon its sensationalism and drama and that circulates within the relations of media competition.³⁵

This vexed position is precisely the plight of the Cambodia survivors.

TELLING THE STORY OF THE *MAHANTDORI:*
HAING S. NGOR'S STORY

A survey of Cambodian American war memoirs confirms this sense of a quite bleak picture. One of the most accomplished, but also memorable and heart-rending, narratives to be published to date was also the first: Haing S. Ngor's *Survival in the Killing Fields* (1987). Ngor was a young doctor in the capital Phnom Penh in Cambodia before the coup by the Khmer Rouge in 1975. After escaping Cambodia in 1979 and repatriating to the United States, he was cast by the renowned director Roland Joffé as the lead character in his 1984 film, *The Killing Fields*, which was based upon the life of the Cambodian photographer Dith Pran, a role for which Ngor went on to win an Academy Award. Despite this success, it is his suffering under Pol Pot that defines his life. His narrative opens:

> I have been many things in life. A trader walking barefoot on paths through the jungles. A medical doctor, driving to his clinic in a shiny Mercedes. In the past few years, to the surprise of many people, and above all myself, I have been a Hollywood actor. But nothing has shaped my life as much as surviving the Pol Pot regime. I am a survivor of the Cambodian holocaust. That's who I am.³⁶

Throughout his life narrative, while Ngor takes care to convey the horrors of his individual experience, he is careful to connect this with the collective suffering of Cambodians:

> I went barefoot. My clothes were rags and my ribs were showing from hunger. To keep the Khmer Rouge from killing me, I had to pretend I was not a doctor. They had already killed most of my family. And my case was typical. By destroying our culture and by enslaving us, the Khmer Rouge changed millions of happy, normal human beings into something more like animals.³⁷

Ngor's narrative adopts the most politically insistent voice to be found in this literature. He uses a curiously detached mode of description at times, often when recalling the bleakest moments of his past, such as the death in childbirth of his wife Huoy and his unborn baby as a result of malnutrition, and the torture and execution of his father and his best friend. The most emotionally charged sections of the story, though, are also the most horrific: his extended accounts of his own torture at the hands of the Khmer Rouge cadres. Ngor underscores this by alerting the reader to the traumatic impact of reading about his torture each time it occurs, before he describes it. For instance, at the start of chapter 21, "The King of Death," he writes:

> A warning: this chapter tells of the very depths of suffering that people like me saw and experienced under the Khmer Rouge regime. It is an important part of the story, but it is not a pleasant part. So if you wish, or if you must, skip this chapter and go on to the next one.[38]

Such warnings occur three times in Ngor's story, and serve to underscore for the reader the traumatic import of the narrative.

There is also a clear sense of revisionism here. For instance, Chapter 26, entitled "The Cracks Begin to Show," opens with this comment:

> Looking back, it seems clear that 1977 was the year the regime began to crack. The Khmer Rouge had tried to reorganize the nation too quickly and radically for the structure to hold. [39]

By underscoring the similarities between narrative accounts of the Khmer Rouge regime, several writers also establish a degree of political as well as personal coalition. Ngor notes that

> We do whatever we can to help heal Cambodia's wounds. There are many of us, volunteering, speaking out, working at all levels, and there is a kinship between us because we all have lived through the same terrible events.[40]

In this manner, the individual reminiscences of each author combine to begin to form a collective record and testimony of this period of atrocity, as well as testimony to this era of environmental destruction.

WOMEN'S PERSPECTIVES: A DAUGHTER OF CAMBODIA

Loung Ung's diptych about her family's life under the Khmer Rouge, *First They Killed My Father: A Daughter of Cambodia Remembers* (2000) and *After They Killed Our Father: A Refugee from the Killing Fields Reunites with the Sister She Left Behind* (2007), warrants separate attention from the other texts discussed here since it deviates from the before/after, victim/survivor binary that Chan has identified as a defining feature of this literature. At first glance, many of the features of Ung's memoir do conform to the typical features of the genre as I have identified them, including a dedication to deceased family members, a map of Cambodia, a family tree, and a framing preface which establishes the connection between Loung Ung's personal story and the collective history of Cambodia:

> From 1975 to 1979—through execution, starvation, disease, and forced labor—the Khmer Rouge systematically killed an estimated two million Cambodians, almost a quarter of the country's population.
>
> This is a story of survival: my own and my family's. Though these events constitute my experience, my story mirrors that of millions of Cambodians. If you had been living in Cambodia during this period, this would be your story too.[41]

Like most other memoirs, the narrative commences in 1975 (which the Khmer Rouge called "Year Zero"), by picturing Loung's pre-revolution childhood in the city, Phnom Penh, as "middle-class" and "well-to-do," relatively idyllic, comfortable and free from tragedy; it proceeds through the family's expulsion from the city and relocation to a hut in the countryside.[42] Ung describes her father's execution when the Khmer Rouge discover that he was an official in the previous government, and, as with other memoirs, she relates her family's gradual slide into malnutrition and edema, dysentery, malaria, and numerous infections. Loung watches her siblings Keav, Geak, and her mother die one by one, and her mother and her brother Kim also endure torture. After Cambodia is liberated in 1979, together with her brother Meng, Ung, like Ngor, escapes to the United States via a boat to Vietnam, then Thailand. Her description of her life post-holocaust in the epilogue also seems to confirm the idea of storytelling as personally cathartic:

> As I tell people about genocide, I get the opportunity to redeem myself. I've had the chance to do something that's worth my being alive. It's empowering, it feels right. The more I tell people, the less the nightmares haunt me. The more people listen to me, the less I hate. After some time, I had talked so much I forgot to be afraid.[43]

Where Ung's memoir differs from others most noticeably, though, is in the presence of a second volume, one which describes her gradual recovery, rehabilitation in the United States, and her reunion with her surviving family in Cambodia. Ung's narrative thereby offers a degree of completion to this collective narrative of tragedy, by figuring the possibilities of an "after," if not quite a "happy ever after," and crucially for my discussion here, by figuring the continental United States as a *healing* environment. Loung Ung repeatedly expresses her desire for and her faith in her new country to heal her: "I'd hoped being Americanized could erase my memories of the war."[44]

In an article on the consequences of Cambodian genocide, Hurst Hannum writes that Cambodian refugees resettled in the United States in a particular pattern:

> People . . . live in places similar to those in which they first settled: urban inner-city locations. . . . Apartment buildings often have a number of Khmer families living in them. This densely populated urban locale has thus become the site of a reconfigured Khmer village in the sense that hundreds of Khmer spanning several generations live in close proximity to each other and rely almost solely on each other for their social and emotional needs.[45]

This recreation of a microcosmic Phnom Penh in the United States establishes a therapeutic community space for recovery for the Cambodian refugees, in which they are able to restore the cultural and social norms of their previous lives, as well as provides a degree of closure to the tragic story of the Pol Pot years. It also provides a safe and nurturing environment for speaking out about the tragic past for these individuals, as Ung paradigmatically summarizes: "I am far from Cambodia now. . . . In America, as my life grows stronger, I am able to rewrite [our] story."[46] Ethnic Cambodian refugee enclaves in the U.S. are not the only healing environment, though. Sucheng Chan notes that the 1990s saw increasing numbers of Cambodian Americans returning to their homeland to participate in its reconstruction—both in terms of its political infrastructure and the physical landscape which had been so damaged under the Khmer Rouge, a full circle move which reminds us once more of the intricate connection between humanity and landscape.[47]

NOTES

1. See, for example, Hurst Hannum, "International Law and Cambodian Genocide: The Sounds of Silence," *Human Rights Quarterly* 11.1 (1989): 82–138.
2. Narratives about Vietnam are closely allied to this body of literature, both in terms of subject matter and the approach to the retelling of the war story and also in terms of the geographical proximity. See Monique T.D. Truong, "Vietnamese American Literature," in *An Interethnic Companion to Asian American Literature*, ed. King-Kok Cheung (New York: Cambridge University Press, 1996), 219–46.
3. *Angkar* and *Mahantdori* are used throughout this chapter as synonyms for the Pol Pot era.
4. E.A. Méng-Try, "Kampuchea: A Country Adrift," *Population and Development Review* 7.2 (1981): 212.
5. Karl D. Jackson, "Cambodia 1977: Gone to Pot," *Asian Survey* 18.1 (1978): 88.
6. It was estimated that by 1979 only ten percent of the rice fields were cultivated and 1979 was one of the worst famine years. See Méng-Try, "Kampuchea," 219.

7. Ibid., 214.
8. Ibid.
9. Ibid., 224.
10. "Speech presented by Comrade Pol Pot, Secretary of the Central Committee of the Communist Party of Kampuchea on the 18th Anniversary of the Founding of the Communist Party of Kampuchea," Phnom-Penh, September 27, 1978. Department of Press and Information, Ministry of Foreign Affairs, Democratic Kampuchea, 1978. http://www.eccc.gov.kh (accessed May 15, 2014).
11. Pol Pot's radio addresses: December 31, 1976, January 4, 1977, and September 27, 1977, quoted in Jackson, "Cambodia 1977," 79.
12. Gay Becker, Yewoubdar Beyen, and Pauline Ken, "Memory, Trauma, and Embodied Distress: The Management of Disruption in the Stories of Cambodians in Exile," *Ethos* 28.3 (2000): 325.
13. Many Cambodian novels deal with this issue, but few have been translated into English.
14. Isabelle Thuy Pelaud notes that most of the first generation of published works by Cambodian and Vietnamese refugees were written in Khmer or Vietnamese and published in Cambodian and Vietnamese language literary journals. Pelaud, *This Is All I Choose to Tell: History and Hybridity in Vietnamese American Literature* (Philadelphia: Temple University Press, 2011), 22–23. Individual narratives are often either self-published or published by small presses and many lack the polish of professionally crafted writing. These narratives also seem to be hampered by their authors' attempts at a kind of cross-cultural brokerage, an anxiety to appeal to multiple readerships.
15. Chileng Pa, *Escaping the Khmer Rouge* (Jefferson, NC: McFarland, 2008), 102.
16. Alexander Laban Hinton, "A Head for an Eye: Revenge in the Cambodian Genocide," *American Ethnologist* 25.3 (1998): 363.
17. Michael Vickery, *Cambodia: 1975–1982* (Boston: South End Press, 1984), 264, 285.
18. The mass forced relocation to the countryside distinguishes the Cambodian story from other attempts to transform the country into a Communist state.
19. Loung Ung, *After They Killed Our Father: A Refugee from the Killing Fields Reunites with the Sister She Left Behind* (London: Mainstream, 2007), 16.
20. This toxicity includes both the contamination of the land by inept agricultural techniques and the residual landmines which littered the landscape, especially in the areas most proximate to the Thai border.
21. Jimmy Carter, "Farewell Address," January 14, 1981, http://www.jimmycarterlibrary.gov/documents/speeches/farewell.phtml (accessed June 20, 2012).
22. "Vietnam Memories in America," in *The Vietnamese American 1.5 Generation: Stories of War, Revolution, Flight, and New Beginnings*, ed. Sucheng Chan (Philadelphia: Temple University Press, 2006), 227. Also see Sucheng Chan, *Survivors: Cambodian Refugees in the United States* (Chicago: University of Illinois Press, 2004).
23. Chan, *Survivors*, 81, 97.
24. Roger Warner, "Foreword," in Haing S. Ngor, *Survival in the Killing Fields* (New York: Macmillan, 1987), 505.
25. Theanvy Kuoch, Richard A. Miller, and Mary F. Scully (Khmer Health Associates), "Healing the Wounds of the Mahantdori," *Women & Therapy* 13.3 (1992): 193.
26. Linda Martín Alcoff and Laura Gray-Rosendale concentrate upon the survivors of sexual abuse but also suggest that "survivor discourse" can more flexibly be adopted to refer to those who have lived through traumatic

experiences. Alcoff and Gray-Rosendale, "Survivor Discourse," in *Getting a Life: Everyday Uses of Autobiography*, ed. Sidonie Smith and Julia Watson (Minneapolis: University of Minnesota Press, 1996), 198–225.

27. Suzette A. Henke, *Shattered Subjects: Trauma and Testimony in Women's Life-Writing* (London: Macmillan, 1998), xiii, xvi. Also see Inga Clendinnen, *Reading the Holocaust* (New York: Cambridge University Press, 1999), and Maria Tumarkin, *Traumascapes: The Power and Fate of Places Transformed by Tragedy* (Melbourne: Melbourne University Press, 2005).
28. Ibid., xii.
29. Ibid.
30. Sidonie Smith and Julia Watson, *Reading Autobiography: A Guide for Interpreting Life Narratives* (Minneapolis: University of Minnesota Press, 2002), 21–22.
31. Ngor, *Survival in the Killing Fields*, 472–73.
32. Smith and Watson, *Reading Autobiography*, 205–6.
33. While reading memoirs of the Khmer Rouge years, I suffered frequent headaches and disturbing dreams.
34. For instance, here is Ngor's dedication in *Survival in the Killing Fields*: "I want to dedicate this book to the memories of my father, Ngor Kea, of my mother, Lim Ngor, of my wife, Chang Huoy (Chang My Huoy), who have died in the most miserable, uncivilized, and inhumane ways under the Khmer Communist regime. I have written this book for the world to better understand communism and other regimes in Cambodia."
35. Alcoff and Gray-Rosendale, "Survivor Discourse," 213.
36. Ngor, *Survival in the Killing Fields*, 1.
37. Ibid.
38. Ibid., 257.
39. Ibid., 310.
40. Ibid., 495.
41. Loung Ung, *First They Killed My Father: A Daughter of Cambodia Remembers* (New York: Harper Collins, 2000), 10.
42. Ibid., 18.
43. Ibid., 277.
44. Ibid., 276.
45. Hurst Hannum, "International Law," 326.
46. Ung, *After They Killed Our Father*, 66.
47. Chan, *Survivors*, 243.

BIBLIOGRAPHY

Affonço, Denise. *To The End of Hell: One Woman's Struggle to Survive Cambodia's Khmer Rouge*. London: Reportage Press, 2005.

Alcoff, Linda Martín and Laura Gray-Rosendale. "Survivor Discourse." In *Getting a Life: Everyday Uses of Autobiography*, edited by Sidonie Smith and Julia Watson, 198–225. Minneapolis: University of Minnesota Press, 1996.

Becker, Gay, Yewoubdar Beyen, and Pauline Ken. "Memory, Trauma, and Embodied Distress: The Management of Disruption in the Stories of Cambodians in Exile." *Ethos* 28.3 (2000): 320–45.

Carter, Jimmy. "Farewell Address." January 14, 1981. http://www.jimmycarterlibrary.gov/documents/speeches/farewell.phtml (accessed June 20, 2012).

Chan, Sucheng. *Survivors: Cambodian Refugees in the United States*. Chicago: University of Illinois Press, 2004.

Clendinnen. Inga. "The History Question: Who Owns the Past?" *Quarterly Essay* 23 (2003): 1–72.

———. *Reading the Holocaust*. New York: Cambridge University Press, 1999.

Hannum, Hurst. "International Law and Cambodian Genocide: The Sounds of Silence." *Human Rights Quarterly* 11.1 (1989): 82–138.

Henke, Suzette A. *Shattered Subjects: Trauma and Testimony in Women's Life-Writing*. London: Macmillan, 1998.

Him, Chanrithy. *When Broken Glass Floats: Growing Up Under the Khmer Rouge*. New York: W.W. Norton, 2000.

Hinton, Alexander Laban. "A Head for an Eye: Revenge in the Cambodian Genocide." *American Ethnologist* 25.3 (1998): 352–77.

Jackson, Karl D. "Cambodia 1977: Gone to Pot." *Asian Survey* 18.1 (1978): 76–90.

Krall, Yung Krall. *A Thousand Tears Falling: A True Story of a Vietnamese Family Torn Apart by War, Communism, and the CIA*. Atlanta: Longstreet Press, 1995.

Kuoch, Theanvy, Richard A. Miller, and Mary F. Scully (Khmer Health Associates). "Healing the Wounds of the Mahantdori." *Women & Therapy* 13.3 (1992): 191–207.

Le, Vui. *The Forgotten Generation: From South Vietnamese to Vietnamese-American*. Bloomington, IN: Universe, 2009.

Méng-Try, E.A. "Kampuchea: A Country Adrift." *Population and Development Review* 7.2 (1981): 209–28.

Ngor, Haing S. *Survival in the Killing Fields*. New York: Macmillan, 1987.

Nguyen, Nathalie Huynh Chau. *Memory Is Another Country: Women of the Vietnamese Diaspora*. Santa Barbara, CA: ABC-CLIO, 2009.

Nguyen, Thi Thu-Lam, with Edith Kreisler and Sandra Christenson. *Fallen Leaves: Memoirs of a Vietnamese Woman from 1940–1975*. New Haven: Council on Southeast Asia Studies, Yale Center for International and Area Studies, 1989.

Nguyen, Thi Tuyet Mai. *The Rubber Tree: Memoir of a Vietnamese Woman Who Was an Anti-French Guerilla, a Publisher, and a Peace Activist*, edited by Monique Senderowicz. Jefferson, NC: McFarland, 1994.

Pa, Chileng. *Escaping the Khmer Rouge*. Jefferson, NC: McFarland, 2008.

Pelaud, Isabelle Thuy. *This Is All I Choose to Tell: History and Hybridity in Vietnamese American Literature*. Philadelphia: Temple University Press, 2011.

Pham, Andrew X. *Catfish and Mandala: A Vietnamese Odyssey*. London: Flamingo, 2000.

———. *The Eaves of Heaven: A Life in Three Wars*. New York: Three Rivers, 2008.

Pol Pot. "Speech presented by Comrade Pol Pot, Secretary of the Central Committee of the Communist Party of Kampuchea on the 18th Anniversary of the Founding of the Communist Party of Kampuchea," Phnom-Penh, September 27, 1978. Department of Press and Information, Ministry of Foreign Affairs, Democratic Kampuchea, 1978. http://www.eccc.gov.kh (accessed May 15, 2014).

Smith, Sidonie and Julia Watson. *Reading Autobiography: A Guide for Interpreting Life Narratives*. Minneapolis: University of Minnesota Press, 2002.

Truong, Monique T.D. *The Book of Salt*. New York: Vintage, 2003.

———. "Vietnamese American Literature." In *An Interethnic Companion to Asian American Literature*, edited by King-Kok Cheung, 219–46. New York: Cambridge University Press, 1996.

Tumarkin, Maria. *Traumascapes: The Power and Fate of Places Transformed by Tragedy*. Melbourne: Melbourne University Press, 2005.

Ung, Loung. *After They Killed Our Father: A Refugee from the Killing Fields Reunites with the Sister She Left Behind*. London: Mainstream, 2007.

———. *First They Killed My Father: A Daughter of Cambodia Remembers*. New York: Harper Collins, 2000.

Vickery, Michael. *Cambodia: 1975–1982*. Boston: South End Press, 1984.

"Vietnam Memories in America." In *The Vietnamese American 1.5 Generation: Stories of War, Revolution, Flight, and New Beginnings*, edited by Sucheng Chan, 219–27. Philadelphia: Temple University Press, 2006.

Warner, Roger. "Foreword." In Haing S. Ngor, *Survival in the Killing Fields* (New York: Macmillan, 1987), 505

6 Ecological Imaginations, the Vietnam War, and Vietnamese American Literature

Cathy J. Schlund-Vials

In the distance, through a scene of withered trees (which had been defoliated now by chemicals as well as bombs), I could see that Bai Gian had not been rebuilt, and that a few remaining temples, pagodas, and wayside shrines—even my old school-house and the guardsmen's awful prison—had been wiped away by the hand of war. Beautiful tropical forests had been turned into a bomb-cratered desert. It was as if the American giant, who had for so long been taunted and annoyed by the Viet Cong ants, had finally come to stamp its feet.

—Le Ly Hayslip, *When Heaven and Earth Changed Places*[1]

An American jeep pulling off the main road suddenly flew in the air and flipped into a somersault like a salmon flying up-current. The blast was so loud and the fire so bright I could see the flames and feel the tremors in the earth from my end of the village, which was quite a few rice fields away.

—Lan Cao, *Monkey Bridge*[2]

One object of ecocriticism, as I see it, is to read in such a way as to amplify the reality of the environment in or of a text . . . so that it becomes a place chiefly interesting because of the human events that unfold in it.

—Robert Kern, "Ecocriticism: What Is It Good For?"[3]

Evoking a Vietnamese American context of war and forced relocation, Le Ly Hayslip's autobiographical *When Heaven and Earth Changed Places: A Vietnamese Woman's Journey from War to Peace* (1989) and Lan Cao's fictional *Monkey Bridge* (1997) inhabit particularly conspicuous positions in the dominant U.S. imagination and within Asian American literary studies. Indeed, as Viet Nguyen notes, "For American readers, Hayslip has become representative of those anonymous millions of Vietnamese in whose name the Vietnam War was fought by both sides. Through her extraordinary personal story, she not only symbolically bears their collective pain but also bears the victim's burden of forgiveness."[4] Whereas Hayslip's memoir has become "symbolically representative" of the war-torn Vietnamese subject and the traumatic contours of the Vietnam War (1959–75), Cao's novel offers, as Jeanne Schinto suggests, an alternative engagement with the conflict as "the first fictional exploration of the Vietnamese experience in America."[5] Schinto perceives that *Monkey Bridge* imaginatively restages the war via "its memorable characterizations, its pattern of images, and the insights that those images invite."[6]

Nguyen and Schinto's observations, which consider cultural and imagistic representations of wartime Vietnamese American subjectivity, serve, in part, to frame this chapter's analysis of *When Heaven and Earth Changed Places* and *Monkey Bridge*, which extends each evaluation to accommodate analogous senses of space. My examination of these texts centers on an ecological pattern of images that is tied to a traumatized Vietnamese American experience and militarized physical environment. When Hayslip describes "withered trees" and "beautiful tropic forests" transformed into "a bomb-cratered desert" by U.S.-manufactured chemicals and munitions, and Cao characterizes an American jeep as a living animal, for example, these writers encapsulate the enduring legacies of U.S. militarization and disastrous American campaigns in Southeast Asia.

At the same time, these images, which engender a re-evaluation of the Vietnam War via environmental costs, render explicit the connection between U.S. war-making, the overt destruction of the Vietnamese landscape, and the representation of the conflict as a multivalent "quagmire." Such relationships are prominently at the forefront of David Halberstam's *The Making of a Quagmire: America and Vietnam during the Kennedy Era* (1965), which gave an important interpretation of the conflict as misguided, mismanaged, and misconstrued foreign policy failure.[7] Halberstam's use of "quagmire" as a means of understanding the contested terrains of mid-century U.S. foreign policy is of specific relevance to this chapter. As an "area of wet, boggy land that gives way under foot," and indicative of "a position or situation which is unpleasant or hazardous; *esp.* one from which it is difficult to extricate oneself," a quagmire is simultaneously spatially vexed and politically unstable.[8] Most significantly, to comprehend the Vietnam War as *quagmire conflict* brings into play an environmental metaphor that captures the wholesale failure of the U.S. project in Southeast Asia.[9]

The Vietnam War involved the *en masse* deployment of approximately 2.15 million Americans to various outposts in the Pacific Rim and Southeast Asia. Out of that number, an estimated 1.6 million soldiers were engaged in active combat, 58,260 killed in action, and another 1,724 reported missing in action.[10] Regrettably, Southeast Asian casualties are far less precise, although the Vietnamese government reported in 1995 that 1.1 million died during the conflict, and an estimated three million perished in Laos and Cambodia.[11]

Admittedly, casualties of war are not limited to the profound loss of human life. Nor does the conflict's disastrous scope end with the April 30, 1975 "Fall of Saigon." Indeed, dire consequences are ecologically evident in present-day considerations about Agent Orange usage. More than twenty-five years after the war's conclusion, the United States and Vietnam reached an agreement in 2001 to study the impact of the toxic defoliant, which to date has affected an estimated one million Vietnamese. The study highlighted the fact that Agent Orange is currently responsible for birth defects in approximately 150,000 Vietnamese children.[12] Most recently, in 2011, the Vietnamese government, armed with U.S. aid, announced that it would begin the initial clean-up phase in areas around former U.S. military bases.[13]

Conceiving of the Vietnam War ecologically as a multivalent quagmire, this chapter begins with an analysis of Hayslip's representation of militarized landscapes and dystopian settings. This is followed by an examination of the devastated Vietnamese countryside in *Monkey Bridge*, a text that engages the war's ecologically catastrophic aftermath through allusions to "scorched earth" policies of the American Civil War and detailed accounts of Agent Orange usage. Such ecological assessments intersect with Robert Kern's view that a central aim in ecocriticism is to "amplify the reality of the environment in or of a text" in order to evaluate the human events that occur within it. This chapter also contributes to the critique of the "absence of Asian American authors" in ecocriticism, which brings to light the field's "general inability to address seriously issues of race and class."[14] By concluding with Michael Herr's *Dispatches* (1977), I return to the ecological notion of "quagmire" and resituate *When Heaven and Earth Changed Places* and *Monkey Bridge* with respect to canonic Vietnam War literature marked by a *haunted* environmental imagination.

RE-ENGAGING MILITARIZED ZONES: *WHEN HEAVEN AND EARTH CHANGED PLACES*

> Twenty-one years ago, almost to the day, a skinny, barefoot farm girl clad in black pajamas, an old overshirt, and a torn straw hat stepped out of the hell of her village onto an antique propeller plane at Danang, and out again onto the ramp at Saigon's Tan Son Nhut airport—America's biggest air base of the war—and into heaven. After the black-and-white life of the countryside, it was as if I had been transported to the Land of Oz—tossed into a kaleidoscope of whirling sound and color.
>
> —Le Ly Hayslip, *When Heaven and Earth Changed Places*[15]

Published at the end of the Cold War, co-written with Jay Wurts, and quickly adapted to film, *When Heaven and Earth Changed Places* is a first-person "return narrative" that fixates on the vestiges of war and possible reunion in the author's country of origin.[16] As primary protagonist and principal author, Hayslip uses a covert trip back to Vietnam in 1986 as a strategic frame that enables a back-and-forth movement between the post-war present and the militarized past. Commencing with the declaration that "[f]or my first twelve years of life, I was a peasant girl in Ky La, now called Xa Hoa Qui, a small village near Danang in Central Vietnam," Hayslip charts her journey "from war to peace" through various settings in Vietnam, such as Ky La, Danang, and Saigon. To a lesser extent, Hayslip also maps her aftermath experiences in the United States, particularly in San Diego, California.[17]

From undisclosed Vietnamese villages to spectacular U.S. airfields, *When Heaven and Earth Changed Places* is a post-conflict memory text located at the environmental intersection of war, gender, and nation. As Leslie Bow rightly surmises, Hayslip's "narratives of life in a war zone and afterward rely upon conventions of realism that appeal particularly to her multiple and shifting positionalities as an engendered subject."[18] Accordingly, as the memoir progresses, Hayslip judiciously details her wartime coming-of-age through four distinct identities: as Viet Cong child soldier, Saigon housekeeper, low-level military base racketeer in Danang, and assimilated Vietnamese American refugee.[19] These roles, which involve encounters with soldiers and occur within spaces of militarized contact, include spatial allusions to "heaven," "earth," and "paradise." This tripartite figuration enables an environmental understanding of utopian beginnings and their contradiction. Hayslip's romanticized characterizations of the Vietnamese countryside collide with nightmarish accounts of militarized zones that contain both enemy combatants and allied troops. Whereas utopian imagery in the memoir bespeaks an idealistic, prewar imagining of space and a largely predictable ordering of place, Hayslip delineates dystopian scenes in relation to inimical forces (e.g., foreign soldiers/Viet Cong troops) and environmental degradation.

Over the course of *When Heaven and Earth Changed Places*, the U.S. military base emerges as a distinct feature of the Vietnamese landscape, and its implied reach signals both utopian possibilities and dystopian actualities. The military base is, on the one hand, a fantastical space capable of remaking and reorienting refugee bodies "out of country." This alchemical facet of militarized space is historically evident in the case of San Diego's Camp Pendleton, where newly drafted U.S. marines trained for deployments during the Vietnam War. In 1975, as the conflict came to a catastrophic close, Camp Pendleton became the first U.S. military base to provide accommodations for Vietnamese evacuees as part of the program "Operation New Arrivals." Such a relocation effort, whereby an estimated 50,000 refugees were transported from Vietnam to the United States, represents the largest humanitarian airlift in American history.[20] As Yen Le Espiritu astutely observes, such "militarized refuge" highlights the contradictory nature of U.S. foreign policy as a practice of overt aggression and combat-driven humanitarianism.[21]

On the other hand, militarized sites concurrently represent past histories of conflict and denote present-day shifts in technological war-craft. This Janus-faced depiction of military space, which brings into play considerations of power and politics, engages multivalent senses of place. As David Wood perceives, military architecture, "whether of the recent or distant past, is caught up in the symbolic landscapes and complexes of meaning that surround constructed forms, and is the visible element of vast networks of socio-technical power."[22] Likewise, Catherine Lutz maintains that the U.S. military base is a recognizable "topography of U.S. power" and a legible "cultural artifact of colonial dominance."[23] Hayslip's conflicting (and conflicted) descriptions of the natural environment and militarized zones render possible an evaluation of *When Heaven and Earth Changed Places* as a topographically-vexed memoir about U.S. foreign policy, the Vietnamese landscape, and the making of Vietnamese American refugees.

These topographical collisions are manifest in the juxtaposition of rural settings and battle-torn environments. For example, while tending to water buffalo in a meadow located at the outskirts of her village, Hayslip's self-ascribed "daydreaming" is interrupted by a peculiar "motor noise":

Like a tiger growling in a cave, the hollow noise became a roar and our buffalo grunted and trotted without prodding toward the trees. Steadily, the roar increased and I looked into the sun to see two helicopters, whining and flapping like furious birds, settle out of the sky toward me.[24]

The setting for Hayslip's remembrance—the Vietnamese countryside—is disturbed by "the sound of trucks and jeeps" and the "roar" of two helicopters. These auditory signifiers extend from and eventually converge on an imagined American military base, which is the assumed origin point for such militarized transport. Hayslip compares the mechanical with the organic in her metaphoric observations that the "motor noise" was "like a tiger growling in a cave" and that the helicopters' "roar" resembled the "whining and flapping" of "furious birds." This interchange between the constructed and natural world, in which animal sound emerges from inanimate object, transforms an idyllic rural environment into a dystopian militarized zone.

The attribution of naturalistic descriptors to militarized U.S. technologies accretes further meaning when situated against the increasingly volatile backdrop of the Vietnam War. Accordingly, Hayslip gestures, with natural metaphors and similes, toward an identifiable war-driven ecology, wherein the mechanistic collides with the organic. Correspondingly, a peaceful Southeast Asian field is transformed into a volatile Vietnam War battleground. These industrial sounds, as militaristic metonyms, signify earthly practices of foreign encroachment that threaten an idealized (or "heavenly") peasant existence.

Such mechanized intrusions are also apparent in Hayslip's descriptions of U.S. soldiers, which emphasize the intense clash of two distinct worlds. The author narrates, "what I feared most were the marines in the fatigues who sometimes stopped by on their way back from the field—smelling like water buffalo, unshaven, with weapons and the reflection of death in their eyes."[25] On one level, Hayslip's portrayal of U.S. military personnel prompts a critical reading of militarized intrusion insofar that soldier-induced apprehension interferes with the mundane registers of country life. On another level, Hayslip's assertion that armed marines resembled domesticated cattle takes on a fatal register via references to firearms and death.

This collocation of mechanistic and organic imagery is not limited to U.S. or even allied South Vietnamese (Republican) troops. These interruptions are equally attributable to Viet Cong forces, who intermittently visit Hayslip's home village to recruit troops and replenish supplies. The presence of the Viet Cong is justified by Hayslip's own position as a likeminded operative. Later, the author suffers socioeconomic need and becomes an American trading partner on a U.S. military base. Notwithstanding Hayslip's shifting geopolitical trajectory within the memoir, the appearance of Viet Cong soldiers—as is the case with U.S. forces—involves analogous characterizations of ecological disruptions of the Southeast Asian landscape by way of mechanized transport. Correspondingly, the utopian, pastoral dimensions of Hayslip's childhood home recurrently give way to more dystopian portraits of burned homes and scattered crops.

The natural world and mechanized realm dizzily and consistently "change places." Illustratively, after a three-day battle between Viet Cong forces and Republican troops, Hayslip notes that the "paddies . . . [were] littered with rubble—upturned trees, shattered rocks, and charred craters where bombs or artillery rounds went astray." This fatalistic landscape is marked by a disturbing tableau of "dead animals," which "lay rotting in the sun—water buffalo with stiff legs and bodies bloated as big as a car; disemboweled pigs and the remains of jungle animals that had run out of the forest to escape the gunfire only to be ripped apart by explosions."[26] The comparison of water buffalo to automobiles reinforces Hayslip's previous conflation of organic native bodies and inanimate military objects. As emblem of automated Fordism, the car image restages the industrial reaches of the U.S. military complex.

Focused on the environmental remnants of war, apparent in disordered ecological formations and animal carcasses, Hayslip's war recollection collapses the space between inanimate object and once-living organism. Such remembrances likewise blur the boundary between dead flora and fauna. To that end, exposed, upended tree roots are interchangeable with the stiff legs of the water buffalo. Moreover, the "shattered rocks" presage the devastated organic remains of both domesticated animals and miscellaneous jungle creatures.

This dramatic destruction of the Vietnamese countryside, which permanently ruptures the sanctity of home, corresponds to what cultural geographer Yi-Fu Tuan terms "landscapes of fear." Such locales, according to Tuan, potently link psychological states to physical environs, and make evident past traumas that continue to haunt present-day subjects.[27] Inclusive of real spaces of "imminent collapse," places of impending death, and chaotic sites of "personalized evil," these imaginaries are circumscribed by, in Tuan's explication, "the feeling that the hostile force, whatever its specific manifestation, possesses will."[28] Such hostilities in the end overwhelm *When Heaven and Earth Changed Places*, which maps the traumatic transformation of the once-familiar Vietnamese countryside into an unrecognizable war-torn environment, and that of a Vietnamese subject into a Vietnamese American refugee.

CIVIL WARS AND ENVIRONMENTAL WASTELANDS: LAN CAO'S *MONKEY BRIDGE*

Whereas *When Heaven and Earth Changed Places* is largely concerned with a presentist reading of the war from a Vietnamese perspective, Lan Cao's fictional *Monkey Bridge* epitomizes what Renny Christopher argues is initially at stake in Vietnamese American writing. Noting the "bicultural stance" of Vietnamese American authorship, Christopher asserts, "Vietnamese exile authors, while becoming 'American,' insist on remaining Vietnamese at the same time."[29] This bifurcated sensibility is evident in the novel's achronological narrative structure, which is split between daughter Mai Nguyen's present-day recollections and mother Thanh's journal entries. It is likewise clear in *Monkey Bridge*'s plot, which hinges on the fragmentation of the family: Mai's grandfather, Baba Quan, fails to meet Thanh at a pre-arranged checkpoint. Consequently, Thanh leaves her father behind amid the chaos of the "Fall of Saigon." As *Monkey Bridge* progresses, Baba Quan's absence haunts both daughter and mother, although for decidedly different reasons.[30] Mai is convinced that her grandfather awaits rescue in Communist Vietnam; Thanh knows that her father was a Viet Cong operative who chose to stay. Such plot elements foreground the novel's admixture of mystery, bildungsroman, war recollection, and immigrant narrative.

Notwithstanding these intergenerational contestations and familial machinations, what dominates the text is its constant environmental engagement with the Vietnam War. *Monkey Bridge* is asymmetrically divided between Mai's first-person remembrances and Thanh's diary entries, which repeatedly utilize "sublime landscape imagery" rooted to the "paradisiacal rice field," as Michelle Satterlee puts it.[31] These idyllic descriptions, which detail peaceful outings on the Mekong River and serene journeys to the Vietnamese countryside, occur alongside increasingly dystopian, wartime accounts of a destroyed landscape. The novel correspondingly produces a contradictory characterization of Vietnam as both romanticized homeland and devastated nation. In so doing, Cao, like Hayslip, tactically uses built and natural environments to explore the complex and contradictory legacies of the war on Vietnamese refugees and Vietnamese Americans.

However, *Monkey Bridge*, unlike *When Heaven and Earth Changed Places*, extends its environmental scope to encompass the traumatic experiences of American veterans, who constitute a late-twentieth century "lost generation." To that end, *Monkey Bridge* begins with an excerpt from T.S. Eliot's *The Waste Land*, which, in its poetic post-World War I connection to wounded masculinity and emphasis on degraded environments partially prefigures the novel's psychological and ecological investments with history and memory.[32] Moreover, the precariousness that haunts the novel's characters, who, to varying degrees, are victims of war-induced relocation and post-traumatic stress, is made legible via the recurrent allusion to "monkey bridges," structures characterized by architectural instability. These bridges, inextricably tied to the rural South Vietnamese landscape, become environmentally and historically significant when considered in relation to the expansive reaches and collateral legacies of the Vietnam War.

The connections between monkey bridges and politicized South Vietnamese space, which collapse that between manmade object and native environs, are evident early in the novel. For example, Colonel Michael McMahon, a close family friend and Vietnam War veteran, tells Mai that these structures were "spindly pedestrian overpasses that hovered thirty meters or so above a web of canals, like a Venice in the tropics. . . . [They] consisted of a thin pole of bamboo no wider than a grown man's foot. . . . A railing was tied to one side, so you could at least hold on to it as you made your way across like a monkey."[33] This description highlights the perilous nature of the bridges, which force a human adult to assume a monkey's movement, while the speaker's status as a U.S. soldier forced to navigate the dangerous terrain of a South Vietnamese jungle atop a bamboo bridge makes evident an ecologically vexed relationship between invasive foreign soldier and indigenous flora and fauna. This contested association with the landscape intersects with a more global reading of the Vietnam War. Specifically, if the American War in Vietnam is largely remembered as a foreign policy quagmire, then monkey bridges metaphorically capture the instability of the larger U.S. Cold War project abroad.

On one level, McMahon's characterization of "Venice in the tropics" collapses, through a seemingly incongruous geographic comparison, the geopolitical spaces between established European center and Vietnamese landscape. On another level, the degree to which monkey bridges connote particular senses of South Vietnamese place facilitates a palimpsestic examination of multiple histories and multivalent politics. Accordingly, the colonel's conflation of European hub with Southeast locale points to an imperial understanding of Vietnam consistent with the tenets of an East-West dyad comprised of a longstanding colonial and militarized relationship with France and the United States. On another level, the structure of the monkey bridge, which connects two disparate points, reinforces the novel's prevailing transnational registers. Such transnational frames are evident in its representation of the interaction between Vietnamese American refugees and Vietnam War veterans in ethnic enclaves such as Little Saigon.

These East/West transnational meditations foreshadow the novel's subsequent North/South consideration of two linked civil war narratives: the Vietnam War and the American Civil War.[34] Notwithstanding *Monkey Bridge*'s preoccupation with notions of place, the allusion to both conflicts militates against a clear sense of refugee emplacement. This unmoored sensibility echoes the haunted experiences of forcibly relocated Vietnamese refugees, who live an uncanny diasporic existence in the United States.[35] For instance, in the months following her relocation and reunion with her mother, Mai relates, "It hardly mattered that all around us ghosts of a different war lingered, the Battle of Fredericksburg, the Battle of Bull Run, Confederate victories secured by Robert E. Lee's Army of Northern Virginia."[36] Mai's characterization of ghostly environs illustrates a war-driven interpretation of the American landscape fixed to a collateral experience with the Vietnam War.

Monkey Bridge employs various haunted topographies that speak to transnational histories of civil war; at the same time, the enduring American narrative is revised to express Vietnamese American experience. Accordingly, the protagonist's spectral allusion to the Battle of Fredericksburg (December 11–15, 1862) and the Battle of Bull Run (July 21, 1861) corresponds to a distinct history of Southern victories that in the end failed to secure Confederate sovereignty. These Civil War "ghosts," which, within the dominant imagination, involve convoluted narratives of family members fighting each other along a north/south axis, become even more significant when set adjacent to Baba Quan's affiliation as a Viet Cong operative. Ecologically, the "scorched earth policy" that was part and parcel of General William Tecumseh Sherman's notorious southern March to the Sea foreshadows a "total war" strategy that was used by the United States during the American War in Vietnam.

At the same time, the protagonist's explicit allusion to Southern victories foregrounds her subsequent meeting with Colonel McMahon, which highlights a different "north versus south" conflict. Seeking McMahon's assistance in locating her grandfather, Mai travels north from Falls Church, Virginia to Farmington, Connecticut. Once there, she is struck by the colonel's "large eat-in kitchen," which "was painted an inconspicuous beige, its walls covered with mementos from Vietnam—a conical straw hat from Danang, large lacquer-and-eggshell paintings, placards with names of places I knew only as battlefields. An Loc, Kontum, Khe Sanh."[37] Though ostensibly innocuous touristic souvenirs, the hat and paintings function as reminders of Vietnam and are emblems of the colonel's various tours of duty. Similar to the previous allusion to Confederate victories, Mai's mention of An Loc, Kontum, and Khe Sanh, the latter of which was abandoned by the U.S. in

July 1968, encompasses two South Vietnamese-U.S. victories and a North Vietnamese victory respectively.[38]

These militarized artifacts, gleaned by a U.S. soldier while on duty during war, metaphorically transform the domestic space of the kitchen into a distant war zone. Moreover, such war mementos assume greater significance when contrasted with the mother Thanh's traumatic recollections of wartime struggle, which repeatedly return to the Vietnamese landscape. As is the case in Hayslip's *When Heaven and Earth Changed Places*, Cao uses organic metaphors to reveal the conflict's disastrous mechanistic realities. Mai's mother relates,

> The elephant had yet to spread its ears or trumpet its loudest, most ominous battle cry. In their final and deadliest charge yet, the elephants rolled out drum after drum painted with orange stripes and sprayed our crops overnight with a special kind of poison, a mixture so powerful that it could command even the most majestic of trees to prematurely drop their leaves.[39]

Comparing the U.S. forces to "elephants," Thanh makes clear their inimical status vis-à-vis the natural environment. Agent Orange as degradation catalyst is defamiliarized and simultaneously appropriated as part of a traditional Vietnamese parable.[40]

The environmental degradation is directly attributable to the United States. Within the novel's narrative, such devastation, wherein "American soldiers poison the land that Baba Quan aimed to protect," signals a potent threat to Vietnamese civilians' economic livelihood.[41] More immediately, the militarized destruction of the landscape prompts migration that eventually motivates the Vietnamese patriarch to become a Viet Cong operative.[42] Such movements ironically presage the involuntary migration of Thanh and Mai, along with their Vietnamese countrymen, to the United States.

As *Monkey Bridge* concludes, the disastrous implications of U.S. foreign policy are foregrounded when Thanh recalls,

> The earthworms, our litmus test, could not live in poisoned soil. And neither could we. That was how the second half of our nightmare began, with the death of our village soil. Soon thereafter, leaflets were dropped from the sky to warn us that our houses would be doused with petrol and burned to the ground so that the Vietcong could no longer be harbored in the village and hidden from view. We were told to pack up and move across the river to a village of concrete surrounded by barbed wire and trenches as deep and wide as the gulf in my own sorrowful soul.[43]

By linking environmental degradation to war-induced devastation, Thanh's description of collateral damage makes visceral the true cost of American war-making with regard to the Vietnamese landscape. The catastrophic use of mechanized force (against organic existence), born out of militarized campaigns, produces an environmentally-driven and emotionally-marked critique of U.S. foreign policy.

CONCLUSION: VIETNAMESE AMERICAN SENSES OF PLACE

Ecological characterizations of space in Hayslip's *When Heaven and Earth Changed Places* and Cao's *Monkey Bridge* foreground remembrance and critique militarization. In so doing, these works engage with "the multiple ways places are metonymically and metaphorically tied to identities."[44] For Vietnamese American refugees, such "senses of place" must, in the aftermath of war and involuntary migration, remain largely "imagined" from an exilic, conflicted subject position. As Monique T.D. Truong avows, such cultural production contains "layers upon layers of contradictions" that necessarily "emerge out of a social and historical moment of military conflict . . . [and] spea[k] of death" while longing for "peace of mind."[45] Correspondingly, Hayslip and Cao articulate an ecological understanding of the Vietnam War that charts the militarized course of in-country conflict and U.S. imperialism.

To be sure, ecological readings of the conflict are by no means limited to Vietnamese American literary production. Such environmental representations are evident in one of the first literary productions about the Vietnam War: Michael Herr's autobiography, *Dispatches* (1977).[46] Reflecting upon the Vietnamese highlands, the former war correspondent-turned-memoirist asserts, "The Puritan belief that Satan dwelt in Nature could have been born here, where even on the coldest, freshest mountaintops you could smell jungle and that tension between rot and genesis that all jungles give off. It is ghost-story country."[47] Focusing on the northern mountain region between Vietnam, Laos, and Cambodia, Herr utilizes the foundational U.S. narrative of Puritanism to interpret the local landscape as diabolical. Eschewing the North American wilderness for the Vietnamese jungle, with a concomitant collapse between colonial New England and postcolonial Southeast Asia, Herr's concluding description of Vietnam as a "ghost-story country" projects Vietnam as an "otherworldly" battleground site. Such Puritanical "senses of place" summon an appraisal of settler politics built on a hostile relationship to "the wilderness" and its indigenous inhabitants.

Set adjacent Herr's haunted text, the paradoxical spatial formations at work in Hayslip's memoir and Cao's novel, which intersect with and diverge from militarized epicenters of war-making and aftermath refuge, make evident each work's analogous negotiation of conflict-driven "landscapes of fear." Both works consistently employ a geographic and architectural vocabulary inclusive of the natural landscape and built environment by which they convey a provocative *ecological* negotiation with the quagmire-like imaginary of the Vietnam War.

Despite their different politics and allegiances, *Heaven and Earth Changed Places* and *Monkey Bridge* mesh imagined and real landscapes of the Vietnam War. Their focus on the physical environment destabilizes the dominant reading of the Vietnam War as a human-centric tale of foreign policy folly and critically encompasses a more expansive militarized landscape. It likewise resituates Vietnamese American literature—and, by proxy, Asian American literature—from the periphery of ecocriticism to its center.

NOTES

1. Le Ly Hayslip (with Jay Wurts), *When Heaven and Earth Changed Places: A Vietnamese Woman's Journey from War to Peace* (New York: Penguin Books, 1989), 195.
2. Lan Cao, *Monkey Bridge* (New York: Penguin, 1997), 243.
3. Robert Kern, "Ecocriticism: What Is It Good For?" in *The ISLE Reader: Ecocriticism, 1993–2003*, ed. Michael P. Branch and Scott Slovic (Athens: University of Georgia Press, 2003), 260.
4. Viet Thanh Nguyen, *Race and Resistance: Literature and Politics in Asian America* (Oxford: Oxford University Press, 2002), 108.
5. Jeanne Schinto, "Invisible Scars," *Women's Review of Books* 14.10/11 (1997): 64.
6. Ibid.
7. David Halberstam, *The Making of a Quagmire* (New York: Random House, 1965).
8. *Oxford English Dictionary*, http://dictionary.oed.com (accessed December 12, 2011).
9. Such "failed" assessments predictably commence with a brief evaluation of human cost.
10. Marilyn B. Young, *The Vietnam Wars: 1945–1990* (New York: Harper Collins, 1991), 319.
11. Andrew Wiest, *The Vietnam War: 1956–1975* (New York: Routledge, 2002), 85.
12. Tom Fawthrop, "Vietnam's War against Agent Orange," *BBC News*, June 14, 2004, http://news.bbc.co.uk/2/hi/health/3798581.stm (accessed December 9, 2011).
13. "Vietnam Begins First Phase of Agent Orange Cleanup," *The Washington Post*, June 17, 2011, http://www.washingtontimes.com/news/2011/jun/17/vietnam-begins-1st-phase-of-agent-orange-cleanup/ (accessed January 1, 2012).
14. Robert T. Hayashi, "Beyond Walden Pond: Asian American Literature and the Limits of Ecocriticism," in *Coming into Contact: Explorations in Ecocritical Theory and Practice*, eds. Annie Merrill Ingram, Ian Marshall, Daniel J. Philippon, and Adam W. Sweeting (Athens: University of Georgia Press, 2007), 58.
15. Hayslip, *When Heaven and Earth Changed Places*, 64.
16. *When Heaven and Earth Changed Places* was the source text for Oliver Stone's 1993 film *Heaven and Earth* (the last production in his Vietnam War trilogy).
17. Hayslip, *When Heaven and Earth Changed Places*, x.

18. Leslie Bow, "Third-World Testimony in the Era of Globalization: Vietnam, Sexual Trauma, and Le Ly Hayslip's Art of Neutrality," in *Haunting Violations: Feminist Criticism and the Crisis of the "Real,"* eds. Wendy S. Hesford and Wendy Kozol (Urbana: University of Illinois Press, 2001), 171.
19. Prior to Hayslip's domestic employment in Saigon, she is brutally raped by Viet Cong soldiers following allegations that she is a traitor. While in Saigon, she has an affair with a married man and gives birth to a son. She is, until the memoir's conclusion, a single mother. Although the term "Viet Cong" ("Vietnamese Communist") was used in South Vietnamese newspapers since 1957, the official name of the Vietnamese Communist party was the "National Liberation Front."
20. Vik Jolly, "Vietnamese Refugee Camp Exhibit Coming to Pendleton," *Orange County Register*, April 7, 2010, http://www.ocregister.com/news/base-243036-exhibit-pendleton.html (accessed November 12, 2011).
21. Taken from a 2010 plenary discussion at the Association for Asian American Studies Conference in Austin, Texas.
22. David Wood, "Territoriality and Identity at RAF Menwith Hill," in *Art and Thought*, ed. Dana Arnold and Margaret Iversen (Malden, MA: Blackwell Publishing, 2004), 142.
23. Quoted in Vernadette V. Gonzalez, "Military Bases, 'Royalty Trips,' and Imperial Modernities: Gendered and Racialized Labor in the Postcolonial Philippines," *Frontiers* 28.3 (2007): 30–31. Also see Catherine Lutz, "Empire is in the Details," *American Ethnologist* 33.4 (2006): 594–611.
24. Hayslip, *When Heaven and Earth Changed Places*, 43.
25. Ibid., 174.
26. Ibid., 79.
27. Yi-Fu Tuan, *Landscapes of Fear* (Minneapolis: University of Minnesota Press, 2003), 6.
28. Ibid.
29. Quoted in Claire Stocks, "Bridging the Gaps: Inescapable History in Lan Cao's *Monkey Bridge*," *Studies in the Literary Imagination* 37.1 (2004): 83.
30. Baba Quan's political allegiances are related to a personal story of betrayal. Unable to pay his land debts, Baba Quan is forced to give his wife to a corrupt landowner in exchange for payment. Thanh is the illegitimate product of a union between a landowner and her mother. This romantic subplot foregrounds the grandfather's absence from the transport location and intersects with a more complex revenge plot involving the landowner's violent murder.
31. Michelle Satterlee, "How Memory Haunts: The Impact of Trauma on Vietnamese American Identity in Lan Cao's *Monkey Bridge*," *Studies in the Humanities* 31.2 (2004): 150.
32. The epigraph is a quotation from T.S. Eliot's *The Wasteland*.
33. Cao, *Monkey Bridge*, 109. Colonel McMahan is referred to as "Uncle Michael" in the novel.
34. Susan Edmonds, in a presentation at the 2009 Annual Modern Language Association convention, first articulated this "civil war" reading via Cao's novel.
35. This is not to suggest that, politically, the aims of the U.S. Civil War and the American War in Vietnam are identical.
36. Cao, *Monkey Bridge*, 31.
37. Ibid., 88.
38. Although both the United States and North Vietnam claimed victory, the abandonment of the base—along with the Tet Offensive that same year—represents a turning point in the war.

39. Cao, *Monkey Bridge*, 244.
40. Cao revises a traditional Vietnamese parable involving elephants and ants. According to the fable, the elephant has the initial advantage of size; however, the ants have the benefit of numbers. The ants, as a result, are able to carry the elephant through the sheer size of their numbers.
41. Stocks, "Bridging the Gaps," 91.
42. Ibid., 91–92. Stocks makes a key observation with regard to Thanh's spine, which, in *Monkey Bridge*, is described as "S-shaped" and "twisted like a crooked coastline," 205. This physiological fact "testif[ies] to the link between herself and the Vietnamese peninsula," 92.
43. Cao, *Monkey Bridge*, 246.
44. Steven Feld and Keith H. Basso, introduction to *Senses of Place*, ed. Steven Feld and Keith H. Basso (Rochester: Boydell and Brewer, 1999), 11.
45. Monique T.D. Truong, "Vietnamese American Literature" in *An Interethnic Companion to Asian American Literature*, ed. King-Kok Cheung (New York: Cambridge University Press, 1997), 219. Even with Truong's provocative engagement with war, recent scholarship on Vietnamese American literature rightly notes that such cultural production has grown beyond immediate rubrics of war and trauma. See Isabelle Thuy Pelaud, *This Is All I Choose to Tell: History and Hybridity in Vietnamese American Literature* (Philadelphia: Temple University Press, 2010).
46. Michael Herr was also one of the screenwriters for Stanley Kubrick's 1987 film *Full Metal Jacket*, which features a military war correspondent (played by actor Matthew Modine).
47. Michael Herr, *Dispatches* (New York: Vintage Books, 1991), 94.

BIBLIOGRAPHY

Bow, Leslie. "Third-World Testimony in the Era of Globalization: Vietnam, Sexual Trauma, and Le Ly Hayslip's Art of Neutrality." In *Haunting Violations: Feminist Criticism and the Crisis of the "Real,"* edited by Wendy S. Hesford and Wendy Kozol, 169–94. Urbana: University of Illinois Press, 2001.

Cao, Lan. *Monkey Bridge*. New York: Penguin, 1997.

Fawthrop, Tom. "Vietnam's War against Agent Orange." *BBC News*, June 14, 2004. http://news.bbc.co.uk/2/hi/health/3798581.stm (accessed December 9, 2011).

Feld, Steven and Keith H. Basso. Introduction to *Senses of Place*, edited by Steven Feld and Keith H. Basso, 3–12. Rochester: Boydell and Brewer, 1999.

Gonzalez, Vernadette V. "Military Bases, 'Royalty Trips,' and Imperial Modernities: Gendered and Racialized Labor in the Postcolonial Philippines." *Frontiers* 28.3 (2007): 28–59.

Gordon, Avery. *Ghostly Matters: Haunting and the Sociological Imagination*. Minneapolis: University of Minnesota Press, 1997.

Halberstam, David. *The Making of a Quagmire*. New York: Random House, 1965.

Hayashi, Robert T. "Beyond Walden Pond: Asian American Literature and the Limits of Ecocriticism." In *Coming into Contact: Explorations in Ecocritical Theory and Practice*, edited by Annie Merrill Ingram, Ian Marshall, Daniel J. Philippon, and Adam W. Sweeting, 58–75. Athens: University of Georgia Press, 2007.

Hayslip, Le Ly (with Jay Wurts). *When Heaven and Earth Changed Places: A Vietnamese Woman's Journey from War to Peace*. New York: Penguin Books, 1989.

Herr, Michael. *Dispatches*. New York: Vintage Books, 1991.

Janette, Michelle. "Guerilla Irony in Lan Cao's *Monkey Bridge.*" *Contemporary Literature* 42.1 (2001): 50–77.

Jolly, Vik. "Vietnamese Refugee Camp Exhibit Coming to Pendleton." *Orange County Register*, April 7, 2010. http://www.ocregister.com/news/base-243036-exhibit-pendleton.html (accessed November 12, 2011).

Kern, Robert. "Ecocriticism: What Is It Good For?" In *The ISLE Reader: Ecocriticism, 1993–2003*, edited by Michael P. Branch and Scott Slovic, 258–81. Athens: University of Georgia Press, 2003.

Lutz, Catherine. "Empire is in the Details." *American Ethnologist* 33.4 (2006): 594–611.

Nguyen, Viet Thanh. *Race and Resistance: Literature and Politics in Asian America*. Oxford: Oxford University Press, 2002.

Pelaud, Isabelle Thuy. *This Is All I Choose to Tell: History and Hybridity in Vietnamese American Literature*. Philadelphia: Temple University Press, 2010.

Satterlee, Michelle. "How Memory Haunts: The Impact of Trauma on Vietnamese American Identity in Lan Cao's *Monkey Bridge.*" *Studies in the Humanities* 31.2 (2004): 138–62.

Schinto, Jeanne. "Invisible Scars." *Women's Review of Books* 14.10/11 (1997): 26.

Stocks, Claire. "Bridging the Gaps: Inescapable History in Lan Cao's *Monkey Bridge.*" *Studies in the Literary Imagination* 37.1 (2004): 83–100.

Tansley, A. G. "The Use and Abuse of Vegetational Concepts and Terms." *Ecology* 16.3 (1935): 284–307.

Truong, Monique, T. D. "Vietnamese American Literature." In *An Interethnic Companion to Asian American Literature*, edited by King-Kok Cheung, 219–48. New York: Cambridge University Press, 1997.

Tuan, Yi-Fu. *Landscapes of Fear*. Minneapolis: University of Minnesota Press, 2003.

"Vietnam Begins First Phase of Agent Orange Cleanup." *The Washington Post*, June 17, 2011, http://www.washingtontimes.com/news/2011/jun/17/vietnam-begins-1st-phase-of-agent-orange-cleanup/ (accessed January 1, 2012).

Wiest, Andrew. *The Vietnam War: 1956–1975*. New York: Routledge, 2002.

Wood, David. "Territoriality and Identity at RAF Menwith Hill." In *Art and Thought*, edited by Dana Arnold and Margaret Iversen, 142–62. Malden, MA: Blackwell Publishing, 2004.

Young, Marilyn B. *The Vietnam Wars: 1945–1990*. New York: Harper Collins, 1991.

7 "Guns, Race, Meat, and Manifest Destiny"

Environmental Neocolonialism and Ecofeminism in Ruth Ozeki's *My Year of Meats*

Youngsuk Chae

Increasing attention is given to the racial and ethnic dimensions of environmental literature as a means of engagement with multiracial concerns and of shifting from the white-centered environmental movement. As Cheryll Glotfelty in her introduction to *The Ecocriticism Reader* states, "Ecocriticism has been predominantly a white movement. It will become a multi-ethnic movement when stronger connections are made between the environment and issues of social justice, and when a diversity of voices are encouraged to contribute to the discussion."[1] Although acknowledging the good intentions of her statement, T. V. Reed finds Glotfelty's remarks "complacent and politically insensitive," and he stresses the "whiteness" of the mainstream environmental movement and its "unwillingness to grapple with questions of racial, class, and national privilege."[2] The need to expand the existing paradigm of environmentalism to embrace diverse voices should not be regarded merely in terms of a supplement to white-dominant ecocriticism. In fact, the connection between environmental problems and the environmental injustice inflicted on the poor, racial minorities, and women is already evident; yet, the discussion of environmental inequity and unequal power relations in environmental problems in national and transnational contexts has not fully unfolded as part of the environmental movement.

Multiracial environmentalism extends the notion of environment to the environmental struggles that transpire in low-income communities and communities of color, as in agendas such as the elimination of lead and occupational hazards and the cleanup of contaminated industrial sites, which are also issues of the environmental justice movement.[3] Of the environmental justice movement, Julie Sze notes that it "challenges the mainstream definition of environment and nature based on a wilderness/preservationist frame by foregrounding race and labor in its definition of what constitutes 'nature.'"[4] The emergence of this movement, according to Daniel Faber and James O'Connor, indicates a shift from "the largely middle-class preservationist-environmental amenities movement" to "working class concerns on workers' health and safety" in the workplace.[5] Moreover, the need to shift paradigms in ecocriticism reflects an increase in environmentally degraded conditions and an uneven distribution of environmental problems to underprivileged people and racial minorities. Laura Pulido's *Environmentalism and Economic Justice*, which focuses on the environmental struggles of Chicano communities in the Southwest, explores how environmental issues intersect with racial ideology, class, and economic forces. Distinguishing mainstream environmentalism from "subaltern" environmentalism—subalternity in terms of "economic marginality" and "structural inequality"—Pulido explains that subaltern environmental movements involving racial minorities and nonunionized immigrant workers address their struggle to make a living as well as their quest for environmental justice for communities of economically and socially marginalized people.[6]

Many racial minorities and immigrants work in unsafe, unhealthy, and discriminatory environments, and they often have no voice with which to speak for themselves. In other words, as Pulido emphasizes, "the environmental problem is embedded within a larger set of unequal economic and social relations."[7] Although many critical racial and ethnic minority literatures disclose environmental hazards and labor exploitation directed against race, ethnicity, and gender, the oppositional stance of such works against the dominant power structure has not been regarded as part of environmental literature. Robert T. Hayashi points out that the "absence of Asian American authors from the field of ecocriticism is part of the field's more general inability to address seriously issues of race and class. . . . Moreover, the field's historical dependence upon 'nature' as the de facto definition of environment has further limited the incorporation of other voices."[8]

Centering on Ruth Ozeki's novel, *My Year of Meats* (1998), this chapter foregrounds the diversity of voices in environmental literature, addressing the close relationship of environmental issues with racial ideology, unequal distribution of power, and economic forces, as well as exemplifying the connections between race, ethnicity, gender, and environmental injustice in local and global contexts. In fact, what is unearthed in ecocriticism's recent shift of focus to the multiracial and transnational realms seems to demonstrate the underlying connection of the environmental crisis and the degraded conditions of "others," and the manner in which the capitalist system and globalization of its commodity markets have precipitated environmentally unethical actions and justified the utilization of "others" as the objects of exploitation and domination. As Ursula K. Heise emphasizes, it is important to note both the underlying economic force responsible for ecocriticism's "transnational turn"[9] and the causative effect of the capitalist logic of profit-making and accumulation in terms of the exploitation and domination of the natural world, women, and underprivileged people within and beyond national boundaries.

My Year of Meats offers a notable example of how multiethnic literature is interwoven with environmental injustice in local and global contexts.

The novel unfolds around two female protagonists: Jane Takagi-Little and Akiko Ueno. Jane, a Japanese American documentarian, works with Japanese crews in the New York office of the television program, *My American Wife!*—a weekly cookery program featuring Americans who share their favorite recipes, usually beef recipes, with a Japanese audience. The program is targeted at Japanese audiences in Japan and is sponsored by BEEF-EX, the United States Beef Export and Trade Syndicate. Akiko, a faithful viewer, is wife of Joichi Ueno, the Japanese advertising agent of BEEF-EX. The novel, set against a political and economic background of the late 1980s when BEEF-EX turned their markets to Asia—especially after Europe banned the import of growth-promoting hormone (DES) injected into U.S. meat in 1989—provides a clear demonstration of how the Asian Americanist critique of U.S.-centered colonial globalization intersects with a critical movement of environmental literature.

My Year of Meats incorporates ecological issues into a larger social and political agenda while unmasking the economic force of environmental injustice. The violent movement of capital beyond national boundaries is part of the capitalist system, and the consequent environmental and biological harms for human beings, nonhuman animals, and nature become the manifest destiny of the system. As Ozeki, through the voice of Jane, states, "Guns, race, meat, and Manifest Destiny all collided in a single explosion of violent, dehumanized activity."[10] The novel shows the clear conjunction between the violence of global capital and environmental degradation; and from an ecological feminist perspective it delineates the disproportionate ecological hazards affecting women, nonhuman animals, and people beyond national boundaries. Ozeki's critique of the capitalist system's profit-oriented logic and environmental injustice to "others" allow us to read global ecological violence as a new form of environmental neocolonialism and to embrace ecological feminism as part of the environmental justice movement in national and transnational contexts.

VIOLENCE OF GLOBAL CAPITAL AND ENVIRONMENTAL NEOCOLONIALISM

Whereas environmental racism, which Robert Bullard defines as racial minorities' disproportionate exposure to environmental hazards and health risks,[11] signifies racial discrimination and inequality that works against minorities, environmental injustice on a global level takes the form of neocolonial exploitation of natural resources, people, and the markets of developing countries. Looking for new commodity markets has been an integral part of the globalizing capitalist system, and globalization as a new form of economic domination and neocolonization of developing countries is in this sense marked by what Arjun Appadurai calls "predatory mobility."[12] As Appadurai claims, "Globalization is inextricably linked to the current workings of capital on a global basis" and is an extension of the political and economic domination of other countries.[13] In many ways, the "predatory mobility" of capital and forced consumption of ecologically hazardous commodities by people in developing countries have been accompanied by environmental destruction with harmful effects on the "other."

The unethical practice of exploiting "others" becomes more prevalent under the capitalist economic system. The economic logic mirrors the view expressed by Lawrence Summers, chief economist of the World Bank, on December 12, 1991, regarding the dumping of toxic waste in less developed countries: "Let Them Eat Pollution."[14] Dumping environmental hazards or toxic chemicals in poor areas has been an ongoing problem since the 1980s,[15] and it has become a global issue. If dumping toxic waste in poor community areas and less developed countries reveals environmental racism and environmental injustice, a late-capitalist form of violence that dumps "goods by corporations at prices below the cost of production"[16] or the capitalist violence that forces other countries to open economic markets for commodities already banned in the U.S. is a form of environmental neocolonialism. Daniel Faber in his book *Capitalizing on Environmental Injustice* explains that the creations of the North American Free Trade Agreement (NAFTA), multinational corporations, and World Trade organization (WTO) have contributed to the elimination or renegotiation of environmental regulations that cause a trade barrier. Faber notes, "free-trade agreements are resulting in a *downward harmonization* of environmental, labor, consumer, and worker health and safety regulations across the world, including the United States."[17] As he explains, capitalist interests have affected governmental and corporate policies, precipitating environmental degradation and ecological harm on land and people in less developed countries.[18] Joshua Karliner calls these transnational corporations "Earth brokers in the global economy" and points to the predatory nature of global corporatization.[19] In a similar vein, Mark Ritchie views transnational corporations' free-trade negotiations as "a new form of colonialism" that accelerates the wealth gap and environmental degradation around the world.[20]

Set against the background of U.S. enforcement of free trade with Japan in order to export contaminated beef, *My Year of Meats* foregrounds the manner in which capitalist violence intersects with biological hazards to people in other countries, women, and nonhuman animals. The novel depicts how "others" become the objects of abuse by global capitalist exploitation through the voice of Jane. Ozeki's protagonist Jane works as a coordinator of the television program *My American Wife!* and she gradually learns about the harmful effects of the growth-promoting hormone DES (or diethylstilbestrol) on women and nonhuman animals while filming candidates for the show. Although it is allegedly known that the Food and Drug Administration (FDA) banned the use of DES in the poultry industry in the 1950s, DES continued to be widely used in beef production.[21] Jane reports:

> In 1954, a ruminant nutritionist at Iowa State College had discovered that if you feed DES to beef cattle they get fat quicker. In fact, the DES-"enhanced" cattle could be "finished" (brought to slaughter weight) more than a month sooner than unenhanced animals, on about five hundred pounds less feed. Obviously this was a good thing for meat producers. DES was trumpeted as a "miracle" and "a revolution in the cattle industry," and without further ado, that very same year, the FDA approved DES for livestock. A year later DES received a patent as the first artificial animal growth stimulant. By the early 1960s, after the ban on implants for chickens, DES was used by more than 95 percent of U.S. cattle feeders to speed up production.[22]

Jane finds out that despite a government ban on DES in 1979, the majority of American cattle feeders still use DES. The European ban in 1989 on U.S. meat forced BEEF-EX to look for new markets.[23] As part of its trade agreement with the U.S., Japan agreed to import DES-injected beef in 1990. Jane explains the economic background behind the creation of the television program: "In 1990, as a result of pressure by the U.S. government, the New Beef Agreement was signed with Japan, relaxing import quotas and increasing the American share of Japan's red-meat market. In 1991, we started production on *My American Wife!*"[24] Working in the New York office for the program, Jane learns that BEEF-EX is the commercial sponsor of the program with its intention "to foster among Japanese housewives a proper understanding of the wholesomeness of U.S. meats."[25]

BEEF-EX uses the media to cover up the fact that the beef is contaminated, while selling idealized images of wholesome American family life in which beef features prominently. In other words, through its sponsorship of the television program, BEEF-EX diverts attention away from the problem of factory farming and instead leaves issues associated with DES-injected meat to the Japanese viewers who might purchase the beef after they watch the show. Regarding the flux of global capital and its influence on the media content through advertising, Zillah Eisenstein in *Global Obscenities: Patriarchy, Capitalism, and the Lure of Cyberfantasy* notes: "Media become part of advertising as products are embedded in storylines and consumer items define media content."[26] BEEF-EX's use of the media to sell U.S. beef to the Japanese audience reveals the manipulative power of what Eisenstein calls "the cyber-media complex of transnational capital."[27]

In the program *My American Wife!* white middle-class American wives with two to three children are considered "ideal" candidates for the show, and beef is prioritized over chicken and pork. The hierarchies the BEEF-EX set for the program content—the so-called "Desirable Things: Delicious meat recipe; Attractive, wholesome lifestyle," and "Undesirable Things: Physical imperfections. Second class peoples"[28]—are based on the BEEF-EX's economic interests, and their instructions for the programs' contents reinforce the white-dominant perspective, revealing its prejudiced views of the poor and people of color. The program associates the image of attractive, white middle-class housewives cooking beef with wholesome American values. The ultimate purpose of the program is to sell more red meat in Japan, while delivering the "traditional family values symbolized by red meat in rural America."[29]

Each episode of the program carries four commercial spots for BEEF-EX. The BEEF-EX commercial with its logo, "Beefland," inserted in between the show segments links the idealized image of America and the American family to the "wholesomeness" of U.S. beef, and the boundary between the fake documentaries of American wives cooking beef and the commercials of BEEF-EX becomes blurred. Eisenstein explains how the corporate interests seep into the media content that reinforces their economic purpose through the visual: "The different components of mainstream commercial media simultaneously construct and reflect the corporatist culture that constitutes mass culture. This culture is consumerist and continuously redefines its patriarchal and racist underpinnings in order to develop new markets in the global economy."[30] The manipulative message of commercial media serves the interests of global capital, as exemplified by the disguising of the real problem with U.S. beef through association with a wholesome American family. BEEF-EX's turn to Asian countries as markets for DES-contaminated beef discloses the dynamic of corporate capitalists' accumulation of profits through economic and racial inequality.

Furthermore, in elucidating the way in which the profit-oriented economic system takes a form of capitalist racism, Ozeki reveals how racial ideology is used to justify violence towards the subordinated. Through interconnections of the meanings of capital, stock, and cattle—"stock as of a human line" and of "a group of animals," and as "the capital invested in corporation"[31]—Ozeki implies the infiltration of capitalists' interests into other races and nonhuman animals as a means to accumulate profits, with racially and economically marginalized groups exploited and abused under the economic system. While filming the Dunn & Son Feedlot in Texas, Jane talks to a white cowboy working for Gale Dunn. He tells Jane that what he is injecting into cows is "Boss's special formula" to keep them disease free, and he says:

"Yup, these cows here's goin' straight to Japan," said the young cowboy conversationally. "I heard they even eat the assholes and everything. Is that where y'all are from?"

The older cowboy spit. "Donny, you just shut yer mouth and don't go sayin' shit you don't know nothin' about."

"Well, that's what Roy down at the packin' plant told me. Straight to Japan, Taiwan, and Korea. You ask me, it's a darn shame, wasting all that good American meat on a bunch of gooks. No offense."[32]

The cowboy's racist notion of a "bunch of gooks" helps justify unethical farming practices and the sale of the contaminated meat to other countries. In other words, racism is extended to justify global environmental injustice, and the racist ideology is a convenient defense for the interests of agribusiness. Through the voice of Jane, Ozeki unmasks the connection between capitalist violence and the consequent disastrous effects on "others."

The ecological hazard and its impacts on nonhuman animals and people in other countries, as uncovered by Ozeki, are associated with capitalism's profit-oriented logic, which is backed by science and technology. Despite the illegality of using DES, Jane learns that most cattle feeders use some form of growth-promoting hormones in feed supplements. Cattle farmers' use of DES to get more profits in a short amount of time suggests an inevitable manifestation of the capitalist economic system. Jane explains:

> Using DES and other drugs, like antibiotics, farmers could process animals on an assembly line, like cars or computer chips. Open-field grazing for cattle became unnecessary and inefficient and soon gave way to confinement feedlot operations, or factory farms, where thousands upon thousands of penned cattle could be fattened at troughs. This was an economy of scale. It was happening everywhere, the wave of the future, the marriage of science and big business.[33]

Through the voice of Jane, Ozeki demystifies the optimistic view of modern science as progress for the human condition and undermines the profit-oriented economic logic that leads to deterioration of the environment and of the conditions of humanity, nature, and nonhuman animals. While filming the Dunn & Son Feedlot, Jane confronts cowboy Gale, who asserts his reason for using growth-enhancing hormones: "Profits so small these days you gotta deal in volume, and without the drugs we'd be finished. The math just don't work out. I'm bringing more head to slaughter than he [Gale's father John Dunn] ever did. If it weren't for the modernizing I accomplished around here—."[34] Gale's idea of modernizing backed by scientific development is essentially an "efficient" way of making profits. In response to Jane's accusation of his use of DES on cattle, Gale defends it as a modern efficient way of "killing two birds with one stone" and justifies his way of farming in terms of "frontier Justice."[35] This justification reveals the ruthlessness of capitalist violence and the unethical actions that violate environmental justice. The profit-oriented rationalist logic infiltrates every aspect of our lives. As Val Plumwood points out, "The regimes of factory farming are the product of this self-maximizing calculus, of the rationalist economy stripped of all ridiculous and corrupting human emotion and compassion."[36] The "self-maximizing calculus" and the violent movement of capital beyond national boundaries are inherent in the capitalist system, and cattle feeders' use of DES to gain more profits and the consequent environmental hazards and biological harms for human beings and nonhuman animals are evident manifestations of the rationalist economic logic.

CAPITALIST PATRIARCHAL VIOLENCE ON WOMEN AND NONHUMAN ANIMALS

Whereas agribusiness and factory farming have brought profits to cattle feeders and the meat industry, their cost-efficiency orientation backed by science and technology negatively affects the environment, nonhuman animals, and women. As Karen Warren argues, there are connections among "unjustified environmental harms to women, other subordinated human groups, and nonhuman nature,"[37] and these "other" groups "suffer disproportionately higher risks and harms than men."[38] The disproportionate environmental hazards and biological harms imposed on women and other subjugated groups suggest a need to understand environmental issues from a feminist perspective. Carolyn Merchant claims that the feminist movement shares a commonality with the ecology movement in the sense that they both are "critical of the costs of competition, aggression, and domination arising from the market economy."[39] In a similar vein, Greta Gaard in *Ecofeminism: Women, Animals, Nature* states that both women and nonhuman animals suffer from environmental hazards and unsafe industrial products, because "toxic pesticides, chemical wastes, acid rain, radiation, and other pollutants take their first toll on women, women's reproductive systems, and children."[40] Ecological feminism, or ecofeminism, according to Gaard, is a response that shows the "connections between the oppressions of women and of nature that are significant to understanding why the environment is a feminist issue, and, conversely, why feminist issues can be addressed in terms of environmental concerns."[41]

Regarding the underlying cause(s) of this oppression of women and nature, and environmental exploitation, ecofeminists have different lines of thought. Merchant explains: "Radical ecofeminism analyzes environmental problems from within its critique of patriarchy and offers alternatives that could liberate both women and nature. Socialist ecofeminism grounds its analysis in capitalist patriarchy and would totally restructure, through a socialist revolution, the domination of women and nature inherent in the market economy's use of both as resources."[42] As Merchant notes, for socialist ecofeminists environmental problems are closely related to capitalism and patriarchy that justify the exploitation of women, nature, and nonhuman animals as well as the economic domination of other countries.[43] Maria Mies also points out the mutually reinforcing relationships of capitalism and patriarchy, calling them one system, "capitalist-patriarchy," and she regards patriarchy as "the invisible underground of the visible capitalist system."[44]

Ozeki's criticism of the profit-oriented economic system and the rationalization behind domination of "others" shares in the socialist ecofeminist perspective,[45] but she develops it by using media in critical ways. Ozeki brings ecofeminist issues to the forefront, exposing the biological harms of DES inflicted on women and nonhuman animals as well as the economic and environmental injustice toward them under the capitalist economic system. The growth-promoting hormone has been used on cattle for fast growth and on pregnant women in order to prevent miscarriage. Jane finds out that she has a deformed uterus due to her mother's ingestion of DES while pregnant, and she learns that for many decades DES has been used for pregnant women in the belief that it would prevent miscarriages and make "bigger and stronger babies." According to research published in 1952, however, DES did nothing to prevent miscarriage and in fact hormone manipulation during pregnancy was dangerous and caused cancer.[46]

Although the harmful effects of DES are foregrounded in the text, Ozeki does not merely criticize cattle feeders' and doctors' administration of DES to nonhuman animals and pregnant women. Rather, she uncovers the exploitative capitalist system and its disastrous effects on women and nonhuman animals, revealing the connection between capitalist patriarchal violence and the degradation of human life and the environment. Jane exclaims, "The conflict that interests me isn't *man* versus *woman*; it's *man* versus *life. Man's* REASON, his industries and commerce, versus the entire natural world."[47] Although acknowledging unequal power relations between men and women, Ozeki does not view men as the main cause of the oppression of women and ecological problems. Rather, through Jane's outcry Ozeki reveals the economic force beneath the Western male-centered dualism and the instrumental reason justifying the domination of women, nonhuman animals, and people in developing countries. Unlike radical ecofeminists' view of patriarchy as the cause of women's oppression and ecological degradation, Ozeki's ecofeminist approach recognizes the multiple factors underlying the problems and discloses the multilayered forms of domination—male-dominant power structure and global capitalism.

Historically, technological advancement and modern Enlightenment ideas have instrumentalized nature and nonhuman animals for the accumulation of profits in the name of the betterment of human life and of progress. Moreover, justification for dominating women as well as unethical utilization of nature and nonhuman animals have been precipitated by the rise of capitalism and colonialism. As Maria Mies and Vandana Shiva note in *Ecofeminism*, new scientific and technical developments are "characteristically patriarchal, anti-nature, and colonial,"[48] and the modern development-oriented ideology, according to their critique, plays a destructive role with regard to the environment, women, and people in developing countries.[49] The problem is that unethical treatments and instrumentalization of "others," as also noted by Plumwood, become intensified under the capitalist system, and those problems are among the inevitable consequences of "capitalist economic rationality."[50] Thus, it is imperative, in Plumwood's words, to distinguish between reductionist rationalism and reason, because "what is prohibited is unconstrained or total use of others as means, reducing others to means."[51]

In alignment with ecofeminists' critique of modern rationalism and development-oriented ideologies, Ozeki's novel challenges the Western male-centered capitalist rationalism that justifies the domination of and violence against women, nonhuman animals, and people in other countries. Approaching from socialist ecofeminist and environmental justice perspectives, Ozeki criticizes profit-oriented global capitalism as well as racist and sexist ideologies that justify the domination of "others." In the novel, the violence of capital, its subsequent environmental damage, and biological harms to women and nonhuman animals, all are vividly depicted in the slaughterhouse where Jane is knocked down. Jane describes a scene in the slaughterhouse where she hears "the death screams of a slaughtered lamb—which is exactly like the cry of a human baby."[52] Jane, who became pregnant by her boyfriend Sloan Rankin, miscarries the baby due to her deformed uterus, and the incidents of slaughtered cows and her aborted fetus occur simultaneously, with the implication that they are both victims of the ruthless violence of capital. Calling herself "the sterile laboratory animal," Jane erases boundaries between women and nonhuman animals and says: "How much of this blood is slaughtered cow and how much is my baby?"[53]

Like a mirror image of Jane's fall on the blood-saturated slaughterhouse floor, the scene of Akiko lying on a hospital bed after being battered by her husband is depicted in parallel. Joichi exemplifies patriarchy's oppression of women and nonhuman animals. As the advertising agent of BEEF-EX, he demands that Akiko should complete a survey questionnaire after she watches *My American Wife!* and also cook beef based on the recipe provided by the wife of the week. This for him is an efficient way of surveying the effectiveness of the program, as well as a way of making Akiko get fattened for pregnancy. Joichi's reasoning resembles the efficiency logic that Gale espouses: "Killing two birds with one stone." Akiko has been treated by Joichi as a tool for furthering his interests. Joichi's reason for marrying Akiko was that he "needed a wife."[54] He does not view Akiko as his equal partner but as a tool to continue his lineage, and her role as a housewife becomes instrumentalized, serving beef and sex for reproduction. As Lori Gruen states, "women and animals serve the same symbolic function in patriarchal society" in that they both are used to "serve and to be served up" for men.[55] In the novel, Akiko cooks meat for Joichi every Saturday after the show, but she keeps purging after she eats beef. She could not contain "any life down inside her,"[56] and this reflects her unconscious refusal to serve the interests of capitalist patriarchy. Akiko feels molested when Joichi is in the house; she wants to be alone. Her dream about following the biblical Moses who holds his hand out to lead her to safety reflects her view of Joichi as an oppressive patriarch. Joichi's belief in U.S. beef, his wish to change his name to the American name "John Wayne," and his force feeding Akiko beef in order to impregnate her reveal the interplay between man's violence and his economic activity as a system of oppression of "others." He is an embodiment of violent capitalist patriarchy.

As the representative of the ad agency in charge of marketing the meats for BEEF-EX, Joichi also censors the content of *My American Wife!* and requests that the production crews follow the U.S. sponsor's instruction. Having received a report from Jane regarding possible candidates for the program, Joichi exercises his power to choose a candidate for the week's wife. Based on the instruction given by BEEF-EX, he chooses a white middle-class woman named Becky Thayer, who owns a Bed-and-Breakfast in Magnolia Springs, and disregards Jane's candidates—the Mexican immigrant family Martinez cooking Texas-style Beefy Burritos, and African American Helen Dawes cooking chitterlings—arguing that Jane's choices are undesirable and unwholesome for the show. Jane confronts Joichi, and she is an oppositional force with respect to him; unlike Joichi, Jane feels a responsibility to depict the underrepresented image of America for the Japanese audience, because she is aware of the impact of "selling off the vast illusion of America to a cramped population on that small string of Pacific islands."[57] Through the challenge Jane poses to Joichi, Ozeki exposes the racist ideology that BEEF-EX is seeking to reinforce through the program contents.

As a DES daughter with a deformed uterus, Jane is aware of the harmful effects of DES on women's reproductive system, nonhuman animals, and the environment, and she uses the media as a way to expose the connections between the exploitative economic force and ecologically degraded conditions of human and nonhuman nature. Jane is interested in showing a true picture of America to the Japanese audience rather than playing the role of a "go-between, a cultural pimp."[58] Jane says, "I had spent so many years, in both Japan and America, floundering in a miasma of misinformation about culture and race. I was determined to use this window into mainstream network television to *educate*. Perhaps it was naïve, but I believed, honestly, that I could use wives to sell meat in the service of a Larger Truth."[59] If BEEF-EX campaigns to cover up the contaminated meat through use of the media, Jane uses the media as a way to reveal the truth behind the meat. Eisenstein describes the manipulative, yet at the same time transformative power of the media as follows:

> These media of discourse present, translate, expose, and cover up the tensions between global corporations and nation-based government. Media simultaneously protect hierarchies of power while also giving them visibility. This visibility is not predetermined in effect. Media

mirrors can challenge the very systems of power of which they are a part. Media are both intimately constructed by corporate interests and the site of negotiation between the cross-pressures of nation and globe.[60]

Whereas Joichi uses the media to serve BEEF-EX and tries to reproduce the existing power structure and ideology as instructed by the Trade Syndicate, Jane through the media attempts to expose the unethical and biologically harmful meat-making processes and tries to subvert the dominant power structure by filming racial minorities, immigrants, and biracial multiethnic Americans for the program.

Contending against Joichi's perspective that reinforces the white-male dominant view of race, class, and gender, Jane subverts the hierarchical orders of instruction, choosing the so-called "othered" groups. Jane calls Joichi's censorship of the program a "wanton capitalist mandate,"[61] and Joichi, while he is drunk, later calls BEEF-EX "a bunch of cowboys pretending to be international traders."[62] Jane, however, realizes that her rage against Joichi is not merely personal; rather, it should be aimed at the nature of the economic system that accumulates profits by exploiting the "other" and at its underlying unethical rationalism of exploitation. Jane discovers that health hazards of meat production impact not only women but also men, since rates of cancer, sterility, impotence, reproductive disorders, and other harmful side effects have increased; and men have also started developing symptoms of elevated voice, as shown in the case of Helen's husband, and of enlarged breasts, in the case of the cattle farmer Gale, who must have gotten estrogen poisoning from the feedlot.[63]

While filming Lara and Dyann—a biracial, lesbian, vegetarian couple, which goes against the interest of BEEF-EX—Jane learns more about the detrimental impact of synthetic hormones on the environment, human body, and female reproductive system and how it correlates with factory farming. Dyann tells Jane that "sperm counts have dropped by about fifty percent in the past fifty years, and this coincides with the start of factory farming and the heavy use of estrogens and other hormones in meat production."[64] Jane also learns that Lara and Dyann became vegetarians for political reasons— not because they do not like beef, but because they know the inhumane and toxic processes involved in meat production. Their decision to become vegetarian implies that the economic force behind the exploitation of non-human animals and the harmful effect of that exploitation on women are connected: their decision is their refusal to be part of the oppressive patriarchal capitalist system. Lara and Dyann personify the ecologically conscious activists who at the individual level challenge the profit-oriented economic system and speak for social and economic justice for the disenfranchised and the marginalized. Through this biracial, lesbian, vegetarian couple, Ozeki delineates the close relationship between environmental problems and feminist issues and articulates the connection between the exploitation of women and nonhuman animals under violent capitalist patriarchy.

GLOBAL SOLIDARITIES AND OPPOSITIONAL
STRUGGLES FOR ENVIRONMENTAL JUSTICE

Ozeki clearly links ecofeminism and the environmental justice movement on local and global levels and uncovers the roots of the current environmental crisis and the exploitation of "others" through her critique of profit-oriented economic forces and capitalist patriarchy. Disproportionate environmental hazards as well as biological harms of artificial growth-enhancing hormones on women, nonhuman animals, and people in other countries constitute global environmental injustice. Ozeki represents oppositional struggles through her critique of the "self-maximizing" economic structure as well as through her emphasis on the importance of the individual's awareness of social and environmental injustice. Furthermore, she challenges oppressive and exploitative capitalist patriarchy through the media, which play an important role in shaping our consciousness and culture in contemporary society.

In *My Year of Meats*, the individual's awareness of patriarchal violence and social and environmental injustice is exemplified through the female characters, Akiko and John Dunn's wife Bunny Dunn, who undergo a gradual transformation from subjugated women to individuals who make choices for themselves and speak against capitalist patriarchal violence and injustice towards women. Both Akiko and Bunny are influenced by the television program that Jane has directed, and their personal transformations clearly reveal the powerful influence of the media in late capitalist society. Akiko is moved by Jane's ideal candidates for the show, Lara and Dyann, because of their courageous decision to lead their own way of life despite many challenges. Watching the show, Akiko finds that she is crying: "These were tears of admiration for the strong women so determined to have their family against all odds. And tears of pity for herself, for the trepidation she felt in place of desire and for the pale, wan sentiment that she let pass for love."[65] Through watching the couple, Akiko learns about an alternative lifestyle for women and motherhood, and she comes to realize her lack of voice in her life and marriage and wants to transform herself from a submissive and passive housewife to a woman who speaks for herself. Having conceived after Joichi violently raped her, Akiko decides to give birth to her baby without him in America: "It's going to be a girl. . . . That's why I'm going to America. It doesn't matter so much for a son, but since she's a girl, I want her to be an American citizen. So she can grow up to become an American Wife."[66] What Akiko says might sound naïve, but her decision is a critique of the sexually oppressive culture and the degraded status of women in society. Her wish for her baby girl to become an American citizen reveals her determination to break away from culturally oppressive practices, hoping for a better future for her baby daughter, and it is her way of challenging the cultural, sexual, and patriarchal violence directed against women. Jane is also sexually assaulted by Joichi, and both Jane and

Akiko are the victims of Joichi's sexual and patriarchal violence.[67] Akiko's reaching out to Jane for help and their resistance against Joichi's violence suggest possibilities for forming solidarities and coalitions among women beyond the boundaries of nation, race, and class, and it demonstrates eco-feminism's interconnectedness in its critical movement against oppressive capitalist patriarchy.[68]

In parallel with Akiko's awakening from patriarchal oppression, Bunny becomes aware of the dangers of DES to human bodies through her five-year-old daughter Rosie, who has suffered hormone poisoning while playing in Gale's feedlot. Bunny wants Jane to spread the word about illegal hormones, agreeing to show Rosie's prematurely developed body "defaced by a wiry tangle of hair" to the camera. Bunny transforms into a person who makes a choice based on what she believes. She tells Jane:

> After you left the house last night I was thinkin' back, and I realized that I ain't never really ever made a single decision in my life, you know. Just kinda drifted from one thing to the next, following the direction these darn things pointed me in, you know? . . . Well, it was like I finally make a choice, talkin' for the camera, and it felt good. Like I was takin' a stand.[69]

Bunny's taking a stand for Rosie and her changing view of Rosie's problem reveal both her raised social consciousness with respect to the biological harms of DES and her transformation as an individual who can make a choice. Bunny wants Jane to spread the word about the illegal hormone and its effects on human nonhuman animal bodies, and Jane feels a responsibility to disseminate a "critical piece of information about the corruption of meats in America out to the world."[70] As Jane realizes, "toxicity in meat, the unwholesomeness of large-scale factory farming, the deforestation of the rain forests to make grazing land for hamburgers" have effects all over creation,[71] and her decision to effect social change through the media by representing toxicity in food and the endangered conditions of human life in late capitalist society is a way of seeking an environmental transformation at individual and societal levels. Furthermore, Jane's politically critical narrative and her indictment of global capital and patriarchal violence suggest that women should become an active "agency"[72] that resists the violence of capitalist patriarchy.

An important perspective that Ozeki projects in her novel concerns her oppositional strategies aimed at ideological apparatuses. The role of the media and its influence in contemporary society are foregrounded throughout the text. Whereas the statement "meat is the message" was what Jane was supposed to deliver as a coordinator of the television program, Jane subverts the message and uses the media to unmask the exploitative capitalist system, the current environmental crisis, and the health risks precipitated by the global capital and corporate interests. She actively uses the television program as an effective medium to show a real picture of America as well as to expose the harmful effects of DES on women and nonhuman animals, and Jane's documentary film on the harmful effects of DES and the case of Rosie gets attention from all the major networks in the U.S. as well as in Europe and Asia. Jane concludes her year of meats:

> I had started my year as a documentarian. I wanted to tell the truth, to effect change, to make a difference. And up to a point, I had succeeded: I got a small but critical piece of information about the corruption of meats in America out to the world, and possibly even saved a little girl's life in the process. And maybe that is the most important part of the story, but the truth is so much more complex.[73]

Undermining the manipulative power of the media backed by capitalist corporate interests, Jane seeks to bring changes in people's view of media-mediated information, raising social consciousness of the "media controversy over reliability in television and the power of corporate sponsorship to determine content and truth."[74]

The novel keenly expresses the need for changes both in the economic system and in social and ideological realms. What is significant about Ozeki's ecofeminism is that unlike socialist ecofeminists who seek political, economic, and social transformations through a socialist revolution, she uses the media as a way to influence people's consciousness, and it reveals her divergent strategies for ecological transformation. Just as many environmentalists' critical voice against the capitalist mode of production raises social awareness of the system, Ozeki's critical engagement with the ideological role of the media exposes the significant influence of the media in late capitalist society. Her attempts to seek changes through the media, by using it as a powerful tool to impact economic and environmental policy, suggest the need to envision further effective environmentalist strategies.

My Year of Meats is an environmentally conscious text, delineating the manner in which unequal social and economic power relations are interconnected with environmental injustice at local and global levels. The multiethnic environmentalism of this text exemplifies the diverse voices of environmental literature, engaging with social and economic inequality against race, ethnicity, and gender. The novel poignantly depicts problems of environmental deterioration, interlinked with the violence of capital as well as profit-oriented and male-centered rationalism that leaves women, nonhuman animals, and people in developing countries as vulnerable victims. Moreover, Ozeki's unmasking of exploitative capitalist patriarchy and the violence of global capital on "othered" groups positions environmental neocolonialism and ecofeminism as part of the environmental justice movement.

All in all, *My Year of Meats* offers a unique manifestation of ecocriticism's shift towards multiethnic and transnational environmental movements and makes clear linkages between environmental injustice and capitalists' exploitation of "others" for profits. Ozeki's critique of male-centered global capitalism and her suggestions regarding the formation of global coalitions to combat capitalist patriarchy and environmental injustice clearly expose the underlying roots of the degradation of the environment. Her calls for ecological awareness and environmental justice on individual, ideological, and structural levels point to effective oppositional strategies as well as a growing critical environmental justice movement in Asian American literature.

NOTES

1. Cheryll Glotfelty, "Introduction: Literary Studies in an Age of Environmental Crisis," in *The Ecocriticism Reader*, ed. Cheryll Glotfelty and Harold Fromm (Athens: University of Georgia Press, 1996), xxv.
2. T. V. Reed, "Toward an Environmental Justice Ecocriticism," in *The Environmental Justice Reader*, ed. Joni Adamson, Mei Mei Evans, and Rachel Stein (Tucson: University of Arizona Press, 2002), 145.
3. Luke Cole and Sheila Foster, *From the Ground Up: Environmental Racism and the Rise of the Environmental Justice Movement* (New York: New York University Press, 2001), 17.
4. Julie Sze, "From Environmental Justice Literature to the Literature of Environmental Justice," in *The Environmental Justice Reader*, 163.
5. Daniel Faber and James O'Connor, "Capitalism and the Crisis of Environmentalism," in *Toxic Struggles: The Theory and Practice of Environmental Justice*, ed. Richard Hofrichter (Salt Lake City: University of Utah Press, 2002), 13. In a similar vein, Soenke Zehle argues that environmental agendas should move beyond the "wild nature," "transcendentalist, and romantic traditions." Zehle, "Notes on Cross-Border Environmental Justice Education," in *The Environmental Justice Reader*, 341.
6. Laura Pulido, *Environmentalism and Economic Justice: Two Chicano Struggles in the Southwest* (Tucson: University of Arizona Press, 1998), 29.
7. Ibid., 40.
8. Robert T. Hayashi, "Beyond Walden Pond: Asian American Literature and the Limits of Ecocriticism," in *Coming into Contact: Explorations in Ecocritical Theory and Practice*, ed. Anne Merrill Ingram, Ian Marshall, Daniel J. Philippon, and Adam W. Sweeting (Athens: University of Georgia Press, 2007), 58.
9. Ursula K. Heise, "Ecocriticism and the Transnational Turn in American Studies," *American Literary History* 20 (2008): 383.
10. Ruth Ozeki, *My Year of Meats* (New York: Penguin, 1998), 89.
11. Robert Bullard. "Anatomy of Environmental Racism," in *Toxic Struggles*, 25.
12. Arjun Appadurai, "Grassroots Globalization and the Research Imagination," *Public Culture* 12.1 (2000): 3.
13. Ibid.
14. John Bellamy Foster, *Ecology against Capitalism* (New York: Monthly Review Press, 2002), 60.
15. Bullard notes that increased toxic-waste sites are found in the areas where poor racial minorities live: "Three out of five African Americans live in communities with abandoned toxic-waste sites; 60 percent (fifteen million) African Americans live in communities with one or more abandoned toxic-waste sites; three of the five largest commercial hazardous waste landfills are located in predominantly African American or Latino American communities, accounting for 40 percent of the nation's total estimated landfill capacity." Bullard, "Anatomy of Environmental Racism," 27.

16. Mark Ritchie points out that the trade agreements by NAFTA, GATT (the General Agreement on Tariffs), and trade-related policies that allow "food-product dumping" destroy "food self-sufficiency in poor countries." Ritchie, "Trading Away the Environment," in *Toxic Struggles*, 217.

17. Daniel Faber, *Capitalizing on Environmental Injustice: The Polluter-Industrial Complex in the Age of Globalization* (Lanham, MD: Rowman and Littlefield, 2008), 177–78.

18. Frederick Buell also points out that "the process of economic globalization" and global treaties such as NAFTA and GATT have been environmentally destructive. Buell, "Nationalist Postnationalism: Globalist Discourse in Contemporary American Culture," *American Quarterly* 50.3 (1998): 571.

19. Joshua Karliner, "The Globalization of Corporate Culture and Its Role in the Environmental Crisis," in *Reclaiming the Environmental Debate: The Politics of Health in a Toxic Culture*, ed. Richard Hofrichter (Cambridge: MIT Press, 2000), 178–79.

20. Ritchie, "Trading Away the Environment," 212.

21. Nancy Langston provides the history of DES regulations as follows: "The FDA banned the use of DES implants in chicken in 1959, while allowing its continued use in cattle feed and for pregnant women. . . . By the 1950s, farmers gave cattle the hormone to promote rapid weight gain, which was a key factor enabling the rapid expansion of industrialized feedlots. . . . In 1971 researchers in Boston reported a cluster of extremely rare vaginal cancers in young women whose mothers had taken DES while they were pregnant. . . . Mothers and children exposed to DES organized to call for research into the drug, and eventually consumers, scientists, and concerned congressional representatives forced the FDA to ban the chemical for most uses." Langston, *Toxic Bodies: Hormone Disruptors and the Legacy of DES* (New Haven: Yale University Press, 2010), ix-x.

22. Ozeki, *My Year of Meats*, 124.

23. Hyun Jin and Won Koo state that Bovine Spongiform Encephalopathy (BSE), widely known as "mad cow disease," was initially discovered in cattle in England in 1986. According to the Economic Research Service of the U.S. Department of Agriculture (USDA), Japan has been the largest export market for U.S. beef since the mid-1980s, and beef import by Japan had increased from December 1991 until March 1996. The Japanese government reported the first case of BSE in 2001. See Jin and Koo, "U.S. Meat Exports and Food Safety Information," *Agribusiness and Applied Economics Report* 514 (2003): 1–2.

24. Ozeki, *My Year of Meats*, 127.

25. Ibid., 10.

26. Zillah Eisenstein, *Global Obscenities: Patriarchy, Capitalism, and the Lure of Cyberfantasy* (New York: New York University Press, 1998), 36.

27. Ibid., 108.

28. Ozeki, *My Year of Meats*, 11–12.

29. Ibid., 8.

30. Eisenstein, *Global Obscenities*, 34.

31. Ozeki, *My Year of Meats*, 365–66.

32. Ibid., 266–67.

33. Ibid., 125.

34. Ibid., 263.

35. Ibid., 279.

36. Val Plumwood, *Environmental Culture* (London: Routledge, 2002), 159.

37. Karen Warren, *Ecofeminist Philosophy* (Lanham, MD: Rowman and Littlefield, 2000), xvii.

38. Ibid., 2.
39. Carolyn Merchant, *The Death of Nature: Women, Ecology, and the Scientific Revolution* (New York: HarperOne, 1989), xx.
40. Greta Gaard, "Living Interconnections with Animals and Nature," in *Ecofeminism: Women, Animals, Nature*, ed. Greta Gaard (Philadelphia: Temple University Press, 1993), 5.
41. Ibid., 4.
42. Carolyn Merchant, "Ecofeminism and Feminist Theory," in *Reweaving the World*, ed. Irene Diamond and Gloria Feman Orenstein (San Francisco: Sierra Club Books, 1990), 100.
43. Ibid., 103.
44. Maria Mies, *Patriarchy and Accumulation on a World Scale: Women in the International Division of Labour* (London: Zed, 1986), 38. The notion of capitalist patriarchy is further explained by Mies and Vandana Shiva. They claim that "the capitalist patriarchal world system emerged, is built upon and maintains itself through the colonization of women, of 'foreign' peoples and their lands; and of nature, which it is gradually destroying." Maria Mies and Vandana Shiva, *Ecofeminism* (London: Zed, 1993), 2.
45. Jennifer Ladino also reads *My Year of Meats* from an ecofeminist perspective and argues that Ozeki's novel prioritizes "women's reproduction over capitalist production": "While her text certainly condemns the oppressive work of patriarchy, it also entertains a desire to connect women and nature in its negotiations of the category of motherhood, which occupies a tenuous position at the nexus of ecofeminism's distinct branches." Ladino, "New Frontiers for Ecofeminism: Women, Nature and Globalization in Ruth Ozeki's *My Year of Meats*," in *New Directions in Ecofeminist Literary Criticism*, ed. Andrea Campbell (Newcastle upon Tyne: Cambridge Scholars Publishing, 2008), 126.
46. Ozeki, *My Year of Meats*, 125.
47. Ibid., 154. Shiva also points out the connections between patriarchal violence, science, and the capitalist economy: "The relationship between reductionism, violence and profits is built into the genesis of masculinist science, for its reductionist nature is an epistemic response to an economic organization based on uncontrolled exploitation of nature for maximization of profits and capital accumulation." Vandana Shiva, *Staying Alive* (London: Zed, 1989), 23.
48. Mies and Shiva, *Ecofeminism*, 16.
49. Ibid., 2–3.
50. Plumwood, *Environmental Culture*, 158–59.
51. Ibid., 22.
52. Ozeki, *My Year of Meats*, 207.
53. Ibid., 303.
54. Ibid., 95.
55. Lori Gruen, "Dismantling Oppression: An Analysis of the Connection between Women and Animals," in *Ecofeminism: Women, Animals, Nature*, 61.
56. Ozeki, *My Year of Meats*, 38.
57. Ibid., 9.
58. Ibid.
59. Ibid., 27.
60. Eisenstein, *Global Obscenities*, 40.
61. Ozeki, *My Year of Meats*, 167.
62. Ibid., 194.
63. In this regard, Chandra Mohanty claims that globalization has "recolonized" both women's and men's lives around the world and urges people

to form a feminist resistance against capitalism. Mohanty, "'Under Western Eyes' Revisited: Feminist Solidarity through Anticapitalist Struggles," *Signs* 28.2 (2003): 515.
64. Ozeki, *My Year of Meats*, 204.
65. Ibid., 181.
66. Ibid., 318.
67. Monica Chiu points out the growing solidarities between Akiko and Jane: "The novel advocates a growing awareness in the two female protagonists of the inextricability of men and meat and how this culturally sanctioned alliance often marginalizes women and poor, instigating a feminist bent from the novel's very masculine connotations of meat." Chiu, "Postnational Globalization and (En)Gendered Meat Production in Ruth L. Ozeki's *My Year of Meats*," *LIT: Literature Interpretation Theory* 12.1 (2001): 112.
68. Shameem Black in this respect claims that the novel searches for a "transnational feminist network of violence against women." Black, "Fertile Cosmofeminism: Ruth L. Ozeki and Transnational Reproduction," *Meridians: Feminism, Race, Transnationalism* 5.1 (2004): 237.
69. Ozeki, *My Year of Meats*, 295.
70. Ibid., 360.
71. Ibid., 334.
72. Cheryl Fish, "The Toxic Body Politic: Ethnicity, Gender, and Corrective Eco-Justice in Ruth Ozeki's *My Year of Meats* and Judith Helfand and Daniel Gold's *Blue Vinyl*," *MELUS: Multi-Ethnic Literature of the United States* 34.2 (2009): 53.
73. Ozeki, *My Year of Meats*, 360.
74. Ibid., 358.

BIBLIOGRAPHY

Adamson, Joni, Mei Mei Evans, and Rachel Stein, eds. *The Environmental Justice Reader*. Tucson: University of Arizona Press, 2002.

Appadurai, Arjun. "Grassroots Globalization and the Research Imagination." *Public Culture* 12.1 (2000): 1–21.

Black, Shameem. "Fertile Cosmofeminism: Ruth L. Ozeki and Transnational Reproduction." *Meridians: Feminism, Race, Transnationalism* 5.1 (2004): 226–56.

Buell, Frederick. "Nationalist Postnationalism: Globalist Discourse in Contemporary American Culture." *American Quarterly* 50.3 (1998): 548–91.

Bullard, Robert. "Anatomy of Environmental Racism." In *Toxic Struggles: The Theory and Practice of Environmental Justice*, edited by Richard Hofrichter, 25–35. Salt Lake City: University of Utah Press, 2002.

Chiu, Monica. "Postnational Globalization and (En)Gendered Meat Production in Ruth L. Ozeki's *My Year of Meats*." *LIT: Literature Interpretation Theory* 12.1 (2001): 99–128.

Cole, Luke and Sheila Foster. *From the Ground Up: Environmental Racism and the Rise of the Environmental Justice Movement*. New York: New York University Press, 2001.

Eisenstein, Zillah. *Global Obscenities: Patriarchy, Capitalism, and the Lure of Cyberfantasy*. New York: New York University Press, 1998.

Faber, Daniel. *Capitalizing on Environmental Injustice: The Polluter-Industrial Complex in the Age of Globalization*. Lanham, MD: Rowman and Littlefield, 2008.

—— and James O'Connor. "Capitalism and the Crisis of Environmentalism." In *Toxic Struggles: The Theory and Practice of Environmental Justice*, edited by Richard Hofrichter, 12–24. Salt Lake City: University of Utah Press, 2002.

Fish, Cheryl. "The Toxic Body Politic: Ethnicity, Gender, and Corrective Eco-Justice in Ruth Ozeki's *My Year of Meats* and Judith Helfand and Daniel Gold's *Blue Vinyl*." *MELUS: Multi-Ethnic Literature of the United States* 34.2 (2009): 43–62.

Foster, John Bellamy. *Ecology against Capitalism*. New York: Monthly Review Press, 2002.

Gaard, Greta. "Living Interconnections with Animals and Nature." In *Ecofeminism: Women, Animals, Nature*, edited by Greta Gaard, 5–12. Philadelphia: Temple University Press, 1993.

Glotfelty, Cheryll. "Introduction: Literary Studies in an Age of Environmental Crisis." In *The Ecocriticism Reader*, edited by Cheryll Glotfelty and Harold Fromm, xv-xxxvii. Athens: University of Georgia Press, 1996.

Gruen, Lori. "Dismantling Oppression: An Analysis of the Connection between Women and Animals." In *Ecofeminism: Women, Animals, Nature*, edited by Greta Gaard, 60–90. Philadelphia: Temple University Press, 1993.

Hayashi, Robert T. "Beyond Walden Pond: Asian American Literature and the Limits of Ecocriticism." In *Coming into Contact: Explorations in Ecocritical Theory and Practice*, edited by Annie Ingram, Ian Marshall, Daniel J. Philippon, and Adam W. Sweeting, 58–75. Athens: University of Georgia Press, 2007.

Heise, Ursula K. "Ecocriticism and the Transnational Turn in American Studies." *American Literary History* 20 (2008): 381–404.

Hofrichter, Richard, ed. *Toxic Struggles: The Theory and Practice of Environmental Justice*. Salt Lake City: University of Utah Press, 2002.

Jin, Hyun and Won Koo. "U.S. Meat Exports and Food Safety Information." *Agribusiness and Applied Economics Report* 514 (2003): 1–19.

Karliner, Joshua. "The Globalization of Corporate Culture and Its Role in the Environmental Crisis." In *Reclaiming the Environmental Debate: The Politics of Health in a Toxic Culture*, edited by Richard Hofrichter, 177–200. Cambridge: MIT Press, 2000.

Ladino, Jennifer. "New Frontiers for Ecofeminism: Women, Nature and Globalization in Ruth Ozeki's *My Year of Meats*." In *New Directions in Ecofeminist Literary Criticism*, edited by Andrea Campbell, 124–47. Newcastle upon Tyne: Cambridge Scholars Publishing, 2008.

Langston, Nancy. *Toxic Bodies: Hormone Disruptors and the Legacy of DES*. New Haven: Yale University Press, 2010.

Merchant, Carolyn. *The Death of Nature: Women, Ecology, and the Scientific Revolution*. New York: HarperOne, 1989.

——. "Ecofeminism and Feminist Theory." In *Reweaving the World*, edited by Irene Diamond and Gloria Feman Orenstein, 100–5. San Francisco: Sierra Club Books, 1990.

Mies, Maria. *Patriarchy and Accumulation on a World Scale: Women in the International Division of Labour*. London: Zed, 1986.

—— and Vandana Shiva. *Ecofeminism*. London: Zed, 1993.

Mohanty, Chandra Talpade. "'Under Western Eyes' Revisited: Feminist Solidarity through Anticapitalist Struggles." *Signs* 28.2 (2003): 499–535.

Ozeki, Ruth. *My Year of Meats*. New York: Penguin, 1998.

Plumwood, Val. *Environmental Culture*. London: Routledge, 2002.

Pulido, Laura. *Environmentalism and Economic Justice: Two Chicano Struggles in the Southwest*. Tucson: University of Arizona Press, 1998.

Reed, T. V. "Toward an Environmental Justice Ecocriticism." In *The Environmental Justice Reader*, edited by Joni Adamson, Mei Mei Evans, and Rachel Stein. 145–62. Tucson: University of Arizona Press, 2002.

Ritchie, Mark. "Trading Away the Environment." In *Toxic Struggles: The Theory and Practice of Environmental Justice*, edited by Richard Hofrichter, 209–18. Salt Lake City: University of Utah Press, 2002.

Shiva, Vandana. *Staying Alive: Women, Ecology, and Development*. London: Zed, 1989.

Sze, Julie. "From Environmental Justice Literature to the Literature of Environmental Justice." In *The Environmental Justice Reader*, edited by Joni Adamson, Mei Mei Evans, and Rachel Stein, 163–80. Tucson: University of Arizona Press, 2002.

Warren, Karen. *Ecofeminist Philosophy*. Lanham, MD: Rowman and Littlefield, 2000.

Zehle, Soenke. "Notes on Cross-Border Environmental Justice Education." In *The Environmental Justice Reader*, edited by Joni Adamson, Mei Mei Evans, and Rachel Stein, 331–49. Tucson: University of Arizona Press, 2002.

Part III

The Environment and Philosophy

8 Hisaye Yamamoto as Radical Agrarian

Sarah D. Wald

The contemporary sustainable food movement often romanticizes an American agrarian tradition. Writers from Wendell Berry to Michael Pollan propose a return to the small family farm as one solution to the industrialization of agriculture. Small family farms, in such works, restore ecological integrity to the land, treat animals humanely, enrich the heteronormative nuclear family, and reduce the exploitation of labor. These visions too often fail to grapple with the racialized relationship to land ownership in the United States. They embrace and naturalize the subject position of the white male farmer and often overlook the subject positions of non-white farmers and farm workers. This chapter suggests the consequences of the contemporary food movement's privileging of whiteness and land ownership through a consideration of Japanese American author Hisaye Yamamoto as a radical agrarian. Yamamoto's nuanced reflections on racialized and gendered labor and property relations reveal the impossibility of contemporary pastoral fantasies to offer equitable food solutions while illustrating the need for an intersectional approach to U.S. racial histories within the sustainable food movement.

Reading Yamamoto as a radical agrarian not only complicates popular understandings of U.S. agrarianism, with its Jeffersonian roots, but also contributes to discussions of Yamamoto's prose within Asian American literary studies. Yamamoto participated in *The Catholic Worker*'s back-to-the-land movement. During the years she wrote her well-known short stories "Seventeen Syllables" (1949) and "Yoneko's Earthquake" (1951), she read about the movement regularly in the pages of *The Catholic Worker*. Just two years after publishing "Yoneko's Earthquake," Yamamoto declined a significant writing fellowship at Stanford University in order to move to a Catholic Worker farm in New York and live alongside Dorothy Day. Scholars have yet to delve into the relationship between Catholic Worker philosophies and Yamamoto's short fiction despite *The Catholic Worker*'s influence on Yamamoto during her most concentrated years of short-story writing. Examining Yamamoto's relationship to *The Catholic Worker* reveals the centrality of agrarianism to her larger political philosophy, including her stated identity as a Christian anarchist.[1]

This chapter offers the first consideration of the relationship between Catholic Worker farming projects and Yamamoto's fictional representations of farming. I contend that Yamamoto's fiction implicitly points to Catholic Worker ideals of collective land ownership and the merging of the scholarly life with manual labor as possible solutions to the psychological and physical violence she depicts, indicating some of the reasons that the Catholic Worker call to cultivation appealed to her. Yet, comparing Yamamoto's short fiction to other Catholic Worker texts also reveals the unrecognized privilege at work in Catholic Worker agrarianism and suggests some of the difficulties Catholic Workers, including Yamamoto, encountered in putting their ideals into practice. To make this argument, I first discuss the Catholic Worker movement's interest in agriculture and examine Yamamoto's growing interest in Catholic Worker philosophies, including her experiences on a Catholic Worker collective farm. This discussion provides the context for my analysis of Yamamoto's short stories and the critique of contemporary U.S. agrarianism and the sustainable food movement that I offer in the final portion of this chapter.

TENETS OF *THE CATHOLIC WORKER*

The Catholic Worker was co-founded by Day and Peter Maurin. As Day wrote in the first issue of *The Catholic Worker*, published on May Day, 1933, "In an attempt to popularize and make known the encyclicals of the Popes in regards to social justice and the program put forth by the Church for the 'reconstruction of the social order,' this news sheet, *The Catholic Worker*, is started."[2] The paper combined anti-capitalist radicalism with Catholic pacifism. Catholic Workers considered themselves conscientious objectors to all wars, and many did not pay federal income taxes as a protest against both war and government. Then, like now, volunteers at Catholic Worker centers around the nation provided food, shelter, and clothes to needy patrons.

During the period in which Yamamoto began reading *The Catholic Worker*, the late 1940s, the paper had more than 66,000 subscribers and was recovering from its wartime loss of supporters over Day's adamant pacifism during World War II. The articles in *The Catholic Worker* advocated racial integration and reported on the arrests of Catholic Workers picketing alongside the National Association for the Advancement of Colored People (NAACP). The paper put reports of lynching and labor struggles side by side on its front page. It followed the rise of McCarthyism and frequently argued against the draft. It contained reports on the U.S. occupation of Japan and bemoaned the hunger and poverty of children across both Europe and Asia in the aftermath of the war. It engaged with environmental discourses by promoting organic farming and critiquing the Soviet Union's reliance on technology to increase agricultural production. According to *The Catholic*

Worker, the scarcity of resources was solved not by technology and industry but by a return to the natural agrarian way of life, voluntary poverty, and the teachings of Christ.

Many of the Catholic Worker movement's core tenets can be traced back to Maurin. Maurin was never as well-known as Day, but Day often credited Maurin as her inspiration. It was Maurin who provided Day with the possibility of reconciling her newly embraced Catholic faith with her social conscience and history of political involvement.[3] It was also Maurin who first suggested that Day start a paper focused on the relationship between Catholicism and social justice. Maurin often expressed the ideas that most appealed to him in blank verse. His "Easy Essays," which *The Catholic Worker* frequently published, were known for their complexity of thought conveyed through repetitive word play. Yamamoto was particularly influenced by these essays, and when asked during interviews about her interest in the Catholic Worker, she referenced Maurin directly.[4]

Maurin was the first and most influential proponent of back-to-the-land projects within *The Catholic Worker*. He originated from a village in the South of France where the local residents worked communal pastures. This experience shaped his political commitment to cultivation. Maurin understood farming not merely as a nostalgic act, but as a solution for many of the social ills he believed capitalism and industrialization caused, including the alienation of individuals from land, the loss of craft and artistry from labor, and destruction of local rural communities as cities grew.[5] He viewed farming as a way of returning a means of production (the land) to a collective social body and also a way of returning dignity to work. Maurin termed his vision of farming, which went hand in hand with *The Catholic Worker* promotion of manual labor and voluntary poverty, "the green revolution."[6]

Maurin's agrarianism may have been rooted in his memory of French peasant life, which he described nostalgically as "precapitalistic," but it was more than just a return to the ways of the past.[7] Rather, he viewed farming as a way of reimagining and reinventing society.[8] Farming communes offered an opportunity to put into action many of the ideas that fueled his interest in Catholic social radicalism. Maurin believed the farms were not just solutions to underemployment and poor labor conditions. He referred to them as agronomic universities, where "The scholars must become workers/ so the workers may be scholars."[9] Maurin believed that intellectuals and laborers needed to learn from each another in order for true education to occur. He envisioned the life of the mind integrated into a life of manual labor, evenly dividing each day between study and labor. There would be little to no separation between the laborer and the scholar. They would not serve as separate classes.

Maurin's vision of the philosopher-farmer coincided with *The Catholic Worker*'s belief that labor conferred a spiritual benefit. Historian Mel Piehl describes "a commitment to satisfying and socially useful labor" as core to Catholic Worker philosophies alongside the pillars of voluntary poverty and pacifism.[10] In an unpublished biography of Maurin, Day explained, "On the farming commune, there was plenty of work for all, another reason why Peter was always extolling the land. People could not live without working. Work was as necessary as bread. But what was needed was a philosophy of labor. Work was a gift, a vocation."[11] One could not lead a fulfilling life without labor, and farm labor offered a particularly uplifting form of labor, ensuring farm residents contributed to their own well-being rather than living off the exploitation of others.

In the 1930s and 1940s, dozens of Catholic Worker farming projects sprung up, inspired by Maurin.[12] In the years leading up to Yamamoto's decision to head to New York, *The Catholic Worker* included articles in almost every issue discussing the benefits of these back-to-the land experiments. These articles emphasized the difficulties of farming endeavors, including practitioners' lack of agricultural knowledge and their frustration over farming failures. Yet, almost all these articles also proclaimed the experience worthwhile and encouraged others to join.[13] An article by agrarian novices Thomas Campbell and his wife is representative. Of their farming experience, they explain:

> We are both brand new, having lived in big cities all our lives and, hence, would like to address ourselves to those who are attempting to make a decision "Shall I—or we—try life on the land? . . . [T]he initial step taken of actually leaving the city and going to the country is an act which will be deep satisfaction in most cases. . . . You cannot read yourself into any worthwhile experience, least of all those connected with the land. So, if you are stopped in the first step, muster your courage and go.[14]

The articles that Yamamoto read in the months and years preceding her decision to go "back-to-the-land" often included pleas about following one's heart and trying out an agrarian lifestyle, regardless of the hardships that would follow.

YAMAMOTO'S ROUTE TO RADICAL AGRARIANISM

Yamamoto had both a personal and a philosophical relationship to agricultural labor. Her family's experiences with agricultural labor contributed to her understanding of the racialized nature of property relations and likely spurred her interest in Catholic Worker collective farming projects. Born in 1921, Yamamoto grew up among Japanese farming communities in Southern California. Her father worked as a farmer.[15] While many of her friends regularly helped out with their families' harvests, she did not. She explained, "I was excused, possibly because I was the only girl in the family, or maybe because I always had my nose in a book."[16] While her friends worked in the fields, she served as a teenage columnist for the English section of one of the local Japanese-language newspapers, *Kashu Mainichi (California Daily News)*. Executive Order 9066, which authorized the military to issue exclusion and internment orders during World War II, interrupted Yamamoto's family life, including her *Kashu Mainichi* column. At that point, Yamamoto's family was growing strawberries on land her father owned through a Japanese farming cooperative, a system likely devised to evade California's Alien Land Law, which prevented Asian immigrants from owning their own land. With internment pending, the cooperative sold the land. Her father received his portion of the cooperative's payment, and instead of profiting from harvesting the crop he planted with his own hands, his family was hired to pick strawberries for wages. Yamamoto's labor was necessary, and she joined her family in the fields. She recalls that the new owner "divided the Mexicans in one group, with a Mexican foreman, and the Japanese in another group, with a Japanese foreman, and that's the way we worked, until we got evacuated."[17] Thus, Yamamoto experienced life both as the daughter of a farmer and, briefly, as a laborer on a larger tract of land under a racialized system of management.

When Yamamoto lost her column at *Kashu Mainichi*, which suspended publication from 1942–47, she found other ways to continue publishing. At the age of twenty, she was interned at the Colorado River Relocation Center in Poston, Arizona, where she stayed for three years.[18] There she wrote for the camp newspaper the *Poston Chronicle*. After leaving the camp in 1945, she began to work at the *Los Angeles Tribune*, an African American newspaper which hired her at least partially in an effort to reach out to returning Japanese Americans after the war. She published increasingly frank articles about racial inequality and the Civil Rights movement in "Small Talk," her *Los Angeles Tribune* column. As historian Matthew Briones argues, Yamamoto's post-war work at the *Los Angeles Tribune* shaped her engagement with questions of race and interracial alliances.[19]

While working at the *Los Angeles Tribune*, Yamamoto first encountered *The Catholic Worker*. It was one of several newspapers to which she was assigned to cull articles of note. Drawn to the philosophies of *The Catholic Worker*, she began bringing the paper home with her.[20] Yamamoto left the *Los Angeles Tribune* in 1948 to concentrate on her writing and raise her adopted son Paul, supported at first by insurance money from her brother Johnny, who was killed in World War II during his service in the celebrated Japanese American 442nd Regimental Combat Team, and then by receiving the John Hay Whitney Foundation Opportunity Fellowship in 1950.[21] Throughout this period, she continued to read *The Catholic Worker*, subscribing for 25 cents a year, or a penny per issue. As Yamamoto explains, "[T]he more I read it, the more I wanted to be part of the movement."[22] Yamamoto also had been corresponding with Catholic Worker activist

Yone U. Stafford. The correspondence began when Stafford sent a letter to the *Los Angeles Tribune* in response to one of Yamamoto's articles. According to Stafford, their exchange of letters was a decisive factor in Yamamoto's decision to move to a Catholic Worker farm.[23] After researching and reading about the Catholic Worker movement for seven years, Yamamoto "finally got up the nerve, in 1952, to write to the Workers to express my desire to join up."[24] She explained, "Dorothy Day didn't jump up and down for joy, but cautiously suggested I meet her later in the year when she was due in Los Angeles on a speaking engagement. I met her at a midnight mass at the Maryknoll Sisters in Boyle Heights, then later for lunch with a couple of others, one of whom was a priest she called a 'fellow renegade.'"[25] After meeting with Day, Yamamoto turned down a prestigious (and funded) opportunity to advance her career as a fiction writer by studying with the prominent poet, literary critic, and Stanford University professor Yvor Winters. Instead, she headed to New York because, as she explained, "My heart chose *The Catholic Worker*."[26]

The 22-acre farm that Yamamoto and her son moved onto was purchased in the late summer/early fall of 1950 and named after Maurin, who passed away in 1949. The farm was in only its third season of Catholic Worker cultivation when Yamamoto arrived, around Labor Day, 1953.[27] By this time, Day often resided at the Peter Maurin Farm, and her grandchildren became Paul's playmates.[28] The farm was not in prime condition. Shortly after Yamamoto's arrival, Catholic Worker Rollande Potvin described it as consisting of "very poor and run down soil. Compared to the farm at Newburgh it is not very productive."[29] The difficulty of the project conferred status; cultivation was not upheld as a form of spiritually beneficial labor because of its ease. Agriculture appealed to Catholic Workers in part because of their belief that humans require meaningful labor to thrive. The physical intensity of the work that the farm required was more important to the project than any agrarian self-sufficiency that could be achieved.

Writing for *The Catholic Worker* became one of Yamamoto's duties at the farm. Her first article in *The Catholic Worker*, "Seabrook Farms—20 Years Later," highlighted the parallels between New Jersey's "worst agricultural strike" in 1934 and more recent walk-outs there by *Nisei* workers.[30] Yamamoto also took over the monthly column containing day-to-day updates on the Peter Maurin farm. She described her farm life as a mishmash of animal tending, housekeeping, and intellectual labor, explaining, "I fed the chickens and rabbits usually, sometimes cooked if there was no one else around to do it, cleaned cupboards, sorted clothing that came in, and wrote for the paper."[31] Her description highlights the gendered nature of labor assignments at Peter Maurin farm. Day celebrated Yamamoto's work ethic, going so far as to label her as the farm's "best example of manual labor."[32] What is perhaps most notable about Day's descriptions of Yamamoto is the way in which Yamamoto's duties seem to exemplify the agronomic university farm ideal that Maurin himself professed. Day explained:

> She works without effort, quietly, efficiently, taking care of rabbits, chickens, washing up the kitchen, dining room, hall, and corridors with a concoction of boiled onion skins and water which Mary Lisi, one of our Italian friends, introduced us to. Our house is spotless, thanks to her, and yet she always has time to type articles, to read, both to herself and to little Paul. What an example of tranquility.[33]

At least in Day's eyes, Yamamoto embodied Maurin's ideal of the scholar-worker.

Yet, Yamamoto's columns consistently register the difficulty of trying to fulfill Catholic Worker ideals in everyday life. They testify to the adversities of communal rural living. As Yamamoto explained, "It is still a daily miracle how we, coming from such diverse backgrounds and thrown together by our common needs, live as one family, struggling to respect one another's personalities."[34] According to her columns, life at Peter Maurin Farm could be quite unpleasant and unproductive. She wrote in one column, "For some reason, Advent—liturgically a season of joyous waiting—turned out to be rather grim at Peter Maurin Farm, with the communal nerves on edge and dissension prevailing."[35] Another time she complained, "Even here at Peter Maurin Farm, where we are actually living on the land, the harassments that come with living in the community often loom larger than the agricultural problems, so that we must occasionally remind ourselves that it is, after all, a farm."[36] Yamamoto later stated that the intensity of the conflicts between community farm members was unexpected, remarking that "Dorothy Day never wrote about the darker aspects of living in community in her column, which had so enchanted me."[37]

The communal tensions Yamamoto found at the Peter Maurin farm were shared by other Catholic Worker projects. Historical theologian Jeffery Marlett, in describing Maryfarm, explained, "Although many, including seminarians, children on vacation, and college students, crowded in during summers, the permanent residents were a motley crew of families, unemployed laborers, and the urban homeless. A more volatile group unprepared for the tensions of communal living could scarcely be found."[38] Catholic Worker William Guachat, who spent over twenty years as part of a Catholic Worker farming collective, complained that participants were often reluctant to become scholar-laborers: "The scholars insist upon being scholarly, and the workers insist upon working physically for weal or woe and the twain never met."[39] The ideals that Maurin described rarely materialized in practice. Race, gender, class, age, citizenship status, and family status continued to mark the division of labor and the process of decision making.

However, there is no evidence that Yamamoto's ultimate departure from Peter Maurin farm resulted from her discontent with the difficulties of communal living. Her departure, rather, appears motivated by love. She returned to California in 1955, following her marriage to Anthony DeSoto, whom she met at Peter Maurin farm. Yamamoto continued to affiliate with Catholic Workers and to believe that small communities could empower the individual disempowered through social injustice. She believed that "government by mutual consent in small groups—communities—is the ideal form of democracy."[40] She published occasionally in *The Catholic Worker* as well as in other venues until her death in 2011. Over thirty years after leaving Peter Maurin farm, Yamamoto professed, "I believe Dorothy Day is the most important person this country has produced."[41]

THE AGRARIANISM OF "SEVENTEEN SYLLABLES" AND "YONEKO'S EARTHQUAKE"

How, then, do we understand Yamamoto's look back at her family's agrarian past on the eve of her move to Peter Maurin farm? In the same years that Yamamoto was reading *The Catholic Worker*'s call for cultivation, she revisited in fiction her own memories and her friends' stories about pre-internment Japanese American agrarian life. Two of her best known stories from this time, "Seventeen Syllables" and "Yoneko's Earthquake," focus on Japanese immigrant families farming in Southern California. The vision of communal farming as spiritually rewarding that *The Catholic Worker* promoted in the 1940s and 1950s contrasts starkly with the representations of racialized and gendered violence in "Seventeen Syllables" and "Yoneko's Earthquake." These short stories represent the economic oppression Japanese immigrants faced and the ways race, gender, and immigration shaped the farm experiences of first generation Japanese immigrants (*Issei*); their second generation children (*Nisei*); and the Japanese, Mexican, and Filipino farm hands they hired. Why would Yamamoto write an indictment of agrarian realities prior to her own experiment in Catholic Worker agrarian idealism?

I suggest that Yamamoto's short fiction, by highlighting the racialized, gendered, and economic violence of her agrarian background, reveals the appeal of Maurin's vision of farming. Consider the explanation she offered for her attraction to Maurin's agrarian ideal:

> Peter Maurin believed in a synthesis of what he called "cult, culture, and cultivation," which meant going back to the land. His ideal was that a person could work out in the fields maybe four days—four hours a day—and then go back to the farmhouse and paint or write or do printing or whatever, all centered around the Catholic Church.[42]

"Seventeen Syllables" and "Yoneko's Earthquake" illustrate the impossibility of combining the status of worker and scholar under the racialized conditions of agricultural production in the United States. The idealistic visions of non-hierarchal communal farming in *The Catholic Worker* appear as implicit solutions to many of the problems Yamamoto explores. This is not to suggest that Yamamoto consciously shaped her short stories to express or respond to any Catholic Worker agrarian ethos. Rather, as Yamamoto acknowledges, an author's politics may shape a text in ways that the author may be unaware. As she explained to one interviewer, "I call myself a Christian anarchist, but I'm not sure my beliefs come through in the stories. If they're part of me, however, some sense of it must be evident. . . . A fiction writer who has a political agenda will probably consciously or unconsciously incorporate it into his work, don't you think?"[43] Her short fiction is in implicit, rather than explicit, conversation with Catholic Worker philosophies.

Maurin's desire for a form of property relations of a scholar-laborer or a philosopher-farmer echoes the central tension in "Seventeen Syllables" between the mother's desire for art and the father's desire for labor, or what Sau-ling Cynthia Wong has called the conflict between necessity and extravagance.[44] In "Seventeen Syllables," the wife Tome Hayashi transforms into the poet Ume in the evenings. As Tome, she contributes to the family's domestic economy: she "kept house, cooked, washed, and . . . did her ample share of picking tomatoes out in the sweltering fields and boxing them in tidy strata in the cool packing shed."[45] In contrast, Ume not only ignores her social obligations to her husband, but also threatens the family's economic well-being. Hayashi's violence in the short story, where he terminates his wife's poetry career, comes at the moment at which Ume's threat manifests itself as explicitly monetary. Tome abandons the tomato harvest when time is of the essence and all help is necessary to salvage the family's investment. Yamamoto writes, "The lugs were piling up . . . and the ripe tomatoes in them would probably have to be taken to the cannery tomorrow if they were not ready for the produce haulers tonight."[46] Shortly after Hayashi informs his daughter, "We've got no time for a break today," Ume rushes off to have tea with Mr. Kuroda, the San Francisco editor bearing her haiku award.[47] Significantly, when Hayashi sends a message to Ume/Tome, it is a reminder about the tomatoes.[48] Hayashi's outrage at Ume is not simply about her creative success or independence, as scholars often contend.[49] He is upset that this success directly interferes with the family's urgent need to harvest tomatoes. That Ume's "life span, even for a poet's, was very brief— perhaps three months at most," suggests the impossibility of Maurin's ideal, the scholar as worker and the worker as scholar, under the economic constraints facing Japanese immigrant farm families, and particularly in the context of the gender dynamics within those families.[50]

Similarly, in "Yoneko's Earthquake," the Filipino farm hand Marpo's transgression is not only his affair with Yoneko's mother, Mrs. Hosoume, but his striving to be more than solely a laborer. Early in the story we are told that Marpo displayed dynamic and varied interests and identities: "Marpo the Christian and Marpo the best hired man, but Marpo the athlete, Marpo the musician (both instrumental and vocal), Marpo the artist, and Marpo the radio technician."[51] This description seems to capture Maurin's ideal of farm labor as allowing a life that engages both body and brain. In contrast, the "old Japanese man" who replaces Marpo after the discovery of the affair has "no particular interests, outside working, eating, sleeping, and playing an occasional game of goh with Mr. Hosoume."[52] Marpo's multiple identities seem directly linked to his inability to perform the duty of farm labor (and only farm labor) in the way in which Hosoume considers appropriate, while the old Japanese man, with "no particular interests," can be more easily reduced to his labor. The racial and economic order in which Marpo toils does not allow the laborer the individuality or humanity for artistry or other forms of creative expression or intellectual engagement to thrive.

In both short stories, Yamamoto describes farm laborers as machine-like and depicts the emergence of human qualities, especially creative and sexual passion, as economically disruptive. Yoneko and her brother Sergio "followed the potato-digging machine and the Mexican workers—both hired for the day—around the field."[53] This statement equates the Mexican laborers with machines because of their capacity to be hired. There is no difference between the renting of a machine and that of employing human labor. Similarly, Rosie, the daughter in "Seventeen Syllables," was capable of working in the fields "as efficiently as a flawless machine."[54] Like Yoneko, she becomes more like a machine than a daughter when she engages in farm labor. Yet, like Marpo, Ume, and Mrs. Hosoume, Rosie's ability to function as a machine is reduced when her passions intrude; as her love interest, Jesus, approaches, "her hands went berserk and the tomatoes started falling in the wrong stalls."[55] Through these descriptions, Yamamoto's texts employ a Marxist critique of wage labor's effect on the experiences of Asian and Latino workers. Under capitalism, the human qualities of the laborers become distractions and inefficiencies. Art and sensuality cannot survive within the racialized economic system of the pre-internment Japanese American family farm. For marginalized individuals, art and sensuality are in direct competition with economic survival.

The forces that foreclose the possibility for Yamamoto's characters to attain economic security and also express their sexuality and creativity are rooted in racialized labor and property relations. Prior to the McCarran-Walter Immigration and National Act of 1952, Asian immigrants, including Japanese immigrants, were unable to naturalize, or become legal U.S. citizens. They were labeled "aliens ineligible for citizenship," a designation which rendered them perpetually foreign and unable to participate in the electoral process. The state reduced the roles of men like the characters Hosoume and Hayashi to their economic function, while the Alien Land Law curtailed their ability to achieve economic success. Because of the Alien Land Law, many Japanese immigrants were forced to lease rather than own their land; others sought ways around the law by putting land in the names of their citizen children or forming corporations which could purchase the land. As Grace Kyungwon Hong contends, Yamamoto's stories reveal the effects of the Alien Land Law through details such as the Hosoume's harvest of crops known for their short term turn-over.[56] Anti-Asian laws affected the crops Hosoume and Hayashi could grow, their ability to invest long-term in a piece of land, and the conditions under which they could hire workers. The economic insecurity of the small family farms in Yamamoto's fiction emerges not only as a general result of capitalism, but specifically from the workings of race in a capitalist system.

Yamamoto's short stories also speak to the effects of denying naturalization to Asian immigrants through the frustration and powerlessness of the stories' patriarchs. Charles L. Crow interprets Yamamoto's harsh depiction of male desire for authority over their wives and daughters as a feminist challenge to patriarchal *Issei* culture.[57] Yet, in "Seventeen Syllables" and "Yoneko's Earthquake," the father's frustrations emerge partially from his powerlessness in the face of the family's economic and political oppression. This was a period in which politicians, newspapers, and members of the general public openly expressed hostility to Japanese immigrants. Legal regulations and cultural manifestations in this period would have prevented Hosoume and Hayashi from embodying the ideal subject or legal citizen of the nation-state. They would also have been excluded in significant ways from U.S. civil society. Consequently, Hosoume and Hayashi perceive their wives' insubordination as jeopardizing each man's sense of self and self-ownership in a nation-state and economic niche where they can legally possess little and where their political and cultural contributions are ignored and denied. Both men resort to violence against their wives because of their feelings of impotence, and perhaps as a result of bodily impotence in Hayashi's case. Their violent reactions stem from their own desires for agency denied by the state and broader society.

The burdens each character carries in "Seventeen Syllables" and "Yoneko's Earthquake" are linked to the capitalist conditions of labor migration and the racist conditions of U.S. property ownership. Cheryl Higashida argues that Yamamoto's short fiction reveals the historical context for the racialized conditions of agricultural production. She contends that it is "the historical conditions of production that are integral" to "the text's subtle protest against racialized patriarchy *and* its sympathetic portrait of a rural *Issei* woman's struggles as a mother, wife, and fieldworker."[58] These historical conditions include Mexican migration to the United States, Filipino migration to both Hawaii and California, Japanese migration to Hawaii and California, the movement of Japanese immigrants from farm workers to farm owners, and Japanese migrants' tensions with the Filipino community.[59] They also include, as Hong argues, the conditions of racialized property ownership that exclude Japanese immigrants, rendering their place in the economic and racial hierarchy always tenuous, just as the Japanese immigrants and Japanese Americans are rendered perpetually foreign.[60]

Given the privileged position a critique of racialized private property holds in Yamamoto's fiction, collective ownership of agrarian land in all likelihood would have held great appeal for her. In "Yoneko's Earthquake" and "Seventeen Syllables," moreover, Yamamoto's characters are prevented from lives that combine manual labor with sexual and creative expression. They face emotional and physical violence when seeking spiritual, sexual, and emotional fulfillment. Yamamoto depicts these forms of fulfillment as a threat to the family's economic survival and to the father's already threatened masculinity. Maurin's farmer-scholar offers the very possibility of the fulfilling life of scholar-worker that so eludes Yamamoto's characters. Her fiction examines many of the problems for which Maurin's agrarian vision appears as a solution.

Yet, significantly, Maurin's writings fail to incorporate the nuanced analysis of race, gender, and sexuality that Yamamoto's fiction provides. For while Maurin viewed agriculture as the solution to the separation of craft and work, Yamamoto's stories reveal the inability of family farming to reconcile labor with art under a system of racialized property relations. While Maurin's investment in Catholic Worker cultivation emerged from his desire to return to the agricultural conditions of his childhood, Yamamoto's short fiction suggests instead the desire to distance herself from the racialized and gendered realities of industrial capital, labor relations, and property ownership that structured her earliest memories and her parents' lives.

AGRARIANISM OF THE MARGINS

Yamamoto was no outsider to *The Catholic Worker*. Considering "Seventeen Syllables" and "Yoneko's Earthquake" as part of the Catholic Worker intellectual tradition broadens our understanding of Catholic Worker agrarianism and remaps the trajectory of American pastoralism, revealing the ways it has never successfully served as an escape from the racialized dynamics of capitalism, but has always been deeply embedded within it. In this chapter, I have argued that Maurin's ideals appealed to Yamamoto precisely because they offered a way of life in which Rosie's mother could harvest tomatoes and have her haiku too. Yet, Yamamoto's fiction points to problems of race and gender about which Maurin's agrarian vision fails to speak, and reports from Catholic Worker farm projects, including Yamamoto's own columns, suggest that the reality rarely matched the ideal. Yamamoto's fiction reveals Maurin's failure to address the economic violence of racist structures in much Catholic Worker agrarian writing. While the Catholic Worker movement under Day's leadership grappled with issues of race, if not always gender, in analyzing urban environments, an anti-racist analysis was seldom tied to discussions of farming life. In contrast, Yamamoto's work suggests the importance of recognizing racial, gender, and sexual hierarchies and structural oppressions in agricultural environments. The family farm in Yamamoto's fiction reveals the ways that racist and sexist structures in an oppressive economic and political system play out in everyday family dynamics. Agrarian utopianism cannot be achieved simply by removing private property without engaging with ways personal histories and interpersonal dynamics remain shaped by psychological and social structures of power.

Yamamoto's short fiction highlights that these issues arise not only in industrial agriculture, but manifest as well on the small family farm. This is an important corrective to the romanticized vision of farm labor that is resurging today. We see this resurgence in the popularity of Wendell Berry's writings, the successful Whole Foods marketing of what Michael Pollan calls "the supermarket pastoral," and in the rise of the local food movement.[61] Many of today's food advocates suffer from the same flaw as Maurin: they too easily envision agrarianism as a solution to industrialization and capitalism without an adequate interrogation of privilege. I have argued elsewhere that Pollan and other local food movement participants perceive workers, particularly immigrant workers of color, as unfortunate consequences of industrial agriculture. Rather than invest in the humanity and agency of marginalized workers, texts such as *The Omnivore's Dilemma* suggest, fallaciously, that with smaller farms, farm labor could be covered by (implicitly white) neighborly volunteers with non-white migrant workers erased from the food system along with pesticides and animal cruelty.[62] As Julie Guthman has pointed out, the idealization of the small family farm fails to deal with such problems as the continued needs for hired farm labor, the sexism and child labor often still part of the family farm regime, and the racist history of land ownership that still shapes the dynamics of who farms and where.[63] Yamamoto's fiction reveals the inequalities and hierarchies present on every farm, no matter how small or family-run. Her work suggests that a successful agrarian vision must address issues of race, class, and gender holistically in order to offer an escape from the various forms of violence in the current system and to create a society capable of achieving Maurin's ideals.

Yamamoto's stories invoke what Janet Fiskio terms an agrarianism of the margins. Fiskio argues against an agrarianism that valorizes the perspective of the "settled landowner" or small farmer over the perspectives of the many migrant agricultural workers.[64] In contrast to Wendell Berry's aesthetics of wholeness, Fiskio proposes an aesthetics of fragmentation found in Helena María Viramontes' novel *Under the Feet of Jesus* (1994) and Scott Hamilton Kennedy's documentary film *The Garden* (2008). Rather than valorizing the rootedness to the land that the intellectual descendants of Jeffersonian agrarianism, including Berry, embrace, these texts envision a sense of place that encompasses migrant communities involved with the various borders of the food system. According to Fiskio, these works reveal "that being settled is a privilege conditioned by class and nation."[65] In *The Garden* and *Under the Feet of Jesus*, place is a process rather than stable locale, and it "is inextricable from networks of social power."[66] Yamamoto presents a similar understanding of place, particularly in her emphasis on the tenuousness of Japanese immigrant land ownership.

Yamamoto's explorations of the contradictions facing Japanese immigrant farmers, barred from citizenship and unable to own land, and the Filipino and Mexican families they sometimes hire, do not suggest that the characters' moral or ethical responsibility emerges from their relationship to the land. Even as farmers, rather than farm workers, Yamamoto's characters lack the ability to naturalize their belonging to the land. In this way, Yamamoto's fiction reveals the privilege at work in Maurin's own vision of the agronomic university. It reveals the confluence of race and citizenship status that kept Filipino migrants, with national ward status; Mexican workers, some with citizenship status; and Japanese immigrants, barred from naturalizing, in a more precarious situation than Maurin, who crossed into the United States from Canada without proper documentation as an unauthorized, but white, migrant. Maurin's political vision does not grapple with the ways different experiences of race, gender, and citizenship status might shape the identities of those attempting to work communal land together.

Yamamoto's writings hold important lessons for an agrarianism inspired by the writings of Berry, Pollan, or Maurin. They suggest the importance of addressing the power dynamics within the farm. This includes the gendered relationship within families and also the racial relationships between farm owner and farm worker. Small farms are not immune to labor exploitation. Indeed, the economic fragility of the small family farm may encourage it. Moreover, we should not consider farms outside of their relationship to the broader political, social, and economic structures. Yamamoto's fictional patriarchs struggle against societal marginalization resulting from Orientalist constructions of the Asian male and powerlessness resulting from their lack of citizenship status. Hosoume's and Hayashi's determination to hold onto control within the family economy results in part from their inability to be fully recognized in the larger society. Yamamoto's fiction shows that the small family farm cannot be used to escape the racial dynamics of agricultural labor. Similarly, as Yamamoto discovered during her time at Peter Maurin farm, collective ownership does not erase the personal and structural experiences of race, gender, and class that shape group dynamics.

The act of farming exists in the broader dynamics of U.S. racial injustice and citizenship inequity. To envision the family farm or the farming collective as an escape from the racial histories of the U.S. that structure property ownership and labor exploitation is to perpetuate and remain complicit in these forms of injustice. Pollan's vision of the small family farm and Maurin's vision of the farming collective, in failing to attend to racial histories or provide an analysis of power and identity, unintentionally enacts a form of symbolic violence by naturalizing the subject position of the white male farmer. Yamamoto's short fiction opens up the possibilities of other subject positions important to a just vision of agricultural labor.

Including Yamamoto's "Yoneko's Earthquake" and "Seventeen Syllables" as part of U.S. agrarianism emphasizes the need to grapple with the historical context for racialized production that shapes contemporary land ownership and food systems patterns. It allows us to develop an American agricultural tradition that places the agrarianism of the margins at its center. Placing Yamamoto's writings in this context, moreover, reveals the centrality of agrarianism to Yamamoto's own political radicalism and Christian anarchism.

NOTES

I would like to express my thanks to Brian Frank, Margaret Konkol, Heather R. Lee, Mindy Richardson, Kyla Zaret, and the editors for their thoughtful and helpful comments.

1. King-Kok Cheung, "Interview with Hisaye Yamamoto," in Hisaye Yamamoto, *"Seventeen Syllables,"* ed. King-Kok Cheung (New Brunswick: Rutgers University Press, 1994), 85.
2. Dorothy Day, "To Our Readers," in *A Penny a Copy: Readings from The Catholic Worker*, ed. Thomas C. Cornell, Robert Ellsberg, and Jim Forest (Maryknoll, NY: Orbis Books, 1995), 3.
3. Mel Piehl, *Breaking Bread: The Catholic Worker and the Origin of Catholic Radicalism in America* (Tuscaloosa: University of Alabama Press, 2006), 23. Dorothy Day and Francis J. Sicius, *Peter Maurin: Apostle to the World* (Maryknoll, NY: Orbis Books, 2004), xiii, xxvii.
4. Cheung, "Interview," 85.
5. William J. Collinge, "Peter Maurin's Ideal of Farming Communes," in *Dorothy Day and The Catholic Worker Movement: Centenary Essays*, ed. William J. Thorn, Philip M. Runkel, and Susan Mourtin (Milwaukee: Marquette University Press, 2001), 386.
6. Maurin's green revolution should not be confused with the term's later and quite separate use to endorse the distribution of synthetic fertilizers, industrial pesticides, and hybrid seed.
7. Day and Sicius, *Peter Maurin*, 105.
8. Collinge, "Maurin's Ideal," 386.
9. Peter Maurin, *Easy Essays* (Eugene, OR: WIPF & Stock, 2003), 27.
10. Piehl, *Breaking Bread*, 97.
11. Day and Sicius, *Peter Maurin*, 81.
12. Piehl, *Breaking Bread*, 129. Jeffrey D. Marlett, "Down on the Farm and Up to Heaven: Catholic Worker Farm Communes and the Spiritual Virtues of Farming," in *Dorothy Day and the Catholic Worker Movement*, 408.
13. Thomas Campbell, "New Beginnings on the Land," *The Catholic Worker* 19.19 (1953): 5; William Guachat, "Reflections on the Green Revolution: The First Twenty Years Are the Hardest," *The Catholic Worker* 29.19 (1953): 5; Jack Thorton, "Five Years on the Land," *The Catholic Worker* 18.13 (1953): 1, 5.
14. Campbell, "New Beginnings," 5.
15. Charles L. Crow, "A MELUS Interview: Hisaye Yamamoto," *MELUS: Multi-Ethnic Literature of the United States* 14.1 (1987): 75.
16. Cheung, "Interview," 76.
17. Crow, "A MELUS Interview," 75–76.
18. Yamamoto briefly departed the camp to work as a cook in Springfield, Massachusetts before the end of internment. However, when her brother Johnny

was killed in Italy, fighting as part of the 442nd Combat Regiment, she returned to Poston to be with her parents.

19. Matthew M. Briones, "Hardly 'Small Talk': Discussing Race in the Writing of Hisaye Yamamoto," *Prospects* 29 (2005): 437.
20. Cheung, "Interview," 81.
21. King-Kok Cheung, introduction to *"Seventeen Syllables,"* ix.
22. Cheung, "Interview," 81.
23. Yone U. Stafford, "Pacifist Conference at Peter Maurin Farm," *The Catholic Worker* 20.3 (1953): 2.
24. Crow, "A MELUS Interview," 77.
25. Ibid.
26. Ibid.
27. Stafford, "Pacifist Conference," 2.
28. Dorothy Day, "Peter Maurin Farm," *The Catholic Worker* 20.11 (1954): 2.
29. Rollande Potvin, "Visit to the Peter Maurin Farm," *The Catholic Worker* 20.5 (1953): 3.
30. Hisaye Yamamoto, "Seabrook Farms," *The Catholic Worker* 20.11 (1954): 3, 6.
31. Cheung, "Interview," 81.
32. Dorothy Day, "Peter Maurin Farm," *The Catholic Worker* 20. 9 (1954): 5.
33. Ibid.
34. Hisaye Yamamoto, "Peter Maurin Farm," *The Catholic Worker* 21.5 (1954): 3.
35. Hisaye Yamamoto, "Peter Maurin Farm," *The Catholic Worker* 21.6 (1955): 3.
36. Hisaye Yamamoto, "Peter Maurin Farm," *The Catholic Worker* 22.1 (1955): 6.
37. Crow, "A MELUS Interview," 78.
38. Marlett, "Down on the Farm," 411.
39. Guachat, "Reflections," 5.
40. Cheung, "Interview," 85.
41. Crow, "A MELUS Interview," 78.
42. King-Kok Cheung, "Hisaye Yamamoto and Wakako Yamauchi," in *Words Matter. Conversations with Asian American Writers*, ed. King-Kok Cheung (Honolulu: University of Hawaii Press, 2000), 365.
43. Cheung, "Interview," 85.
44. Sau-ling Cynthia Wong, *Reading Asian American Literature: From Necessity to Extravagance* (Princeton: Princeton University Press, 1993), 13–14.
45. Hisaye Yamamoto, "Seventeen Syllables," in *"Seventeen Syllables,"* 23.
46. Yamamoto, "Seventeen Syllables," 32.
47. Ibid., 33.
48. Ibid., 35.
49. For example, Elaine Kim explains, "In 'Yoneko's Earthquake' and 'Seventeen Syllables,' the husbands are hard-working and serious but unable to tolerate their wives' efforts to create beauty and poetry. They ultimately crush their wives and shackle them to a life of endless toil behind them, not necessarily because they are evil, but because they cannot tolerate independence of any kind in their wives." Kim, "Hisaye Yamamoto: A Woman's View," in *"Seventeen Syllables": Hisaye Yamamoto*, 115.
50. Yamamoto, "Seventeen Syllables," 23.
51. Hisaye Yamamoto, "Yoneko's Earthquake," in *"Seventeen Syllables,"* 44.
52. Ibid., 54.
53. Ibid., 55.
54. Yamamoto, "Seventeen Syllables," 33.
55. Ibid.
56. Grace Kyungwon Hong, "'Something Forgotten Which Should Have Been Remembered': Private Property and Cross-Racial Solidarity in the Work of Hisaye Yamamoto," *American Literature* 71.2 (1999): 291.

57. Charles L. Crow, "The *Issei* Father in the Fiction of Hisaye Yamamoto," in *"Seventeen Syllables,"* 119–20.
58. Cheryl Higashida, "Re-Signed Subjects: Women, Work, and World in the Fiction of Carlos Bulosan and Hisaye Yamamoto," *Studies in the Literary Imagination* 34.1 (2004): 37.
59. Ibid., 38.
60. Hong, "Something Forgotten," 292, 295–96.
61. Michael Pollan, *Omnivore's Dilemma: A Natural History of Four Meals* (New York: Penguin, 2007), 137.
62. Sarah D. Wald, "Visible Farmers/Invisible Workers: Locating Immigrant Labor in Food Studies," *Food, Culture, and Society* 14.4 (2011): 569.
63. Julie Guthman, *Agrarian Dreams: The Paradox of Organic Farming in California* (Berkeley: University of California Press, 2004), 174.
64. Janet Fiskio, "Unsettling Ecocriticism: Rethinking Agrarianism, Place, and Citizenship," *American Literature* 84.2 (June 2012): 308.
65. Ibid., 311.
66. Ibid., 312.

BIBLIOGRAPHY

Briones, Matthew M. "Hardly 'Small Talk': Discussing Race in the Writing of Hisaye Yamamoto." *Prospects* 29 (2005): 435–71.
Campbell, Thomas. "New Beginnings on the Land." *The Catholic Worker* 19.19 (1953): 5.
Cheung, King-Kok. "Interview with Hisaye Yamamoto." In Hisaye Yamamoto, *"Seventeen Syllables,"* edited by King-Kok Cheung, 71–86. New Brunswick: Rutgers University Press, 1994.
———. Introduction to *"Seventeen Syllables,"* edited by King-Kok Cheung, 3–7. New Brunswick: Rutgers University Press, 1994.
———. "Hisaye Yamamoto and Wakako Yamauchi." In *Words Matter. Conversations with Asian American Writers*, edited by King-Kok Cheung, 343–82. Honolulu: University of Hawaii Press, 2000.
Collinge, William J. "Peter Maurin's Ideal of Farming Communes." In *Dorothy Day and The Catholic Worker Movement: Centenary Essays*, edited by William J. Thorn, Philip M. Runkel, and Susan Mourtin, 385–98. Milwaukee: Marquette University Press, 2001.
Crow, Charles L. "A MELUS Interview: Hisaye Yamamoto." *MELUS: Multi-Ethnic Literature of the United States* 14.1 (1987): 73–84.
———. "The *Issei* Father in the Fiction of Hisaye Yamamoto." In Hisaye Yamamoto, *"Seventeen Syllables,"* edited by King-Kok Cheung, 119–28. New Brunswick: Rutgers University Press, 1994.
Day, Dorothy. "To Our Readers." In *A Penny a Copy: Readings from The Catholic Worker*, edited by Thomas C. Cornell, Robert Ellsberg, and Jim Forest, 3–4. Maryknoll, NY: Orbis Books, 1995.
———. "Peter Maurin Farm." *The Catholic Worker* 20.9 (1954): 2, 3, 5.
——— and Fancis J. Sicius. *Peter Maurin: Apostle to the World*. Maryknoll, NY: Orbis Books, 2004.
Fiskio, Janet. "Unsettling Ecocriticism: Rethinking Agrarianism, Place, and Citizenship." *American Literature* 84.2 (2012): 301–25.
Guachat, William. "Reflections on the Green Revolution: The First Twenty Years Are the Hardest." *The Catholic Worker* 19.19 (1953): 5.
Guthman, Julie. *Agrarian Dreams: The Paradox of Organic Farming in California*. Berkeley: University of California Press, 2004.
Higashida, Cheryl. "Re-Signed Subjects: Women, Work, and World in the Fiction

of Carlos Bulosan and Hisaye Yamamoto." *Studies in the Literary Imagination* 34.1 (2004): 35–60.

Hong, Grace Kyungwon. "'Something Forgotten Which Should Have Been Remembered': Private Property and Cross-Racial Solidarity in the Work of Hisaye Yamamoto." *American Literature* 71.2 (1999): 291–310.

Kim, Elaine. "Hisaye Yamamoto: A Woman's View." In Hasaye Yamamoto, *"Seventeen Syllables,"* edited by King-Kok Cheung, 109–17. New Brunswick: Rutgers University Press, 1994.

Marlett, Jeffrey D. "Down on the Farm and Up to Heaven: Catholic Worker Farm Communes and the Spiritual Virtues of Farming." In *Dorothy Day and The Catholic Worker Movement: Centenary Essays*, edited by William J. Thorn, Philip M. Runkel, and Susan Mourtin, 406–17. Milwaukee: Marquette University Press, 2001.

Maurin, Peter. *Easy Essays.* Eugene, OR: WIPF & Stock, 2003.

Piehl, Mel. *Breaking Bread: The Catholic Worker and the Origin of Catholic Radicalism in America.* Tuscaloosa: University of Alabama Press, 2006.

Pollan, Michael. *Omnivore's Dilemma: A Natural History of Four Meals.* New York: Penguin, 2007.

Potvin, Rollande. "Visit to the Peter Maurin Farm." *The Catholic Worker* 20.5 (1953): 3.

Stafford, Yone U. "Pacifist Conference at Peter Maurin Farm." *The Catholic Worker* 20.3 (1953): 2.

Thorton, Jack. "Five Years on the Land." *The Catholic Worker* 18.13 (1953): 1, 5.

Wald, Sarah D. "Visible Farmers/Invisible Workers: Locating Immigrant Labor in Food Studies." *Food, Culture, and Society* 14.4 (2011): 567–86.

Wong, Sau-ling Cynthia. *Reading Asian American Literature: From Necessity to Extravagance.* Princeton: Princeton University Press, 1993.

Yamamoto, Hisaye. "Peter Maurin Farm." *The Catholic Worker* 21.5 (1954): 3, 5–8; 21.6 (1955): 3; 22.1 (1955): 6.

———. "Seabrook Farms." *The Catholic Worker* 20.11 (1954): 3, 6.

———. *"Seventeen Syllables,"* edited by King-Kok Cheung. New Brunswick: Rutgers University Press, 1994.

9 A Geomantic Reading of Asian Diasporic Literature

Stephen L. Field

Fengshui, sometimes known as *geomancy*, is an example of Chinese wisdom whose ethos has entered the American psyche to join the likes of kungfu even though no cinematic blockbuster has appeared to popularize its mystique.[1] Scarcely evident outside of East Asia until the last decades of the twentieth century, there are now numerous accounts of its practice in Asian diasporic literature. For example, many Western readers are familiar with such "pop" fengshui warnings as the following, articulated in Amy Tan's novel, *The Joy Luck Club*: "'Wah!' cried the mother upon seeing the mirrored armoire in the master suite of her daughter's new condominium. 'You cannot put mirrors at the foot of the bed.'"[2] Yet, most tend not to understand the cosmological world view that lies behind such behavior.

According to Robert T. Hayashi, "How the specific cultural and religious contexts of Asian immigrants and their descendants have impacted their views of the American environment and their interaction, shaping, and expressions of it remains unexplored."[3] Fengshui is just such a context, and the exploration of its use in literary expression is the aim of this chapter. Simply speaking, the goal of fengshui theory is the proper siting of a building within the environment. Furthermore, aesthetic considerations aside, the metaphysical aspect of the fengshui environment always determines the physical. This chapter will examine writings influenced by such a world view and, by doing so, will attempt to develop a "geomantic" theory of literature. Reminiscent of geocriticism, which links the imaginary space of the text to its real world referent, the geomantic reading will analyze the literary environment against the cosmological world view of the character or author.[4]

A minimum analysis of the geomantic world view requires that we understand how the built environment of fengshui is comparable to a constructed space whose builder or whose dweller therein has no knowledge of fengshui. The chapter will thus begin with a Western perspective on building—that of German philosopher, Martin Heidegger, who equated dwelling with "being." According to Heidegger, before a house can be a dwelling its natural environment and the cultural background of the people who inhabit it must merge. This creates a metaphysics of place, which may then be used to analyze literary spaces to determine if they reflect this oneness.[5] For our purposes, then, a geomantic reading will look for that "spirit" of a place which marks its inhabitants as dwellers.

Since the focus of this chapter is the created spaces of selected contemporary Asian diasporic novels, it is the cosmology of fengshui which serves as the metaphysical background for such authors. The chapter will thus continue with a detailed analysis of the art of fengshui, beginning with an account of Form School theories, which are based on the geological formations of the environment surrounding the dwelling. Then the theories of the Compass School will be described—the school most familiar to Western aficionados with its elemental orders and flows of *qi*. In order to illustrate the practical application of the various principles, passages from novels will be cited. Close readings of the novels will not be offered; instead, citations are chosen to the extent that they support a geomantic reading of literature.

Eight novels are discussed in the course of this chapter: *The Joy Luck Club* (1989), *The Hundred Secret Senses* (1995), and *The Bonesetter's Daughter* (2001) by Amy Tan; *Fixer Chao* (2001) by Han Ong; *The Money Dragon* (2002) by Pam Chun; and *The Feng Shui Detective* (2000), *The Feng Shui Detective's Casebook* (2003), and *Mr. Wong Goes West* (2008) by Nury Vittachi. Tan's *The Joy Luck Club* is the most frequently cited, not only because of the numerous references to the practice of fengshui within its covers, but also because Tan's own life is informed by fengshui precepts according to her autobiographical work, *The Opposite of Fate* (2003). Her world view as revealed in her works is analyzed in the section titled, "The Wind and Water Cosmology of Amy Tan." As readers of this chapter will discover, the cosmology of Tan's fictional world does not always conform to the traditional view of her forebears. An author for whom the geomantic perspective is the central theme of his works is Sri Lankan native and Hong Kong expatriate, Nury Vittachi. His comedy-crime series follows the escapades of the Singaporean sleuth and fengshui master, C. F. Wong. Vittachi's detective novels, with their focus on the daily life of a fengshui consultant, form an interesting counterpoint to the works of Tan. The final section of the chapter explores the concept of "balance" in the works of Vittachi and Tan, as it pertains to the geomantic world view.

HEIDEGGER'S HUT

Martin Heidegger wrote his most famous work of philosophy, *Being and Time* (1927), in his cabin in the Black Forest region of Germany. Describing his mountainous environment, he noted that "the wind, shifting quickly, grumbles in the rafters of the cabin" and "the mountain brook in night's stillness tells of its plunging over the boulders."[6] Years later, Heidegger imagines a farmhouse in that valley "on the wind-sheltered mountain slope looking south, among the meadows close to the spring," around which he constructed his philosophy of dwelling.[7] Those even remotely familiar with the ideal fengshui locale will recognize something akin to the "dragon lair" in this idyllic setting. We must therefore ask, if Heidegger's *Schwarzwaldhof* (Black Forest farmhouse) were built instead on the slopes of Dawu Mountain in Black Forest township, Jiangsu Province, China, would the fortune of its inhabitants be any different?

Heidegger points out in his essay that the high German root of the word for "building" (*Bauen*) means "to dwell." Although the original sense of the verb *bauen* has been lost, he says, it was clearly related to cultivation as well as construction, as if dwelling "preserved and nurtured" our being. Moreover, since the dwelling is the primary relationship between humans and the space they occupy, and since human beings cannot fail to dwell, Heidegger believed that dwelling "is *the basic character* of Being."[8] In other words, to build is to dwell and to dwell is to be. The Black Forest farmhouse embodies that original attitude of cultivation, as if the peasants who built it, by their very dwelling in that space, made the house grow up around them. In Heidegger's words, "the self-sufficiency of the power to let earth and heaven, divinities and mortals enter *in simple oneness* into things, ordered the house."[9] It is this "oneness" that marks the Black Forest site as a dragon lair. For that is in reality what the geomancer seeks to accomplish: the "syncing" of the dwelling site and its inhabitants with the natural environment, so that Heaven (the astrophysical realm), Earth (the geophysical realm) and humans (the metaphysical realm) coincide. This analysis of Heidegger's farmhouse looks beyond his European locale to find a metaphysical grounding of the physical space and, as such, is a geomantic reading.

As Hayashi also notes, "The few investigations of environment, or of place, within Asian American literary criticism discuss place more as a process than as a locale."[10] His notion of "place" is noteworthy for its absence, or rather its "displacement," and is more a verbal construct than a nominal one since Asian Americans are often characterized as struggling to "establish, find, and maintain . . . roots in America, while retaining those of somewhere else."[11] This chapter will also concentrate on the process of placement—that is, how Asians struggle to locate themselves properly in spaces, both native and diasporic. However, rather than Hayashi's "politics of place," it is more particularly a metaphysics of place that a geomantic reading will require. A metaphysical placement cannot be conducted at the expense of locale, since the locus for any cosmological reticulation is always a place, either fictional or real. Similarly, the resident of any locale is not able to establish roots unless the cultural foundations are present. From a Heideggerian perspective, the natural ("earth and heaven") and the cultural ("divinities and mortals") must merge before the place can become a dwelling.[12] Lastly, the fengshui process is universal—its efficacy is the same in any environment regardless of national boundary, as long as the practitioner believes in its rules.

Belief is clearly important in the practice of fengshui. A novel whose premise relies on such belief (or its absence) is *Fixer Chao* (2001). Filipino

American Han Ong's novel describes the exploits of gay Filipino hustler, William Narciso Paulinha, who masquerades as the famed fengshui master, William Chao, in order to dupe the rich and famous of Manhattan. After being exposed as a charlatan, William asks himself at the end of the novel, "How could it have been fraud if I myself believed?"[13] Characters in many of the novels analyzed here question the efficacy of fengshui practice. As Patricia Hamilton says about the daughters in her study of *The Joy Luck Club*, "They reject as nonsense the fragments of traditional lore their mothers try to pass along to them."[14] Amy Tan, on the other hand, "endorses the mothers' traditional Chinese worldview because it offers the possibility of choice and action in a world where paralysis is frequently a threat."[15] Fortunately, belief in fengshui is not necessary for the reader of fiction to derive ultimate meaning. That is because fengshui is an art, and its individual practice, like literature, is a work of art. From the vantage of an aesthetic worldview we do not have to judge the reality of a phenomenon in order to derive meaning from it.

THE ART OF FENGSHUI

So, we must ask ourselves, what is the art of fengshui? It would be the most venerable example of environmental planning in the world were it not for the fact that its scope is the individual rather than the community. The only "community" within the traditional fengshui purview is the family or clan, so the concept of protecting the environment for the good of the world is not a major consideration in a geomantic world view. The sole significance of the environment surrounding a site is its influence upon the fortunes of the family that lives there or whose ancestors are interred there.

Family, indeed, is an integral component of any understanding of traditional fengshui practice. An Asian American novel that quite authentically adheres to the geomantic world view is Pam Chun's *The Money Dragon* (2002), a story based on the history of one of the first Chinese families to immigrate to Hawaii. The book's protagonist, Lau Ah Leong, after making his fortune in Hawaii (thus his designation, the Money Dragon), returns to Canton to build a mansion for his family. Here he discusses the building site with his first son:

> You know the property across the river, the one with paddy fields down the Dragon mountain? The *fengshui* is propitious for my new house. See the *ch'i*? Calm flowing water to the south brings wealth. Four main doors, one facing each of the cardinal directions: north, east, west, and south. Ten separate outdoor toilets—one for each son and his family. One hundred and eighteen bedrooms for all my wives, sons, grandchildren, and great-grandchildren to come.[16]

Foci such as dragon-shaped mountains, water flowing to the south, and attention to the cardinal directions mark this site as geomantic.

Fengshui also determines the location of the patriarch's final resting place: "Ah Leong's funeral site was chosen for its auspicious location. It was on the highest hill in Manoa Cemetery, on a gentle slope backed by the mountains. . . . He could see all the lands he had owned and watch the ships coming into Honolulu Harbor as he had done so often when he was alive."[17] Although fengshui is not mentioned in this scene, which appears in the penultimate chapter of the book, its principles are clearly being followed. From a cosmological perspective, burying Ah Leong with his back to the mountains and his face toward the water is not strictly for aesthetic reasons. Instead, it was believed that the geological formations that surrounded the burial site interacted with the tomb to ensure that the spirit of the patriarch was content in the afterlife. Called "Form School" after the topography that is the object of its scrutiny, this is also the branch of geomancy that governed the siting of cities in imperial China. Before we delve into the theories of this school, it is important to note that contemporary Western notions of fengshui do not normally recognize such an anthropocentric world view. The concept of ancestral worship, while meaningful in the diasporic community, has not captured the attention of the American public like the concept of *ch'i* (qi) with its resemblance to the "force" of *Star Wars* fame. Primarily for this reason, fengshui in America is more an environmental perspective than a religious belief.

THE FORM SCHOOL THEORY OF GEOMANTIC ANALYSIS: THE DRAGON LAIR

Let us now take a closer look at the principles underlying the sort of geomantic environments described by Chun in *The Money Dragon*. Scholars believe that the earliest practice of what eventually would be known as fengshui was to orient the homes of the dead rather than the homes of the living. The term itself appears first in a passage from the *Book of Burial*, which dates to the fourth century CE:

> *Qi* rides the wind [*feng*] and scatters, but is retained when encountering water [*shui*]. The ancients collected it to prevent its dissipation, and guided it to assure its retention. Thus it was called *fengshui*.[18]

Fengshui may literally indicate "wind and water," but this is merely shorthand for an environmental policy of hindering the wind and hoarding the waters. Blocking the wind is necessary to prevent the dissipation of the natural flow of qi along the ground, while flowing water attracts qi like a magnet. The most auspicious burial site, therefore, is one that encourages water to linger in its vicinity yet with sufficient windbreaks—all for the purpose of gathering that ineffable substance called qi.[19]

Etymologically, *qi* means steam or vapor (as in clouds), but by the time of Confucius (sixth century BCE) had come to mean an animating force in the atmosphere manifested in various meteorological phenomena. On earth, it was compared to blood flowing in veins. By the time the *Book of Burial* was written over a thousand years later, qi had become the life force quested by fengshui masters in the geophysical environment. From the opening chapter of the *Book of Burial* comes this important passage: "Truly, life is accumulated *qi*. It solidifies into bone, which alone remains after death. Burial returns *qi* to the bones, which is the way the living are endowed."[20] The corpse is interred to receive the influence of the qi flowing in the earth. The process whereby the bones are energized is called "mutual resonance," for which the standard proof given by the ancient philosophers is this: if a string on one lute is plucked, the same string on a nearby lute will simultaneously vibrate. It follows, then, that the qi of the interred ancestor and the qi of the living descendants are related. Therefore, when the vital, life-giving qi of the burial site surrounds the bones, they are energized like a dead battery being recharged, and the lives of the descendants are thereby endowed with good fortune.

The challenge for fengshui masters, both ancient and modern, is the location of qi since, as a substance, it is invisible. The following passage from the *Book of Burial* gives valuable clues regarding its detection: "Where the ground holds auspicious *qi*, the earth conforms and protrudes. When [arterial] branches hold accumulated *qi*, water conforms and accompanies them."[21] The elevation of topographical features is the result of the underground presence of qi. Such "arteries" are thus conduits of qi which, as it accumulates in the terrain, also manifests the outward flow of water. From a fengshui point of view, qi originates in the forces of mountainous heights, slowly winds around as it decreases in altitude, and finally runs its course in the hills and knolls of the lowlands. When such a terrain can be traced from its highland origin to its lowland terminus, this is the optimum manifestation of qi. The *Book of Burial* describes such topography as follows:

> Where contour ceases and features soar high, with a stream in front and a hill behind, here hides the head of the dragon. The snout and forehead are auspicious; the horns and eyes bring doom. The ears obtain princes and kings; the lips lead to death or injury from weapons.[22]

This is the "dragon lair," pictured here as if a dragon slumbers in its cave, head protruding. In another passage, a second guardian appears: "The dragon and tiger are what protect the district of the lair."[23] And the environment is complete with four directional guardians: "Bury with the Cerulean Dragon to the left, the White Tiger to the right, the Vermilion Bird in front, and the Dark Turtle in back."[24]

If the topography of a particular locale conforms to these descriptions, then qi will be generated along the flow of terrain, and the appearance of water at the terminus will be proof of the coalescence of that qi. This water is the means by which the qi generated by the dragon can be harnessed to revive the spirit of the interred bones. Thus, the grave of Ah Leong—like his estate in Canton—is located with a dragon mountain to the back with flowing water in front. This will insure that the fortunes of his son, Tat Tung, whose wife is the narrator of the story, continue to rise.

One of the most representative accounts of this cosmological world view appearing in Asian American literature is from Tan's *The Hundred Secret Senses*. The protagonist in the story, Olivia Yee, has returned to China at the request of her half-sister, Kwan. In this scene, Kwan tells Olivia about the origins of her home village, Changmian, in the Guilin district of southern China (famous for its rugged karst topography):

> We stare in silence at the mountains, and then Kwan nudges me. "Now maybe you see dragon," she says. "Two side-by-side dragon. Yes?"
>
> I squint hard. Kwan grabs my shoulders and repositions me. "Squeeze-close eyes," she orders. "Sweep from mind American ideas. Think Chinese. Make you mind like dreaming. Two dragon, one male, one female."
>
> I open my eyes. It's as though I'm viewing the past as the foreground, the present as a faraway dream. "The peaks going up and down," I say, tracing in the air, "those are their two spines, right? And the way the two front peaks taper into those mounds, those are their two heads, with the valley tucked between their two snouts."
>
> Kwan pats my arm, as if I were a student who has recited her geography lessons well. "Some people think, 'Oh, village sit right next to dragon mouth—what bad *fengshui*, no harmony.' But to my way thinking, all depend what type dragon. These two dragon very loyal, good *chi*—how you say in English, good *chi*?"
>
> "Good vibes," I say.[25]

Not only does Kwan specifically describe the landscape of Guilin in terms of undulating dragons, she correctly points out that the mouth of the dragon is an inauspicious locale (note the dragon's "lips" in the *Book of Burial* passage quoted above). And, as with the dragon mountain of Pam Chun's Canton, the Guilin dragons watch over the family of the story's narrator.

THE COMPASS SCHOOL THEORY OF GEOMANTIC ANALYSIS: THE COSMOLOGY OF QI

Admittedly, the search for topographical dragons and tigers is not the branch of fengshui that Westerners normally encounter. More well-known is the Compass School version, named after the familiar *luopan* or geomantic compass. Its theories are based on the cosmology of *wuxing*, the five categories of qi with the elemental designations of water, metal, fire, earth, and wood. Strictly speaking, rather than being constituent material elements of the cosmos, these categories refer instead to agents of change or phases that regularly metamorphose into one another. Two such orders of transmutation are presented in Figure 9.1.

To conduct a geomantic reading, the fengshui practitioner juxtaposes the element corresponding to the birth year of the prospective occupant with the corresponding element of the direction faced by the front door of the prospective dwelling. The prevailing qi in the environment naturally would "flow" through the dwelling's entrance and thus merge with the natal qi of the dweller. This interaction of human and place "conjures up a star spirit, which visits good or bad fortune upon the person who by chance or choice resides in that space at that time."[26] Good fortune is indicated when the two exhibit a relationship of mutual production, while bad fortune is indicated when the two exhibit a relationship of mutual conquest. For example, let us imagine that a person with the natal element wood wanted to build a house facing the direction north, which has the phase water. In the mutual production order of the five elements, water nourishes wood, so this conjunction would indicate good fortune. On the other hand, suppose the same person wanted to build a house facing the direction southwest. The direction southwest has the phase earth. In the mutual conquest order of the five elements, wood saps earth, so the conjunction would indicate bad fortune.

Compass School fengshui can analyze the auspice of any sector of a person's dwelling by scrutinizing the qi of the direction faced by that sector of the house. In the Eight-House school—the most popular brand practiced in the world today—each of eight sectors has a designation that names the "house" whose front door opens toward that direction (Xun, Li, Kun, etc.), as well as a "star" that governs that house (four, nine, two, etc.).[27] Figure 9.2 gives the names of each of the eight houses, its numerological star, its

Mutual Production Order	Mutual Conquest Order
Earth harbors metal (ores)	Earth dams water
Metal condenses water (on bronze)	Water quenches fire
Water nourishes wood (plants)	Fire melts metal
Wood feeds fire	Metal cuts wood
Fire builds earth (as ashes)	Wood saps earth

Figure 9.1   Production and Conquest Orders of the Five Elements

characteristic element, and its direction. Chinese cosmological maps conventionally place south at the top.

In order to see the principles of Eight-House fengshui in operation, examine a passage from *Mr. Wong Goes West* by Sri Lankan author, Nury Vittachi. In this scene, fengshui consultant C. F. Wong, protagonist of Vittachi's novels, is being given a tour of the new Chek Lap Kok airport in Hong Kong. During the tour, he asks the guide where the front door of the airport is:

> For Wong, it was a natural question to ask: how could you understand the fengshui of a building without knowing where the front door was? The main door of the house had to be aligned with the most positive direction for the director of the group of people who used the building. For example, if the most senior man had a *kua* number of seven, a northeast facing door would make the house prosperous, while a southwest door would see the property expanding in size; other directions would be less positive.[28]

Gua (or *kua*, meaning *Yijing* trigram) number seven indicates the House of Dui, whose element is metal. The halls (or rooms) of Gen, in the northeast, and Kun, in the southwest, both belong to the element earth, which "harbors" the ores of metal. Thus, both of these directions generate the natal element of the "most senior man" who inhabits the house. When the element of a direction "generates" the qi of the person dwelling in that locale (rather than destroying that qi), good fortune will result.

This passage could pertain as much to a residence as to a business, since Eight-House fengshui theories are equally valid for places of commerce. In the following passage from the same novel, Wong is evaluating

Wood SE 4 XUN	Fire SOUTH 9 LI	Earth SW 2 KUN
Wood EAST 3 ZHEN	5	Metal WEST 7 DUI
Earth NE 8 GEN	Water NORTH 1 KAN	Metal NW 6 QIAN

Figure 9.2   Map of Eight-House Fengshui

the penthouse office of a new client, the chairman of Skyparc Airside Enterprises, who hopes to sell British aircraft to China:

> Using details of Sir Nicholas Handey's birth—he was born in the Year of the Monkey, 1932—Wong decided that west-southwest was his most positive direction. He was able to make slight adjustments to the room easily, to give power to the chairman's seat.[29]

Here, Master Wong adjusts the boardroom for a man born in the House of Kun, belonging to the element earth. West-southwest is the direction halfway between the element earth and the element metal which it engenders. As with the "most senior man" above, since earth generates metal, rather than destroying it, good fortune will result.

In Vittachi's first novel, *The Feng Shui Detective*, which is set in Singapore, Wong encounters the following situation when conducting a reading of an apartment:

> The block was a rectangular construction on an almost square podium, and belonged to the K'un orientation, with its door facing southwest. The main room faced due west of the center. This was one of the more prosperous directions for the main living space, and was known as the Direction of the Celestial Physician.[30]
>
> There was a potential clash with the flow of *ch'i* moving from the kitchen to the second bedroom which was directly opposite, but nothing that couldn't be fixed with the judicious placing of suitable objects to catch and divert any unsuitable rush of water or fire energy.[31]

Here, the ideal fengshui orientation for the owner's dwelling needs to match the element of his or her birth. Since Wong identifies the apartment as a Kun House we must assume that the birth element of its owner, Dr. Leiber, a dentist from New York, is earth. This automatically isolates four sectors of the house as lucky and four as unlucky. This is because the earth of the southwest and northeast sectors produces metal, the element of west and northwest. On the other hand, the shaded sectors of the house in the Eight-House diagram above are unlucky because wood saps earth, fire melts metal, metal cuts wood, and earth dams water. According to Wong's geomantic analysis of the apartment, the kitchen and second bedroom are located in the north and south sectors of the apartment. Although we are not informed about the directions of the rooms, we may presume that the kitchen (with its stove) resides in the south, the direction of fire. The mention of a clash of elements refers to the destruction of fire by water. However, a "rush" of water qi from the bedroom to the kitchen can be counteracted by placing "suitable objects" in the path. Such objects normally destroy the harmful element; so, for example, clay pots might be positioned next to the kitchen door because earth dams water and clay is a form of earth.

As the narrative continues, Wong becomes puzzled by the fengshui of the apartment: "Was there something outside he had missed? He scanned the horizon for the twentieth time. Although there was no obvious geological dragon guarding the premises, nor was there anything overtly negative."[32] Here, Wong also makes use of Form School theories ("geological dragon"). Still perplexed, the geomancer suddenly smiles, realizing that "the flat *smelt* wrong . . . the heady tang of something like paraffin, the sharp odor of carbon, and the sour smell of ash. 'The house is on fire,' he explained." A fire had mysteriously been set just outside the front door, blocking escape. With no fire extinguisher, with burglar bars on all the windows, and with no time for the fire department to arrive, it falls to Wong to save the day:

> He walked into the heart of the burning living room with the paper in his left hand. "This apartment qualifies as a K'un dwelling because it faces southwest. But its water sources come from the south," he shouted over the crackling of the flames. "Just here, in fact."[33]

He picks up a hammer and beats on the wall until it fractures, exposing a water pipe on which he continues to hammer until a torrent gushes into the room and extinguishes the fire.

Chun also partakes of Compass School theories to describe the dwelling of Phoenix, the narrator of *The Money Dragon*.

> I looked for a clean, quiet area, friendly neighbors, and a big house with the right *fengshui*. It had to have the proper elements around it to promote the beneficial flow of that vital cosmic energy force, *ch'i*. I considered each home's orientation to the water, the mountains, and the surrounding buildings. Was it in harmony with the trees and the turn of the road? I studied what way the rooms faced and how the rooms flowed one to the other.[34]

"Beneficial flow" would thus imply the mutual production of elements. When Phoenix located the house on Circle Lane, palms (wood) graced the entry and a mango tree (wood) shaded the side yard. This probably identified the residence as a House of Xun, belonging to the element wood. Thus, before moving in to the new house, she installed a new stove in the kitchen as if she knew that "wood feeds fire," thus generating good fortune.

THE WIND AND WATER COSMOLOGY OF AMY TAN

Tan's world view is also informed by the Compass School of fengshui. She describes her own house in this fashion:

> And the location of my study is particularly auspicious, according to Chinese principles of *fengshui* ("wind and water"). Its three bay

windows overlook neighborhood rooftops and face north toward water and mountains.[35]

Based on her year of birth—1952—Tan was born under the element of wood in the direction of East. The standard evaluation for such an individual (from the online consultancy, "Fengshui Readings by Master Ten Li") is as follows:

> The study, office, or den/living room should be located in the north portion of the house, the direction of water. Since water nourishes wood in the mutual production order of the five elements, the time you spend in this room will be rejuvenating.[36]

Perhaps more telling is the following admission regarding her writing of *The Joy Luck Club*:

> In any case, originally I had titled the book *Wind and Water*, after the Chinese philosophy of harmony with nature. And originally there were going to be five sections to the book, three stories for each of the five elements found in harmonious nature: earth, fire, wood, water, and metal.[37]

While Hamilton does an admirable job of analyzing the "elemental" basis of characterization in *The Joy Luck Club*, it is worth noting that Tan significantly enlarges the concept of fengshui in this statement.[38]

What she does is shift the focus from the local to the cosmic, that is, from the specifics of an individual's dwelling to his or her relationship with nature. In Tan's world view, *feng* and *shui* are apparently surrogates for *yin* and *yang* whose interaction represents balance and harmony in traditional Chinese philosophy.[39] Evidence of this is illustrated by the words of Rose Hsu Jordan describing her parents' naiveté before the tragic drowning of her brother: "It had given them the confidence to believe their luck would never run out, . . . that all the elements were in balance, the right amount of wind and water."[40] It is as if the image of dark yin chasing light yang in the conventional Daoist Taiji symbol has been replaced in Tan's cosmos by a whirl of wind and a swirl of water. In traditional Chinese cosmology, the image of whirling and swirling is precisely how ancient poets depicted the chaos state.

> When Heaven and Earth were yet unformed,
> All was ascending and flying, diving and delving.[41]

Tan may be implying that fengshui can cure chaos.

In fact, wind is not one of the five elements as is implied in Rose's statement. Wind and water do not need to be in balance in order for good fortune to accrue at a dwelling site. According to the *Book of Burial*, wind strips away the life-giving qi, so the proper site should be sheltered from its ingress.

On the other hand, life-giving qi accumulates in water, so water should be encouraged to flow nearby. Ong makes a similar claim in *Fixer Chao*. In this scene, William Chao is conducting research for his new "profession":

> I cracked open the first of the library books. The first lines my eyes lit on said: "The term Feng Shui literally translates as 'wind-water.' These are two elements thought to be essential to the life of any living thing, and are equivalent to what the Chinese call 'chi'—'energies' or 'currents'— through which Feng Shui operates."[42]

Perhaps Ong conflates wind with "air," since the latter is one of the Aristotelian elements.[43] While wind may be a manifestation of qi in a meteorological sense, it is not considered to be an element. Nevertheless, the amelioration of the metaphysical concept of wind is striking in Tan's fiction, and it bears further analysis.

In "The Red Candle" chapter of *The Joy Luck Club*—the tale of Lindo Jong's fated marriage into the Huang family of Taiyuan—much of the young girl's character is expressed in cosmological terminology. Lindo's childhood village borders the Fen, a tributary of the Yellow River that drains the "great plain" that gives the region its name. As an alluvial basin, the Taiyuan area was subject to flooding, so rural residents would have been well aware of the fengshui of their dwellings, particularly the bends of a river (or the bends of a road in the modern cityscape), which, like the peaks of a mountain range, are considered to be environment-influencing dragons. As Lindo explains, "Our house sat on a little hill. We called this hill Three Steps to Heaven, but it was really just centuries of hardened layers of mud washed up by the Fen River."[44] Such an apotropaic designation of the hill compound in a real world scenario would be evidence that the residents suspected the water dragon would eventually destroy their land. Disaster irrevocably struck, and the family was forced to migrate to the south, leaving Lindo with the Huangs, whose "house sat higher up in the valley."

On her wedding day, while sitting at a dressing table watching an approaching thunderstorm through an open window, Lindo ponders her arranged marriage. She even contemplates throwing herself into the river that had destroyed her family, but reconsiders:

> And then I realized it was the first time I could see the power of the wind. I couldn't see the wind itself, but I could see it carried the water that filled the rivers and shaped the countryside. . . . I had on a beautiful red dress, but what I saw was even more valuable. I was strong. I was pure. I had genuine thoughts inside that no one could see, that no one could ever take away from me. I was like the wind.[45]

In a reversal of orthodox fengshui symbolism, it is the wind that confers potency and water that withdraws it in Lindo's life. By the publication of her fourth novel, *The Bonesetter's Daughter*, which in its entirety contains only one cryptic reference to fengshui, Tan seems to acknowledge that her understanding is a reversal of conventional wisdom. In this novel, Lu Ling, the mother of the story's protagonist, has just asked her husband "why did the way of heaven lead to" the death of her parents. His answer, that there was no reason, led her to ponder, "When wind and water changed places, I tried to convince myself that there was no reason for this as well."[46] In other words, accepting the amelioration of wind to the detriment of water required a certain amount of persuasion on the part of Lu Ling.

Wind, in fact, is a persistent image of power in *The Joy Luck Club*. Lindo taught her daughter, Waverly, "the art of invisible strength," which really was how to understand the wind. "Wise guy, he not go against wind," Lindo advised.[47] When Waverly eventually discovers her talent for playing chess, the wind "whispered secrets" to her. Water, on the other hand, is the harbinger of death in the novel. In Rose's account of her brother's death by drowning, her mother An-mei makes the startling admission: "An ancestor of ours once stole water from a sacred well. Now the water is trying to steal back. We must sweeten the temper of the Coiling Dragon who lives in the sea."[48]

In another account of the lethal quality of water, Ying-ying St. Clair, when just a small child of four, almost drowned in Tai Lake when she fell off a floating pavilion on an outing to view the full moon of the Mid-Autumn Festival. She was saved by fishermen who put her on the shore to await her family's search for her. The near-death experience, combined with the fear of abandonment following her rescue, is so traumatic that Ying-ying never fully recovers. "I never believed my family found the same girl," she claims.[49] When she was a young girl, because of her disobedient habit of wearing her hair loose, her mother scolded her, saying, "You are like the lady ghosts at the bottom of the lake."[50] When she was sixteen, she was seduced by a friend of the family and eventually married the man, describing the seduction as "a large wind [blowing] in from the north." But eventually the same wind "blew [her] husband . . . out the back door" when he left her to live with another woman. Ying-ying "became like the ladies of the lake" and "floated like a dead leaf on water."[51]

Ten years later, working as a clerk in a Shanghai boutique, Ying-ying met and married Clifford St. Clair and "willingly gave up [her] *chi* . . . and became an unseen spirit."[52] In her new life in San Francisco, in her daughter Lena's estimation, she "had the mysterious ability to see things before they happen."[53] Furthermore, a significant portion of her clairvoyance stems from geomantic skills. As Lena notes,

> One time when I was growing up in San Francisco, she looked at the way our new apartment sat too steeply on the hill. She said the new baby in her womb would fall out dead, and it did.

When a plumbing and bathroom fixtures store opened up across the street from our bank, my mother said the bank would soon have all its money drained away.[54]

So, a woman with a surfeit of wind and water becomes adept at fengshui—this is an unorthodox interpretation of Chinese cosmology, but is indicative of Tan's brand of Chinese philosophy. In the intersection of cultures that marks the work of many Asian American authors, the fictional world view is often more a transformation than a translation. In the terminology of Heidegger, while it is possible to *inhabit* a place where the local "gods" are not one's own, a person cannot *dwell* there.[55] In order to make the environment one's own, the dweller may seek to recapture or recreate the culture of origin, but that quest might in turn be influenced by the new environment. The resulting equilibrium is neither the original nor the adopted culture.

THE SEARCH FOR BALANCE IN AMY TAN AND NURY VITTACHI

Tan admits that her stories are about "the search for balance in [her] life."[56] Balance is a key word in her cosmology, and she playfully juxtaposes its common meaning with its metaphysical import. In *The Hundred Secret Senses*, protagonist Olivia Yee's half-sister, Kwan, hears this advice from a ghost: "Lao Lu say cannot just balance checkbook, see how much you got left. Must balance life too."[57] But her notion of balance is also intricately tied to her personal understanding of fengshui. In *The Joy Luck Club*, Rose, in reference to her pending divorce, has the following insight:

> Even if I had expected it, even if I had known what I was going to do with my life, it still would have knocked the wind out of me.
> When something that violent hits you, you can't help but lose your balance and fall.[58]

Here the loss of balance is the loss of wind, but "wind" in this context is breath, and breath is another rendition of that ineffable concept of qi.[59] While the wind and water of fengshui are not constituent elements like the fire and water of *wuxing*, they are certainly atmospheric forces. In one of its earliest textual references qi is described as being composed of the six meteorological categories of cold and heat, wind and rain, and darkness (yin) and light (yang).[60] If wind and rain are heavenly qi, it should follow that wind and water are the manifestations of qi on earth. Thus, Tan's "balance" is not only a harmony between wind and water, but also a cosmic equilibrium between the forces of heaven and earth.

Vittachi also refines his geomantic philosophy down to an elixir of "balance" in *Mr. Wong Goes West*:

> As he had aged, CF [sic] Wong had become increasingly aware that the most complex mental constructions were rooted in the simplest of truths. The entire art and science of environment optimisation lay in a single word: balance.
>
> It was a simple concept to understand, but not an easy one to realise. He'd learned that the most powerful place was the point at which the most extreme opposites lay in exact, tense counterpoint.[61]

To illustrate this point, Vittachi has his protagonist describe a scene from his childhood.

> The old man called it the Fire Dragon's Back. . . . On the left were the snowy wastes and high mountains of the Tibetan plateau. On the right were green fields and rolling, verdant hills, which eventually become the yellow grey of the plains of the Takla Makan desert. Winter on one side, summer on the other. Cold and heat. Yin and yang.
>
> "We call this the Point of Balance," Rinchang said.[62]

This unique environment, a place that balances the six atmospheric forces—cold and snow and darkness on the left, and heat and wind and light on the right—is the back of a dragon mountain, but not just any dragon mountain. The geographical setting is the Kunlun Mountains north of Tibet and the source of the Yellow River. Moreover, Kunlun is also a paradise realm in Chinese mythology, the cosmic pillar that separates the heaven from the earth. Vittachi could not have chosen a more appropriate setting for his balance point. It is at this cosmic location that he situated the novel's denouement. Skyparc, the specially designed Airbus 380 "flying business park," was heading from Hong Kong to London, when Wong learned that it was taking the route over China:

> "Does the route matter? Surely the destination is the key thing?" Sir Nicholas asked.
>
> "Every person has directions which are lucky at some times and unlucky at some times. This plane . . . it is good luck for this plane to travel east or southeast, but bad luck to travel northeast."[63]

The pilot refuses to change the flight plan, and the plane continues on its scheduled route. When terrorist bombs damage the landing gear and start a fire in the luggage compartment, Wong remembers the mountain ridge from his childhood and promptly informs the pilot to change course. Minutes later, Skyparc crash-lands in the deep snow of the dragon's back.

It is not merely serendipitous that Vittachi guided his doomed aircraft to the back of a dragon on top of a mythical mountain. In the Chinese sky, the celestial equator is circumnavigated every twenty-four hours by four great zodiacal constellations—the Cerulean Dragon (equivalent to Scorpius, Libra, and Virgo in the Greek conception of the sky), the Vermilion Bird, the White Tiger, and the Dark Turtle. When the southern sky is viewed at dusk in successive seasons, each of these great stellar deities supersedes the other as the year progresses.[64] In ancient China, the rising of the "Horn" (of the Cerulean Dragon) in the east marked the beginning of the year.

However, the stars did not always rise in the east and set in the west. In the mythical past, Kunlun's nine-tiered summit stood in the center of the world, a pathway up to Heaven where deities descended and shamans ascended, and where any human who could climb its heights was granted immortality. In those halcyon days, all four deities adorned the night sky together as if the dragon, phoenix, tiger, and turtle followed one after another along the earthly horizon in their celestial journey. The *Book of Burial* states, "The Dark Turtle hangs its head; the Vermilion Bird hovers in dance; the Cerulean Dragon coils sinuously; the White Tiger crouches down."[65] But eventually, the blurring of the line between mortal and immortal sowed turmoil on the earth. The Water Lord—champion of the toiling masses—vied with the Lord of Fire—grandson of the Yellow Emperor—for dominion over the Earth. Lord Water lost the battle and, in his rage, toppled Kunlun Mountain and called forth the waters to inundate the land. After this great cataclysm, the rivers of China thereupon flowed eastwards, and the stars flew thence forward toward the west.

Now, let us note once again the description of the ideal geomantic site according to Form School theory: "Bury with the Cerulean Dragon to the left, the White Tiger to the right, the Vermilion Bird in front, and the Dark Turtle in back."[66] We must ask ourselves, why are the celestial deities embracing the earthly environment of the burial site as if it were the locus of that paradise of yore? Assuming the observer is looking south, this configuration of the prelapsarian sky would represent the spring equinox (and thus the symbol of birth and growth) were it possible to actually visualize the entire zodiac in this fashion. When the fengshui master locates the dragon and tiger in his local environment, he has constructed a veritable paradise by recovering heaven on earth. Perhaps Wong says it best:

The two hills, their fingers touching behind the house, formed a perfect Dragon and Tiger embrace, protecting the house and encompassing it with the best fortune imaginable. Further behind the house were tall trees and, beyond, a much larger mountain.

Wong picked out the elements that made the location so magical. "Green dragon one side, white tiger other side. At back is black turtle. *Ming t'ang* in front. Truly here is heaven."[67]

THE GEOMANTIC READING

To conclude, for Tan balance is a cosmic equilibrium between heavenly qi or wind, and earthly qi or water. For Vittachi, the Point of Balance is the cosmic pillar, the point equidistant between heaven and earth, between fire and water, between dark and light. As such, the Fire Dragon's Back was the most auspicious dragon lair on earth, and it is no wonder that the jetliner crashes atop the mountain without suffering a single casualty.

As we have seen, geomantic "balance" is the philosophical objective of characters in the works of various Asian diasporic authors. That is, they locate themselves in physical space by controlling the disposition of qi in the environment. A German philosopher also claimed that peasants in his native land exhibited a similar goal—to build a house by letting "earth and heaven, divinities and mortals enter *in simple oneness* into things." Heidegger's oneness, like Tan's balance, requires an awareness by the dweller of some ineffable other, "divinities" in his case.[68] In the lives of their fictional surrogates these writers seek to harmonize the dwelling site and its inhabitants with the natural environment by means of metaphysical principles. At the very least, the geomantic reading can assist the reader in understanding the metaphysics of place in selected Asian American and other Asian diasporic novels. It is hoped that the reader has also gained a more universal perspective that will bring the geomantic world view to bear on other cultures and their literatures. In the words of canonical Asian American author, Maxine Hong Kingston, "I'm not alone; people here and people who've/ migrated everywhere are doing this work of/ influencing wind and water (fengshui)."[69]

NOTES

The author would like to thank the editors for their constructive comments, which greatly contributed to improving the final version of this chapter.

1. In the orthography of *pinyin* ("spell-sound")—the romanization system developed by the People's Republic of China in the 1950s, words of more than one Chinese syllable are spelled without hyphens or spaces. Thus, *fengshui* is the proper spelling of the two-syllable term rather than *feng shui* or *feng-shui*. The term "geomancy" was borrowed by nineteenth-century missionaries to translate the Chinese term. Originally a Greek term applied to an Arabian system of divination ('*ilm al-raml*, or "sand science"), *geomancy*—divination by the earth—actually makes more sense as a description of fengshui than as a name for '*ilm al-raml*.

2. Amy Tan, *The Joy Luck Club* (New York: G.P. Putnam's Sons, 1989), 147.

3. Robert T. Hayashi, "Beyond Walden Pond: Asian American Literature and the Limits of Ecocriticism," in *Coming into Contact: Explorations in Ecocritical Theory and Practice*, ed. Annie Merrill Ingram, Ian Marshall, Daniel J. Philippon, and Adam W. Sweeting (Athens: University of Georgia Press, 2007), 70.

4. Geocriticism "focuses on the spatial representations within the texts," and explores "the overlapping territories of actual, physical geography and an author's or character's cognitive mapping in the literary text." Robert T.

Tally, "Geocriticism and Classic American Literature" (2008), *Faculty Publications-English*, Paper 14, http://ecommons.txstate.edu/englfacp/14 (accessed November 24, 2012).

5. As geomantic criticism is reminiscent of geocriticism, so too is a metaphysics of place suggestive of "the spirit of place" first discussed by D. H. Lawrence: "The spirit of a place is a great reality. The Nile valley produced not only the corn but the terrific religions of Egypt. China produces the Chinese, and will go on doing so. The Chinese in San Francisco will in time cease to be Chinese, for America is a great melting pot." Lawrence, *Studies in Classic American Literature* (New York: Viking, 1964), 5–6.

6. Martin Heidegger, "The Thinker as Poet," in *Poetry, Language, Thought*, trans. Albert Hofstadter (New York: Harper and Row, 1971), 8, 10.

7. Heidegger, "Building Dwelling Thinking," in *Poetry, Language, Thought*, 160. According to Adam Sharr, "He considered the philosophy of Todtnauberg to be that of forests, brooks, rocks, mist, meadows, and winds. For Heidegger, these were elemental motions—the core of philosophy 'up there,' a palpable verity that outreached irrelevances he perceived in life 'below.'" Sharr, *Heidegger's Hut* (Cambridge: MIT Press, 2006), 73.

8. Ibid., 160.

9. Ibid.

10. Hayashi, "Beyond Walden Pond," 63.

11. Ibid.

12. Peter Critchley, "Martin Heidegger: Ontology and Ecology" (2004), http://www.academia.edu/705387/Martin_Heidegger_Ontology_and_Ecology, 3–4 (accessed November 21, 2012).

13. Han Ong, *Fixer Chao* (New York: Farrar, Straus and Giroux, 2001), 370.

14. Patricia L. Hamilton, "*Feng Shui,* Astrology, and the Five Elements: Traditional Chinese Belief in Amy Tan's *The Joy Luck Club*," *MELUS: Multi-Ethnic Literature of the United States* 24.2 (1999): 126.

15. Ibid., 127.

16. Pam Chun, *The Money Dragon* (Naperville, IL: Sourcebooks, 2002), 120.

17. Ibid., 277.

18. *The Zangshu* or *Book of Burial* by Guo Pu (276–324), trans. Stephen Field, II. A. 2–4, http://www.fengshuigate.com/zangshu.html (accessed July 28, 2011).

19. Chinese syllables originally spelled *ch'i* in nineteenth-century Wade romanization, are now spelled *qi* in *pinyin*. Both Wade and *pinyin* are still accepted in scholarly publications, although *pinyin* is the international standard. Some writers omit the apostrophe in *ch'i* (as does Amy Tan), although strictly speaking this is incorrect orthography.

20. *Book of Burial*, I. B. 6.

21. Ibid., IV. A. 7–8.

22. Ibid., VI. B. 1–6.

23. Ibid., VII. B. 2.

24. Ibid., VIII. A. 1.

25. Amy Tan, *The Hundred Secret Senses* (New York: G.P. Putnam's Sons, 1995), 269.

26. Stephen L. Field, *Ancient Chinese Divination* (Honolulu: University of Hawaii Press, 2008), 82.

27. The stars are actually numbers in a "magic square" where all rows, columns, and diagonals add up to fifteen (see Figure 9.2, the Map of Eight-House Fengshui). For this reason, Eight-House fengshui is also known as Nine-Star fengshui. The numbers and the names of the houses are derived from the eight *gua* (or *kua*) "trigrams" of the *Yijing* or *Book of Changes*.

28. Nury Vittachi, *Mr. Wong Goes West* (Sydney: Allen and Unwin, 2008), 62.
29. Ibid., 93
30. Each of the eight halls also has a designation that indicates its auspice. Auspicious halls, in descending order are Life Breath, Extended Years, Celestial Physician, and Guardians. Unlucky halls are Shortened Life, Five Ghosts, Six Curses, and Accidental Injury.
31. Nury Vittachi, *The Feng Shui Detective* (New York: St. Martin's Press, 2002), 2.
32. Ibid., 6.
33. Ibid., 13.
34. Chun, *The Money Dragon*, 147–48.
35. Amy Tan, *The Opposite of Fate: A Book of Musings* (New York: G.P. Putnam's Sons, 2003), 233.
36. Stephen Field, "Fengshui Readings by Master Ten Li," http://www.fengshuigate.com/MasterTen/reading.html (accessed July 28, 2011).
37. Tan, *The Opposite of Fate*, 302–3.
38. Hamilton, "*Feng Shui*, Astrology, and the Five Elements," 132. With Hamilton's essay as a handbook, it might even be possible to find traces of the original story plan, since she outlines the birthdates and astrology of many of the characters in the book.
39. "*Qi* is the universal fluid, active as Yang and passive as Yin, out of which all things condense and into which they dissolve." A.C. Graham, *Disputers of the Tao: Philosophical Argument in Ancient China* (La Salle, IL: Open Court, 1989), 101.
40. Tan, *The Joy Luck Club*, 121–22.
41. John S. Major, *Heaven and Earth in Early Han Thought: Chapters Three, Four, and Five of the Huainanzi* (Albany: State University of New York Press, 1993), 62.
42. Ong, *Fixer Chao*, 60.
43. Ancient Chinese cosmologists posited five elements (or phases of qi) that constituted the cosmos: earth, metal, water, wood, and fire. Ancient Greek philosophers posited four elements: earth, water, air, and fire, to which Aristotle added a fifth element, aether.
44. Tan, *The Joy Luck Club*, 52.
45. Ibid., 58.
46. Amy Tan, *The Bonesetter's Daughter* (New York: Ballantine, 2008), 267–68.
47. Tan, *The Joy Luck Club*, 89.
48. Ibid., 129.
49. Ibid., 82.
50. Ibid., 243.
51. Ibid., 246–49.
52. Ibid., 251.
53. Ibid., 149.
54. Ibid.
55. Critchley, "Martin Heidegger," 4.
56. Tan, *The Opposite of Fate*, 302.
57. Tan, *The Hundred Secret Senses*, 25.
58. Tan, *The Joy Luck Club*, 120–21.
59. In the sixth century BCE *Analects* of Confucius, the term was used to indicate the blood and breath of the human body. See Field, *Ancient Chinese Divination*, 8.
60. Field, *Ancient Chinese Divination*, 8–9. This is *tianqi*, or heavenly qi. In modern Chinese the same term refers simply to "weather."
61. Vittachi, *Mr. Wong Goes West*, 2–3.

62. Ibid., 27.
63. Ibid., 165. The ellipsis in this quote appears in the original text.
64. The celestial equator is equivalent to the horizon at the north and south poles; for the rest of the world it is canted upward from the horizon like the nested rings of a gimbal, depending on how far the observer resides from the poles. In the northern hemisphere, this celestial ring makes a great arc across the southern sky, and so the stars of the zodiac rise in the east and set in the west.
65. *Book of Burial*, VIII. A. 2.
66. Ibid., VIII. A. 1.
67. Vittachi, *The Feng Shui Detective's Casebook* (Sydney: Allen & Unwin, 2006), 167.
68. Just as qi has no religious connotation in Chinese philosophy, Heidegger's divinities are not to be confused with anthropomorphic gods, per se. As one component of the "fourfold" (earth and heaven, divinities and mortals), the divine is the counterpoint to what is mortal, and is inherent in the world around us.
69. Maxine Hong Kingston, *I Love a Broad Margin to My Life* (New York: Alfred A. Knopf, 2011), 209.

BIBLIOGRAPHY

Chun, Pam. *The Money Dragon*. Naperville, IL: Sourcebooks, 2002.

Critchley, Peter. "Martin Heidegger: Ontology and Ecology," 2004. http://www.academia.edu/705387/Martin_Heidegger_Ontology_and_Ecology, 3–4 (accessed November 21, 2012).

Field, Stephen L. *Ancient Chinese Divination*. Honolulu: University of Hawaii Press, 2008.

———. "Fengshui Readings by Master Ten Li." http://www.fengshuigate.com/MasterTen/reading.html (accessed July 28, 2011).

———. "An Overview of Ancient Fengshui." http://www.fengshuigate.com/overview.html (accessed July 28, 2011).

———, translator. *The Zangshu* or *Book of Burial* by Guo Pu (276–324). http://www.fengshuigate.com/zangshu.html (accessed July 28, 2011).

Graham, A. C. *Disputers of the Tao: Philosophical Argument in Ancient China*. La Salle, IL: Open Court, 1989.

Hamilton, Patricia L. "*Feng Shui*, Astrology, and the Five Elements: Traditional Chinese Belief in Amy Tan's *The Joy Luck Club*." *MELUS: Multi-Ethnic Literature of the United States* 24.2 (1999): 125–45.

Hayashi, Robert T. "Beyond Walden Pond: Asian American Literature and the Limits of Ecocriticism." In *Coming into Contact: Explorations in Ecocritical Theory and Practice*, edited by Annie Merrill Ingram, Ian Marshall, Daniel J. Philippon, and Adam W. Sweeting, 58–75. Athens: University of Georgia Press, 2007.

Heidegger, Martin. *Poetry, Language, Thought*, translated by Albert Hofstadter. New York: Harper and Row, 1971.

Kingston, Maxine Hong. *I Love a Broad Margin to My Life*. New York: Alfred A. Knopf, 2011.

Lawrence, D. H. *Studies in Classic American Literature*. New York: Viking, 1964.

Major, John S. *Heaven and Earth in Early Han Thought: Chapters Three, Four, and Five of the Huainanzi*. Albany: State University of New York Press, 1993.

Ong, Han. *Fixer Chao*. New York: Farrar, Straus and Giroux, 2001.

Sharr, Adam. *Heidegger's Hut*. Cambridge: MIT Press, 2006.

Tally, Robert T. "Geocriticism and Classic American Literature" (2008). *Faculty Publications-English*, Paper 14. http://ecommons.txstate.edu/englfacp/14 (accessed November 24, 2012).

Tan, Amy. *The Bonesetter's Daughter*. New York: Ballantine, 2008.

———. *The Hundred Secret Senses*. New York: G.P. Putnam's Sons, 1995.

———. *The Joy Luck Club*. New York: G.P. Putnam's Sons, 1989.

———. *The Opposite of Fate: A Book of Musings*. New York: G.P. Putnam's Sons, 2003.

Vittachi, Nury. *The Feng Shui Detective*. New York: St. Martin's Press, 2002.

———. *The Feng Shui Detective's Casebook*. Sydney: Allen & Unwin, 2006.

———. *Mr. Wong Goes West: A Feng Shui Detective Novel*. Sydney: Allen & Unwin, 2008.

10 Environment for "A Free Life"

King-Kok Cheung

> To Nan's amazement, when the sweltering summer set in, the geese
> didn't leave for the North as they were supposed to do. Instead, they
> perched in the shady bushes on the other shore. . . . Nan realized
> that these Canadian geese had grown fat, lazy, and comfortable, no
> longer possessed of the instinct for migration.
>
> —Ha Jin, *A Free Life*

This description of disruption to Canadian geese migration appears in
the middle of Ha Jin's *A Free Life* (2007), an immigrant tale that traces
a Chinese family's adjustment to the United States, particularly Nan Wu's
meandering trek to be a poet while supporting his wife and son. Although
the reflection about the geese has little to do with the plot of the novel, it
nevertheless captures Jin's idea of a propitious ambience for artists: instead
of behaving like the Canadian geese that opt for security and comfort, they
must stretch their wings and scale new heights. Nan Wu, an aspiring poet,
risks letting his talent rust away unused; he has to unfetter himself from
various chains—political, economic, domestic, and psychological—that
constrain his literary ambition. In the novel, ecological and linguistic milieu
are inextricably linked: a free life involves finding a healthful environment
that permits Nan to write without political or financial anxieties and root-
ing himself in a new semantic soil that allows him to shed received values
and re-make himself ontologically. The solitude Nan espouses at the end of
the novel harkens to three different strains: the reclusiveness of traditional
Chinese writers who live close to nature to escape from politics and commerce; the dissension of contemporary Chinese thinkers who question state
power; and the nonconformist spirit championed by American literary—
also pastoral—figures such as Emerson, Frost, Whitman, and Faulkner.[1]

Given that Jin has traveled a route similar to Nan's in order to arrive
at his position as a writer who publishes in an adopted language, one cannot help sighting autobiographical traces in the novel, especially regarding
authorial struggle and aesthetic philosophy. Both Jin and Nan were doc-
toral students at Brandeis in 1989 who decided to stay in the United States

after the Tiananmen crackdown; both went on detours as night watchman and chef before entering a new linguistic territory; both have become persona non grata to the Chinese government. Although the novel is carefully crafted and many details are undoubtedly invented, it is dedicated to Jin's wife and son who expressly "lived this book." At various junctures, I will juxtapose passages from *The Writer as Migrant* (Jin's collection of essays) and *A Free Life* to bring out certain writerly parallels between Jin and Nan. The immigrant journey for both of them doubles as a stylistic expedition: their attempt to find a place under the American sun is also a metanarrative about finding their way in a sea of English letters.

I am not the first to construe language terrestrially. Costica Bradatan, for instance, observes: "To practice writing is to grow roots into [a] language. . . . Literary virtuosity almost always betrays a sense of deep, comfortable immersion into a familiar soil."[2] It is therefore painfully unsettling for a writer to switch to a different linguistic medium—an uprooting as radical as emigration. But the experience can also be regenerative, for language is not merely a means of expression but also "a mode of subjective existence" and "a constitutive part" of oneself; therefore, "to abandon your native tongue and to adopt another is to dismantle yourself . . . and then to put yourself together again, in a different form."[3] In undergoing a double— physical and linguistic—exile, Jin and his protagonist also refashion themselves ontologically. For both, the serene landscape etched deeply in their psyche by traditional Chinese poetry and painting can now be found only outside their homeland. They publish in English not only to avert Chinese censors but also to remake themselves, to blaze an individual trail. Jin's recourse to bilingual grafting throughout the novel illustrates that the poetic mind is its own place which knows no national borders. The re-visioning of Chinese and American tropes deliberately detach the expressions from their national moorings, a figurative move in keeping with the notion of freedom in the novel, which is as much about writing in an open climate as breathing clean air, migrating geographically as transmigrating ontologically, and exploring a second tongue as finding a new home.

This chapter analyzes the correspondences between ecological, linguistic, and moral landscapes, between geographical and rhetorical crossings, and between pastoral and existential solitude in Nan's dual odyssey. The first section compares the reclusive and transcendentalist traditions and how both forms of pastoral writing caution against the pitfalls of power, wealth, and society. The second section examines the confluence of ecological and political climate that impels Nan to remain in the United States and to write in English. The third section foregrounds the transpacific materialism that depredates the environment in China and stalls Nan's artistic development in America. The fourth section reveals how both the Chinese tenet of parental sacrifice and the commonplace conception of the American Dream reinforce the compulsive accumulation of wealth to the detriment of higher pursuits. The last section parses the tripartite solitude exemplified by Nan and demonstrates how his cross-stitching of Chinese and American expressions opens up the possibility of a geographical and literary homeland across national borders.

CHINESE RECLUSIVE IDEAL AND TRANSCENDENTAL APPRECIATION OF NATURE

Recent ecocriticism has brought to the fore the relationship between landscape and power, exposing how colonialism and the concomitant economic exploitation of indigenous people have devastated their native terrain.[4] But Ursula K. Heise is mindful that "neither environmentalism nor ecocriticism should be thought of as nouns in the singular"; "the assumptions that frame environmentalist and ecocritical thought in the United States cannot simply be presumed to shape ecological orientations elsewhere."[5] In Chinese literature there are many mentions of local government posing environmental threats similar to those associated with colonialism. Ecological and ethical well-being, moreover, are viewed as interdependent, so that an earthly paradise must be situated as far as possible from centers of power and commerce. Jin's novel, in conjoining ecological and political malaise, in inveighing against greed and material accumulation, and in embracing solitude and self-reliance, resonates with this Chinese tradition as well as with the Emersonian ideas of nature and solitude which inform subsequent American pastoral texts.

Before analyzing *A Free Life*, I will sketch what I perceive to be the Chinese and American imprints on its concept of freedom. According to Sinologist Li Chi, the reclusive ideal "never ceased to haunt the mind of the Chinese literatus [and] monopolize much of the spirit of Chinese poetry."[6] Tucked away in remote mountains and hidden hamlets, the idyllic refuge is not only free of air pollution but—perhaps more importantly—unencumbered by power play and petty economic competition. Many traditional Chinese writers regard living in harmony with the natural world as a release from government and trade. For example, in "Peach Blossom Spring"—a well-known fable written by Tao Qian 陶潜 (also known as Tao Yuanming 陶渊明, 365–427 CE) of the Six Dynasties[7]—a fisherman traverses a grove aflame with peach blossoms that ends in a natural spring. He then comes upon a village founded dynasties ago by refugees from wars, draft, taxation, economic rivalry, and political persecution. There are no potentates controlling the populace in this egalitarian community, where villagers make their living by farming and raising cattle. After the fisherman returns to his prefecture he informs the magistrate of the unique village (against the wishes of its inhabitants), but it cannot be located again. Peach Blossom Spring, Tao implies, exists only in the imagination.

Chen Guangchen considers Tao's village to be "a kind of 'ecotopia' that . . . occupies a central place in the Chinese human-nature relationship."[8] In the fable, as in much of traditional Chinese literature, the ruling class is responsible for most of the ills in society; officials often reek of toadyism, rapaciousness, and oppression. This far-reaching opprobrium is encapsulated in an adage: "Avoid the court in life and hell in death [生不入官门，死不入地狱]." Both officialdom and wealth (which tend to go in tandem) are deemed corrupting, unworthy of a poet's pursuit and adverse to artistic integrity. Rural life, Chen observes, is set against political tyranny, with attendant literary implications: "Nature is an escape from politics, as much as nature writing is an escape from literature serving propaganda purposes. Behind this rhetoric is yet another conflict . . . between the Confucian ideal of the literati's social responsibility and the Taoist pursuit of individual freedom."[9] Chen succinctly pinpoints the political and cultural ramifications of nature writing—as a means to avoid subsuming literature to ideology and to affirm artistic independence.

Western pastoralism, as Leo Marx points out, is similarly grounded in "the presumed opposition between the realm of the collective, the organized, and the worldly on the one hand, and the personal, the spontaneous, and the inward on the other."[10] The closest American parallel to the Chinese reclusive ideal is Emerson's ruminations about solitude and nature, which have inspired much of subsequent nature writing: "If a man would be alone, let him look at the stars. The rays that come from those heavenly worlds will separate him and what he touches. . . . The stars awaken a certain reverence, because though always present, they are inaccessible."[11] The passage suggests that solitude is a sublime experience accessible to the responsive mind in nature's presence. Emerson, like the Chinese reclusive poets, marvels at the healing power of the natural world on the workaday soul: "To the body and mind which have been cramped by noxious work or company, nature is medicinal and restores their tone. The tradesman, the attorney comes out of the din and craft of the street, and sees the sky and the woods, and is a man again."[12] Imperial opulence pales beside natural splendor: "Give me health and a day, and I will make the pomp of emperors ridiculous. The dawn is my Assyria, the sun-set and moon-rise my Paphos."[13]

Unlike the Chinese poets who are content to lead a self-effacing pastoral existence, however, Emerson sees nature as "thoroughly mediate" and ancillary to the "realized will" of a human being—"the creator in the finite."[14] He opines that each individual must learn to "detect and watch that gleam of light which flashes across his mind from within, more than the lustre of the firmament of bards and sages," and to answer to his inner calling without being beholden to public approbation.[15] "Society is a joint-stock company," Emerson quips, "in which the members agree, for the better security of his bread to each shareholder, to surrender the liberty and culture of the eater. The virtue in most requests is conformity. Self-reliance is its aversion." Hence the oft-quoted corollary: "Whoso would be a man must be a nonconformist. . . . Nothing is at last sacred but the integrity of your own mind."[16] For Emerson self-reliance and solitude are allied, but the latter is not contingent on isolation: "the great man is he who in the midst of the crowd keeps with perfect sweetness the independence of solitude."[17]

What Stanley Cavell calls Emerson's "aversive thinking,"[18] his resistance against the pressure to conform, has a marked impact on contemporary Chinese intellectuals, including Nobel laureates Gao Xingjian and Liu Xiaobo, both of whom affiliate solitude and self-reliance and are displaced (exiled and incarcerated respectively) by mainland China for their dissident views. Liu, the 2010 Nobel Peace Laureate, asserts: "Solitude implies independence, self-reliance; it means not following the crowd. . . . For Chinese intellectuals, solitude must start with a complete negation of the self, because throughout our long feudal history, Chinese intellectuals were never independent thinkers . . . but 'court literati.'" The Emersonian echo is evident when he continues: "Whoever wants to possess the universe must first possess an independent self."[19] Gao Xingjian, recipient of the 2000 Nobel Prize in Literature, likewise sees loneliness as an affirmation of one's personal worth—"a prerequisite for freedom"—and decries the dehumanization that takes place under both communism and capitalism.[20] As Belinda Kong rightly contends, Gao uses *Taowang (Escape)* (1989), (his drame à clef about the Tiananmen Incident) not to lend support to the pro-democracy movement but to limn his "philosophy of existential flight."[21]

Whether figured as a "joint-stock company" with dividends for the shareholders, a cultural bureaucracy abetting careerism, or a panopticon policing its citizenry, society for Emerson, Liu, and Gao represents collective pressure that threatens to smother the individual. Jin, who mentions Emerson repeatedly in *A Free Life*, also joins the two Chinese Nobel laureates in decrying state power, through his protagonist: toward the end of the novel Nan rises above conventional values of property and fame, bucks against the nation-state, embraces the mind as his poetic touchstone, and dares the world to whip him with its displeasure.

POLITICAL QUAGMIRE

A Free Life evinces the inverse relationship between state power and ecological well-being, between affluence and wholesome living, and between the trappings of the American dream and self-fulfillment. Nan's agonistic stance toward the Chinese Communist government recalls conventional distrust of the ruling class. His generation lived through a tumultuous period in China, when many intellectuals suffered ruthless persecution during the Cultural Revolution and again during the 1989 Tiananmen crackdown. Nan relates how both he and his wife Pingping feel sick for days after watching *Doctor Zhivago*, for the movie reminds them of the life in China where "human lives had been worthless."[22] Nan himself has encountered direct setbacks on account of the Chinese authorities. The political fallout of Tiananmen ricochets into his life thousands of miles away in the United States, transforming him from foreign student to immigrant laborer overnight. Being a student at Brandeis University in 1989, he was unfairly implicated in a scheme to kidnap Chinese delegates' children, resulting in the revocation of his passport. He fumes about the tormenting officials and the expectations that one be obedient. After settling down in the United States, Nan and Pingping remain constantly reminded of their obligation as Chinese expatriates. Nan, who had thought that his family could sever themselves from the Chinese community and just live a "reclusive" life soon realizes that "China would never leave them alone."[23] The wistful comment conveys his sense of unremitting political harassment.

Perhaps in part as a reaction to Mao's guidelines established in Yan'an in 1942 about the social and political function of literature, Nan is adamantly opposed to subordinating poetics to politics. Maintaining that poetry should "transcend history and . . . outlast politics," he is annoyed by the conflation of nationalist fervor and literary arts by an emigrant poet who declares that the entire body of his poetry is worth less than "'*one drop of the blood shed by the martyrs in Tiananmen Square.*'"[24] Nan's views certainly dovetail with the author's. In *The Writer as Migrant* Jin mentions that although he once saw himself as a spokesperson for the oppressed Chinese, he has since recognized the limits of art as social struggle. He regrets that a calamitous event such as the Anti-Rightist Movement in China in the late 1950s has not been memorialized in a lasting literary work, without which "sufferings and losses will fade considerably in the collective memory, if not altogether." He continues:

> What was needed was one artist who could stay above immediate social needs and create a genuine piece of literature that preserved the oppressed in memory. Yes, to preserve is the key function of literature, which, to combat historical amnesia, must be predicated on the autonomy and integrity of literary works inviolable by time.[25]

Both Jin and Nan refuse to be tethered by nationalism. When Danning Meng, Nan's friend, insists that decent human beings must always love their homeland, Nan testily retorts: "*I spit at China, because it treats its citizens like gullible children.*"[26] In an almost verbatim echo of the author, who avers that "loyalty is a two-way street" and feels "betrayed by China,"[27] Nan tells Danning: "*China has betrayed me, so I refuse to remain its subject anymore.*"[28] In Nan's view there is nothing natural about attachment to a nation, especially one that coerces the masses into submission and brutalizes those who balk at its authority. By refusing to pledge allegiance to a country that does not treat its citizens as independent thinkers and does not allow writers to express themselves freely, Nan indicates that it is the environment and not any abstract interpellation that governs his choice of abode. This belief will eventually lead to a radical redefinition of "homeland."

For both Jin and Nan, China's tight control over culture through restraining creative and journalistic expressions that cast a negative light on the regime has been especially debilitating. Jin expatiates on how such proscription hobbles creativity in an article entitled "The Censor in the Mirror," noting that the damage is "not only what the Chinese Propaganda Department does to artists, but what it makes artists do to their own work"—turning themselves into eponymous censors.[29] His own Chinese editor told him in 2004 that his novels *The Crazed* (with the Tiananmen Incident as backdrop) and *War Trash* (about the Korean War) could not be published in China owing to their sensitive subject matter. After the Shanghai censorship office rejected his collection of short stories *Ocean of Words* in 2005, the editor abandoned the project of publishing Jin's work in China altogether.[30] Elsewhere Jin has revealed that he along with a few poets in China thought that the Chinese language has been "polluted by revolutionary and political jargon, had reached the stage where changes must be made."[31] His words connect national and linguistic crisis, political and literary contagion.

Jin no doubt draws on his own experience when he has Nan address the difficulties of continuing to write in Chinese and publishing in China. Nan stops submitting works to China for publication after an editor there has asked him to delete several lines judged politically sensitive; he learns about a group of novelists in Toronto whose manuscripts were often rejected in China on the grounds of the subject matter. Friends of his who have repatriated end up writing hackneyed or tepid work due to official censorship or the dictates of the publishing marketplace. Danning, for example, writes to Nan that he is "living in a net."[32] Even though Danning later becomes a popular writer in China, he remains frustrated because the authorities want to make writers "*less subversive and more inconsequential.*"[33] The national government, by hamstringing creative effort, has turned the country into a cultural desert that produces only arid works peripheral to lived experience.

When Danning visits the Wus in Georgia, he not merely admires the countryside scenery but also connects it with honest living and enduring art. He tells Nan that he is prohibited from seeking spiritual enlightenment in a church or temple. He confides that he is like a fish seeking "clean" water.[34] The simile links cultural bureaucracy with muddy waters, from which a fellow cannot emerge unadulterated. Expecting Danning's desperation to last as long as he holds his official position, Nan jibes at the current regime by inverting Mao's famous saying ("Failure is the mother of success"): "success was the mother of failure."[35] Danning's and Nan's musings replicate those of traditional reclusive poets, who associate the metropolis with moral and political decadence and extol nature as a haven that enables its inhabitants to rise above power, fame, and fortune. Ironically, for these two writers the *locus amoenus* rendered by Chinese poetry and painting can now be found only outside their ancestral country.

The specter of literary censorship deters Nan from continuing to write in his mother tongue. He attributes his periodic depressions to his inability to publish in Chinese or establish himself as an English poet. He tries to cheer himself up by calling forth two lines by Bai Juyi (白居易 772–846 CE), a Tang poet, which evoke the grass re-growing after a fire. Nan then extrapolates that he must go on, "like the invincible grass with blades," thinking of Whitman.[36] In a notable act of literary code-mixing, Nan not only appropriates Bai's conceit about the resilience of nature to refer to his own poetic genius—dormant seeds pending auspicious elements to burgeon—but mingles the wild grass of the Chinese prairie with Whitman's leaves of grass in the New World. Though no explicit mention is made of *Song of Myself*, the reference to the American bard jostles the reader's memory of the other vegetation pullulating and "growing among black folks as among white."[37] Nan/Jin has surreptitiously added yellow folks to the racial spectrum. Through such linguistic cross-pollination Nan begins to fashion his own hybrid aesthetics.

Meanwhile, the political strictures in his native country compel Nan to write in English—an unnerving gambit for him. He attributes his state as a migrant writer to the turmoil in his motherland. When he visits China twelve years after emigration, he feels alienated even in his hometown. He is literally sickened by the smog and nauseated by the similarly hazy political climate. The connection between environmental and political effluence is further stressed when he is asked to bring the ashes of a dissident scholar to the New World because the former patriot *"wanted to be buried in a clean place."*[38]

TRANSPACIFIC MATERIALISM

A Free Life aligns urban squalor with moral turpitude; greed (along with state power) poses a major social and ecological hazard, as it does in traditional Chinese poetry. Danning tells Nan that in addition to the problem of censorship in China, the people there are overly concerned about making money. While staying with his family in Harbin, Nan and his brother Ning visit a riverbank nearby. There had been a park there, but "now most of the plants were gone" and there were stalls.[39] Ning, who is thinking of emigrating to Australia, views the deterioration of their green neighborhood into a concrete bazaar as mirroring a general ethical degeneration: *"Millions and millions of Chinese have lung problems, because China has no lungs any more—all the forests are gone."*[40] Like Danning, Ning correlates topos and ethos. He divulges that bureaucratic corruption and human avarice have become endemic in China, jeopardizing both the natural environment and the physical and moral health of its citizenry. Rampant disease and deceit come along with the toxic territory.

Not that America is averse to material gains. Well before Danning denounces the worship of wealth in China, Nan has passed a similar judgment on the United States, where one's worth is a function of how much wealth one has. Recalling a man who labels his profession as "millionaire" in a lonely hearts section of the *Boston Herald,* Nan infers, "Money was God in this place."[41] When he has to withdraw from his graduate study to become a breadwinner, he frets that he cannot market himself. Knowing he can never be free to write without financial stability, however, he undergoes a commonplace immigrant struggle by taking up sundry jobs—security guard, night watchman, busboy, assistant editor, and sous-chef. The drudgery wears him out physically and mentally. At one point he is so tired of working for hire and the accompanying indignities that he begs a traffic cop to shoot him.

Nan is particularly uneasy about the commodification of art. He wonders why Edward Neary, a distinguished American poet, would behave like a businessman who harps on about power and money. He is surprised that Nick Harrison, his poet friend, should cavil about the sale of his books and his speaking fees. He deplores the ways in which Bao Yuan, a painter, tries to get rich by churning out a painting a day. If state power keeps writers under the thumbs of bureaucrats, the lure of profit has driven some artists to produce corporatized art that is no less stymied.

Although Nan shares traditional Chinese poets' reservations about earthly riches, he has also learned from his American experience that poverty is anything but uplifting, exploding the myth held by Chinese reclusive poets (and some American nature writers) that art could improve under adverse conditions; rather, need has a blunting effect on his poetic sensibilities, just as prolonged hard work has stymied his poetic development. During a visit to the Museum of Chinese Immigrant Culture, he is dismayed by the dearth of artwork, concluding that arduous labor and art do not go together. His own poetic endeavor has to take a back seat when the Wus buy a restaurant business and put a down payment on a brick ranch in Georgia, necessitating an extensive interruption in his writing. The family work so hard that they attain the classic American dream in several years. Their former landlady from Boston is impressed that they have gained so much in less than ten years, and thinks it could not happen anywhere but America.

But instead of taking pride in their success, Nan becomes despondent, feeling as if "the American dream was shoddy, a hoax."[42] He soon realizes it is his failure to go after his own dream that has robbed him of a sense of fulfillment. He is disgusted with himself for putting things off. When Nan comes across a quotation from Faulkner (in a book entitled *Good Advice on Writing* but originally from his acceptance speech of the Nobel Prize)— "The writer must teach himself that the basest of all things is to be afraid"— his self-loathing intensifies. It dawns on him that for years he has been afraid to write and has made up excuses about it.

Through this wrenching epiphany, Nan questions the Asian modality of parental sacrifice and the philistine aspect of the American dream. Many immigrant parents, the Wus included, travail around the clock for the benefit of the next generation. Nan puts it wryly: "The first generation was meant to be wasted, or sacrificed, for its children."[43] The imagery of seeds, used earlier to encrypt poetic genius, here signifies offspring; Nan finds it taxing to tend to both forms of seedlings simultaneously. His friend Shubo, on hearing Nan chide himself for his lack of literary productivity, tells him that writing poetry as a profession should be reserved for immigrants' grand-children and reiterates the Chinese bromide that Chinese survive through each generation's concern about the next generation. Nan counters that sac-rifice is just a rationale. When Shubo adds that even Ben Franklin's father dismissed most verse-makers as beggars and forbade his son to be a poet, Nan snaps back, *"Then Franklin's dad was a major American philistine."*[44] Jin suggests that no one—Chinese or American—should eschew his or her vocation out of parental obligation or pusillanimous pragmatism.

Furthermore, while parental devotion has always been exalted as noble and altruistic in East Asian cultures, the novel pries into its underside. erin Khuê Ninh has pointed out how some Asian parents unconsciously—or per-haps even consciously—use their sacrifice as a form of capitalist investment and end up trying to control the lives of their children, who are supposed to show their gratitude through obedience.[45] This theme plays out in the lives of several of the novel's characters. Nan, formerly a college instructor in China, was scorned by his father for being unable to procure decent hous-ing for his family. Danning's daughter, who loves painting, is dissuaded by her parents from majoring in fine arts and asked to specialize instead in ad designing, which is more likely to lead to a lucrative profession. Pingping similarly disregards her son Taotao's desire to major in French and urges him to become a doctor. Parental sacrifice, then, can sometimes turn out to be a form of economical manipulation, as crippling as political control or economic hardship. Such generational transaction, Jin implies, can thwart the aspirations of both parents and children.

Nan's ambivalence about being fixated on the next generation may seem at odds with the ecological wisdom that everyone is connected and that we must preserve our planet for posterity. Yet parental enterprise that amasses wealth and property to the detriment of both the environment and self-fulfillment may, in fact, harm the biosphere as well as intergenerational atmosphere.

"FILTHY LUCRE" AND "DIRTY ACRE"

Nan sees his pecuniary preoccupation as largely responsible for derailing his literary progress. He has set out to do *"something moneyed people can't do,"*[46] but at some point he becomes dazzled by dollar signs. While he had no choice but to put his nose to the grindstone at the beginning, he contin-ues to work long hours after the family restaurant business has taken off. He now excoriates himself. Like the Canadian geese in the epigraph, which have arrested their inborn abilities as migratory birds in exchange for being fed daily, Nan has ensconced himself in the family business (ironically called the Gold Wok) instead of exercising his faculties and taking wing as a poet.

Upon reading Faulkner's aforementioned remonstrance against fear, Nan undergoes a "paroxysm of aversion" verging on a nervous breakdown. Removing all the banknotes from the cash register of the restaurant, he proceeds to ravage the altar for the God of Wealth, for whom the Wus have been making regular offerings. This dramatic scene registers Nan's revolt against the transpacific idolization of mammon. By desecrating the Chinese God of Wealth and destroying American bills, Nan recants his blind devotion to household livelihood.

Nan's incendiary act may be regarded as both an exorcism and a rebirth—abjuration of his mercenary self and resuscitation of the poet in him. The Gold Wok has turned into an albatross for the born-again Nan, who now rouses himself from the addictive dream of economic prosperity. Thus, it is almost a blessing in disguise when the Wus are forced to sell their restaurant business after Pingping suffers a back injury. Because her condition calls for expensive medical treatment, Nan finds a job as a front desk clerk at the Sunflower Inn that offers adequate medical insurance for the family. He is glad to be free at last of the restaurant. Despite reduced family income he is able to find the quiet setting and repose of mind needed to read and write poetry during his night shift, instead of toiling like an automaton to climb the economic ladder. Sitting by himself at the front desk from 11 p.m. to 7 a.m., Nan comes to a new understanding of the American dream as "something to be pursued only": "To be a free individual, he had to go his own way . . . to be brave enough to devote himself not to making money but to writing poetry."[47] Unlike immigrant tales that glorify the American dream or bemoan its elusiveness, *A Free Life* impugns the economic impetus that drives the conventional dream and redefines it as a process of self-actualization.

Nan's rebirth is also bound up with his literary initiation in a foreign tongue. Bradatan believes that the process of literary switching to another language is not unlike a rebirth. Nan's unlearning of Chinese values such as parental sacrifice and uncritical patriotism and his determination to pursue his own American dream by writing poetry at the risk of utter failure is inextricable from this performative dimension of language, from his plunge into English letters—a move that is fraught with perils even as it allows for a new mode of subjective existence. In immersing himself in a different vocabulary Nan has spouted, as it were, an alternative self that accesses the world afresh.

HOME OF SOLITUDE

The resolution of Nan's psychic crisis may be encapsulated in the word "solitude" in its variant strains—pastoral reclusiveness, political dissidence, intellectual individualism, and linguistic marginality. The transition from the *Gold* Wok to the *Sunflower* Inn harks back to traditional Chinese poets' retreat from political and commercial embroilment to a life close to nature. For Nan, however, sitting at the front desk alone, writing, is sufficient for composure. He appreciates having Pingping with him. As the repeated references to his spouse imply, Nan's idea of a secluded existence—in contrast to the cocooning of Emily Dickinson—comports with the Chinese tradition in which poets who sequester themselves from public life still enjoy being around their families.

What Nan appreciates most about his current occupation is the freedom to apply himself in the absence of distractions. His preferred *modus operandi* is not unlike the author's. Jin discloses in a personal vignette that he dreamed of being a stonemason.[48] Nan comes close to being Jin's alter ego. Both masonry and carpentry use natural resources; associating writing with these crafts concords with the pastoral convention that poetry issues most spontaneously from a natural source. Perhaps the life of a clerk at the appositely named Sunflower Inn writing poetry during predawn hours is the closest approximation Nan can achieve to the work of a stonemason—an image reminiscent of the unobtrusive figures (often emaciated, presumably on account of their Spartan fare) appearing amid rocks and pines in Chinese paintings, connoting free living. Nan, who tries to live an austere life by curbing his hearty appetite after selling the restaurant, is able to recreate in an urban setting the tranquil and ascetic lifestyle relished by Chinese literati and by Jin. Despite or because of his alienation and deracination from his native land, Nan takes after his reclusive forebears.

Nan's seclusion does not entail an actual mountain retreat, though it is clear from Danning's remarks earlier that the bucolic surrounding of the Wus' residence in Georgia plays a salubrious role. An appendix attached to the novel proper entitled "Poems by Nan Wu" suggests that the ambience of the Sunflower Inn and Nan's renewed appreciation of his household indeed behoove his art.[49] On Christmas Eve Nan is able to pen a verse for Pingping, much to his own surprise. The poem, entitled "Belated Love," ends with the line "My love, I've come home"—a tacit acknowledgment of Pingping's abiding companionship, which might have kept Nan's solitude from congealing into loneliness and transformed it into a boon.[50] Jin suggests that as long as a poet has a peaceful niche in which to compose (and, one might add, a wife in the offing), an obsession with bills and property can sabotage creativity. At this point in the novel, Nan has learned that making a living must not displace making a life. He turns down a promotion to motel manager that would bring a big pay raise not just out of paternal duty (to pick up his son from school in the afternoon) but also in favor of his nightly vigil, which affords him quiet time and relieves him of the need to ingratiate himself.

The mentality that Nan admires can be glimpsed in a poem entitled "A Eulogy." The poem's equation of a palace with a mere dwelling and valorization of pure air over social stature are consonant with traditional Chinese pastoral. Nan's poem also alludes to "Yueyang Lou Ji [岳阳楼记]," a well-known verse by Fan Zhongyan 范仲淹 (989–1052 CE)—a prominent statesman, educator, and literary figure during the Song dynasty. Nan's lines about being unflappable in the face of disaster or triumph echo Fan's couplet: "Not gratified by external gains, not distressed by personal losses [不以物喜, 不以己悲]." But if Nan subscribes to Fan's stoic stance, he undercuts the Chinese doyen through his insistence on putting one's kin above one's country, thereby upending Fan's hortative clincher: "Place the concerns of the country before your own; put your own welfare behind that of the country [先天下之忧而忧, 后天下之乐而乐]."[51]

Much as the physical quietude cherished by Nan has roots in traditional Chinese poetry, the restive independence he embraces sets him apart from a Confucian scholar or an insouciant Taoist. His refusal to allow the country to control the individual and his resolve to set the terms of his own life by braving a new linguistic frontier have a definite American ring, reverberating especially to Emerson's cadences. He learns from writers such as Whitman, Thoreau, Emerson, Faulkner, and Frost that he must heed his own metier without dreading public censure or hankering after popular acclaim. As indicated earlier, Jin is not alone among Chinese intelligentsia to draw on American individualism for artistic inspiration and personal fulfillment. Gao Xingjian defends artistic autonomy from the encroachment of politics and maintains that literature must not "tolerate having restrictions imposed upon itself . . . for the sake of the nation or the party, the race or the people."[52] Liu Xiaobo, who urges intellectuals to desist from serving those in power, avows: "I am myself, nothing more. I worship no one and am no one's lackey; I'm a perpetual loner."[53] Jin, likewise a staunch proponent of intellectual and political individualism, frequently articulates his sentiments through Nan. At a meeting of Chinese expatriates, Nan denounces the exaltation of country and race above the private self as "*the first principle of fascism*" and speaks out fervently against jingoism, contravening the Communist preachment and the opinion prevalent among his Chinese compatriots.[54]

Nan, like his creator, also is forging an individualist path on the literary front. As Bettina Hoffman points out, Jin abides neither by the artistic goal of *Künstlerroman* to create beauty nor by the social commitment of many American writers of color who try to express a communal vision.[55] Committed to producing works that possess more strength than beauty, Nan blends his bicultural legacies to herald a migrant poetics. Just as he modulates the trope of rustic solitude according to his urban situation and takes liberties with Chinese texts, his assimilation of American aphorisms, as Arnold Pan astutely points out, is "never a one-way street, since his cultural familiarity with idiom and language are re-routed and interpreted through an immigrant experience."[56] The authorial "fear" against which Faulkner admonishes, for example, becomes for Nan the angst of blazing his trail through foreign words; unlike the great American authors, his challenge is compounded by his adopted medium. His aforementioned redefinition of the American dream—as "something to be pursued only"—similarly issues from his *sui generis* explications of Emerson and Frost: to be free, he had "to give up the illusion of success" to become reconciled to his status as an immigrant and an English language novice.[57]

His words closely echo Jin's own soul-searching before the author decided to use English as his creative medium: "I had to ask myself whether I could accept failure as the final outcome . . . which meant having wasted my life without getting anywhere."[58] In place of the robust confidence of Emerson, who proclaims, "Speak your latent conviction, and it shall be the universal sense,"[59] Nan evokes the tangible loneliness of groping in the margins. He sees his solitude as an existential condition for those relegated to the linguistic fringes. His invocation of Emerson to reflect his own tenuous plight is doubly ironic. Nan was told by a Chinese historian "not to '*parrot that so-called New England sage*' who was a racist and always despised the Chinese."[60] The way Nan bends the poet-prophet's pronouncement to the measure of his own Chinaman's chance can thus be considered as either a tribute or retribution.

Frost's pregnant question concerning "what to make of a diminished thing" similarly is recast as a poignant self-reference by Nan—an unknown poet wielding a second tongue. Although Nan echoes Emerson's conviction that the individual supersedes any collective and that the mind alone suffices as self-validation, his credo stems from his precarious situation as a "linguistic immigrant" subject to the sharp tongues of Chinese and English critics.[61] Mei Hong, a fellow Chinese expatriate, accuses Nan of betraying China and its language.[62] No less scathing is the taunt of an English editor, who insinuates that Nan, a non-native English writer, cannot possibly enrich American Literature, let alone the timbre and texture of its poetry.[63]

Nan's response, in his journal, advances a more inclusive view of the language's flexibility, its assimilation of foreign elements. On a metanarrative level, Nan already has answered the editor's sardonic question by infiltrating American English with his peculiar constructs, modeling a form of linguistic deterritorialization. Both by adapting Chinese lines into English lyrics and by imbuing well-known lines by Faulkner, Frost, and Emerson with shades peculiar to his own struggle as a émigré writer, he has inflected the "standard" lexicon with singular tonalities. The colloquy of Chinese and American poetics and the infusion of Chinese immigrant sensibility into American texts dissolve cultural borders, keeping the ethnic legacy alive while expanding the American heritage.

Nan's solitary stance, brought on by a shift into another tongue and posited as a prerequisite to independence, is likewise a syncretic variation on the Chinese reclusive ideal and American rugged individualism. Having accepted his limbo state between languages, and the possibility of falling into the abyss, Nan begins to sense a certain linguistic and ontological liberation in passing through the void. Jin himself has disclosed in an interview that English gives him "a lot of freedom, but of a different kind, closer to solitude," that the language allows him to be "independent and work alone."[64] *A Free Life* suggests that the optimal habitat for a poet is not so much restorative as invigorating; the "self-made man" is not someone who has "made it" in monetary terms, but someone who dares to be his own person: to chase after a personal ideal, spurn worldly profit and glory, and make something of himself against formidable odds. Jin does not downplay the importance of legal citizenship, economic independence, and domestic harmony, all of which contribute to Nan's equanimity. But he cautions against single-minded accumulation of wealth, the craving for public veneration, and the abandonment of personal objectives in the name of domestic responsibility or political expediency or at the risk of intellectual or moral bankruptcy. Just as industrial pollution jeopardizes one's health, so desires for money, reputation, or power can stifle the creative impulse and keep a free life at bay. Having overcome the menaces to self-trust that prevent him from pushing his limits, Nan seems to have succeeded in cultivating the kind of infrangible selfhood lauded by Emerson: "Think alone, and all places are friendly and sacred. The poets who have lived in cities have been hermits still. Inspiration makes solitude anywhere."[65] Nan, who used to simmer at work and at home, now cherishes both localities. What accounts for the transformation is not solely the milieu but also his ability to "think alone."

The novel concludes with imagery that aligns pristine, if austere, snowy nature with Nan's newfound strength as poet. "Belated Love," "Homeland" (another poem by Nan), and the novel proper all end with the same word—"home." In the last essay of *The Writer as Migrant*, entitled "An Individual's Homeland," Jin meditates on the title's two meanings—as one's provenance and as "the land where one's home is at present."[66] In his mind, the term involves "arrival more than return" since "your homeland is where you build your home."[67] While acknowledging that relocated writers never can dislodge themselves utterly from their past, he warns against the nostalgia that deprives emigrants of "a sense of direction and prevents them from putting down roots anywhere."[68] He concludes the essay using the first person plural: "no matter where we go, we cannot shed our past completely—so we must strive to use parts of our past to facilitate our journeys. As we travel along, we should also imagine how to rearrange the landscapes of our envisioned homelands."[69] He answers the challenge of rearranging the linguistic contours of the new homeland in *A Free Life*, in which the past winds its way to the present in the form of cultural heritage. Rather than wallowing in nostalgia Nan, like the author, has chosen to savor the solitude of displacement and settle down in an environment that let him breathe freely. After being virtually exiled from his native land, then adrift and tongue-tied in the New World, he has finally arrived at a place where he can feel more or less at home, both physically and linguistically.

NOTES

1. There is actually a fourth strain, that of the *Künstlerroman*. See Bettina Hofmann, "Ha Jin's *A Free Life*: Revisiting the *Künstlerroman*," in *Moving Migration: Narrative Transformations in Asian American Literature*, ed. Johanna C. Kardux and Doris Einsiedel (Münster: LIT Verlag, 2010), 199–212. I will not reiterate Hoffman's detailed analysis of that aspect of Jin's novel. Emerson, Frost, Whitman, and Faulkner are all discussed under the rubric of pastoral writers in Leo Marx, "Pastoralism in America," in *Ideology and Classic American Literature*, ed. Sacvan Bercovitch and Myra Jehlen (New York: Cambridge University Press, 1986), 36–67.
2. Costica Bradatan, "Born Again in a Second Language," *New York Times*, August 4, 2013, http://opinionator.blogs.nytimes.com/2013/08/04/born-again-in-a-second-language/?emc=eta1&_r=0 (accessed August 4, 2013).
3. Ibid.
4. See, for example, Elizabeth DeLoughrey and George B. Handley, eds. *Postcolonial Ecologies: Literatures of the Environment* (New York: Oxford University Press, 2011); Elizabeth DeLoughrey, "Ecocriticism: The Politics of Place," in *The Routledge Companion to Anglophone Caribbean Literature*, ed. Michael A. Bucknor and Alison Donnell (London: Routledge, 2011), 265–75; W.J.T. Mitchell, *Landscape and Power* (Chicago: University of Chicago Press, 1994).
5. Ursula K. Heise, *Sense of Place and Sense of Planet* (New York: Oxford University Press, 2008), 9.
6. Li Chi 李祁, "The Changing Concept of the Recluse in Chinese Literature," *Harvard Journal of Asiatic Studies* 24 (1962–63): 235.
7. Tao Qian, "Peach Blossom Spring," in *Anthology of Chinese Literature*, ed. Cyril Birch (New York: Grove Press, 1965), 1: 167–68. Tao himself—a provincial governor as well as a renowned poet—resigned from the Jin court at thirty to become a farmer, as recorded in "Two Poems on Returning to Dwell in the Country," in *Anthology of Chinese Literature: From Early Times to the Fourteenth Century*, trans. William Acker, ed. Cyril Birch (New York: Grove Press, 1965), 182–83.
8. Chen Guangchen, "Personal Landscape: Shen Congwen and Gao Xingjian's Autobiographical Writings," in *Ecology and Life Writing*, ed. Alfred Hornung and Zhao Baisheng (Heidelberg: Universitätsverlag Winter, 2013), 178.
9. Ibid., 179. On how the trope of nature is variously embraced by Taoists and Confucians, see also Joseph R. Levenson and Franz Schurmann, *China: An Interpretive History* (Berkeley: University of California Press, 1969), 110–16.
10. Marx, "Pastoralism," 44.
11. Ralph Waldo Emerson, "Nature," in *The Portable Emerson*, ed. Carl Bode and Malcolm Cowley (New York: Penguin, 1979), 9.
12. Ibid., 14.
13. Ibid., 14–15.
14. Ibid., 28, 43.
15. Emerson, "Self-Reliance," in *The Portable Emerson*, 139.
16. Ibid., 141.
17. Ibid., 143.

18. Stanley Cavell, "Aversive Thinking: Emersonian Representation in Heidegger and Nietzsche," *New Literary History* 22.1 (1991): 135.
19. Liu Xiaobo, "On Solitude," in *New Ghosts, Old Dreams: Chinese Rebel Voices*, ed. Geremie Barmé and Linda Jaivin (New York: Random House, 1992), 207–9.
20. Gao Xingjian, "The Necessity of Loneliness," in *The Case for Literature*, trans. Mabel Lee (New Haven: Yale University Press, 2007), 164, 165.
21. Belinda Kong, *Tiananmen Fictions outside the Square* (Philadelphia: Temple University Press, 2012), 13.
22. Ha Jin, *A Free Life* (New York: Vintage, 2009), 516. Italics in the original indicate that the conversations are conducted in Mandarin/Putonghua.
23. Ibid., 235.
24. Ibid., 95.
25. Ha Jin, *The Writer as Migrant* (Chicago: University of Chicago Press, 2008), 29, 30. See also King-Kok Cheung, "The Chinese American Writer as Migrant: A Restive Manifesto," *Amerasia Journal* 38.2 (2012): 2–12.
26. Jin, *A Free Life*, 96.
27. Ha Jin, "Exiled to English," *New York Times*, May 31, 2009, WK9. Jin also discusses his own belief in reciprocal loyalty in *The Writer as Migrant*, 31–32.
28. Jin, *A Free Life*, 96.
29. Ha Jin, "The Censor in the Mirror," *American Scholar* 77.4 (2008): 26.
30. Ibid., 26. Although the *American Scholar* essay names *Under the Red Flag* as the rejected book, Jin informs me that it was in fact *Ocean of Words* that was nixed. Email correspondence June 12, 2013.
31. Ha Jin, "Exiled to English," *Sinophone Studies: A Critical Reader*, ed. Shu-mei Shih, Chien-hsin Tsai, and Brian Bernards (New York: Columbia University Press, 2013), 118.
32. Jin, *A Free Life*, 409, 423, 257.
33. Ibid., 532.
34. Ibid., 602.
35. Ibid., 603.
36. Ibid., 409.
37. Walt Whitman, "Song of Myself," in *Leaves of Grass*, 1st (1855) Edition, ed. Malcolm Cowley (New York: Penguin 1976), 29.
38. Jin, *A Free Life*, 568, 570.
39. Ibid., 552–53.
40. Ibid., 555. Nobel Laureate Mo Yan also exposes similar "local riches-through-ruse" activity in Chinese villages; see Mo Yan, "Bull," *New Yorker*, November 20, 2012, 67.
41. Jin, *A Free Life*, 66.
42. Ibid., 418.
43. Ibid., 419.
44. Ibid., 420, 421.
45. erin Khuê Ninh, *Ingratitude: The Debt-Bound Daughter in Asian American Literature* (New York: New York University Press, 2011).
46. Jin, *A Free Life*, 42.
47. Ibid., 619.
48. Ha Jin, "A Stonemason," *Amerasia Journal* 38.2 (2012): 1.
49. Jin self-consciously models his text after Pasternak's *Doctor Zhivago*, which also includes poems by the protagonist at the end of the novel proper. Nan's penchant to draw lessons from quotidian events in *A Free Life* is also in keeping with Emerson's instruction to take a numinous lesson from each material event.

50. Jin, *A Free Life*, 620.
51. Fan Zhongyan 范仲淹, "Yueyang Lou Ji [岳阳楼记]," http://hn.rednet.cn/c/2012/07/26/2692358.htm (accessed July 26, 2012), my English translation. On the various ways Jin uses English to reflect Chinese culture, see Hang Zhang, "Bilingual Creativity in Chinese English: Ha Jin's *In the Pond*," *World Englishes* 21.2 (2002): 305–15.
52. Gao Xingjian, "Without Isms," in *The Case for Literature*, trans. Mabel Lee (New Haven: Yale University Press, 2007), 67.
53. Liu, "On Solitude," 208–9.
54. Jin, *A Free Life*, 496.
55. Hofmann, "Ha Jin's *A Free Life*," 185.
56. Arnold Pan, "Belonging Across Cultures: Immigration and Citizenship in *A Free Life*," *Amerasia Journal* 38.2 (2012): 24.
57. Jin, *A Free Life*, 619.
58. Ibid. Jin, "Exiled to English," 119.
59. Emerson, "Self-Reliance," 138.
60. Jin, *A Free Life*, 55. What the Chinese historian fails to notice is that Emerson, who had read many Confucian classics, delivered a speech in which he deems China "old, not in time only, but in wisdom." See Emerson, "Speech at Reception of Chinese Embassy," in *The Works of Ralph Waldo Emerson* (New York: Hearst's International Library Co. Publishers, 1914), 3: 523.
61. Jin also addresses the challenges of writing in an adopted language in *The Writer as Migrant*, 31–60. I am indebted to my student Matthew Miranda for the term "linguistic immigrant."
62. Jin, *A Free Life*, 496. Jin addresses this question of national betrayal in *The Writer as Migrant*, 31–60. I suggest that Jin is indeed establishing a "migrant pedigree" in that book when he discusses the works of Conrad, Nabokov, Kundera, and Naipaul. See Cheung, "Chinese American Writer," 10. Yingjian Guo reveals that "Jin is not included in the list of Chinese American authors" in Mainland China. Guo, "*A Good Fall*: Surviving the Internationalized Net," *Amerasia Journal* 38.2 (2012): 14.
63. Jin, *A Free Life*, 626, 628.
64. Steven G. Kellman, "Interview with Ha Jin," in *Switching Languages: Translingual Writers Reflect on Their Craft*, ed. Steven G. Kellman (Lincoln: University of Nebraska Press, 2003), 83.
65. Emerson, "Literary Ethics," in *Essays and Lectures*, ed. Joel Porte (New York: Library of America, 1983), 58.
66. Jin, *The Writer as Migrant*, 65.
67. Ibid., 84.
68. Ibid., 63.
69. Ibid., 86.

BIBLIOGRAPHY

Barmé, Geremie R. "Confession, Redemption, and Death: Liu Xiaobo and the Protest Movement of 1989." In *The Broken Mirror: China after Tiananmen*, edited by George Hicks, 52–99. Chicago: St. James, 1990.

———. *In the Red: On Contemporary Chinese Culture*. New York: Columbia University Press, 1999.

Bradatan, Costica. "Born Again in a Second Language." *New York Times*, August 4, 2013. http://opinionator.blogs.nytimes.com/2013/08/04/born-again-in-a-second-language/?emc=eta1&_r=0 (accessed August 4, 2013).

Cavell, Stanley. "Aversive Thinking: Emersonian Representation in Heidegger and Nietzsche." *New Literary History* 22.1 (1991): 129–60.

Chen, Guangchen. "Personal Landscape: Shen Congwen and Gao Xingjian's Autobiographical Writings." In *Ecology and Life Writing*, edited by Alfred Hornung and Zhao Baisheng, 177–97. Heidelberg: Universitätsverlag Winter, 2013.

———. "Slanted Allusions: Transnational Poetics and Politics of Marilyn Chin and Russell Leong." *positions: east asia cultures critique* 21.1 (2014): 237–62.

Cheung, King-Kok. "The Chinese American Writer as Migrant: A Restive Manifesto." *Amerasia Journal* 38.2 (2012): 2–12.

DeLoughrey, Elizabeth. "Ecocriticism: The Politics of Place." In *The Routledge Companion to Anglophone Caribbean Literature*, edited by Michael A. Bucknor and Alison Donnell, 265–75. London: Routledge, 2011.

——— and George B. Handley, eds. *Postcolonial Ecologies: Literatures of the Environment*. New York: Oxford University Press, 2011.

Emerson, Ralph Waldo. "Literary Ethics." In *Essays and Lectures*, edited by Joel Porte, 52–62. New York: Library of America, 1983.

———. "Nature" and "Self-Reliance." In *The Portable Emerson*, edited by Carl Bode and Malcolm Cowley, 7–50, 138–64. New York: Penguin, 1979.

———. *Society and Solitude: Twelve Chapters*. Boston: Fields, Osgood & Co, 1870; Ann Arbor: University of Michigan, 2008.

———. "Speech at Reception of Chinese Embassy." 1868. In *The Works of Ralph Waldo Emerson*, vol. 3, 523–25. New York: Hearst's International Library Co. Publishers, 1914.

Fan, Zhongyan 范仲淹. "Yueyang Lou Ji [岳阳楼记]." http://hn.rednet.cn/c/2012/07/26/2692358.htm (accessed November 5, 2012).

Gao, Xingjian. "Without Isms" and "The Necessity of Loneliness." In *The Case for Literature*. Translated by Mabel Lee, 64–77, 164–66. New Haven: Yale University Press, 2007.

Guo, Yingjian. "*A Good Fall*: Surviving the Internationalized Net." *Amerasia Journal* 38.2 (2012): 13–18.

Heise, Ursula K. *Sense of Place and Sense of Planet*. New York: Oxford University Press, 2008.

Hofmann, Bettina. "Ha Jin's *A Free Life*: Revisiting the *Künstlerroman*." In *Moving Migration: Narrative Transformations in Asian American Literature*, edited by Johanna C. Kardux and Doris Einsiedel, 199–212. Münster, Germany: LIT Verlag, 2010.

Jin, Ha. "The Censor in the Mirror." *American Scholar* 77.4 (Autumn 2008): 26–32.

———. "Exiled to English." *New York Times*, May 31, 2009, WK9. Reprinted in *Sinophone Studies: A Critical Reader*, edited by Shu-mei Shih, Chien-hsin Tsai, and Brian Bernards, 117–24. New York: Columbia University Press, 2013.

———. *A Free Life*. New York: Vintage, 2007.

———. "A Stonemason." *Amerasia Journal* 38.2 (2012): 1.

———. *The Writer as Migrant*. Chicago: University of Chicago Press, 2008.

Kellman, Steven G. "Interview with Ha Jin." In *Switching Languages: Translingual Writers Reflect on Their Craft*, edited by Steven G. Kellman, 81–84. Lincoln: University of Nebraska Press, 2003.

Kong, Belinda. *Tiananmen Fictions outside the Square*. Philadelphia: Temple University Press, 2012.

Levenson, Joseph R., and Franz Schurmann. *China: An Interpretive History*. Berkeley: University of California Press, 1969.

Li, Chi 李祁. "The Changing Concept of the Recluse in Chinese Literature." *Harvard Journal of Asiatic Studies* 24 (1962–63): 234–47.

Liu, Xiaobo. "On Solitude." In *New Ghosts, Old Dreams: Chinese Rebel Voices*, edited by Geremie Barmé and Linda Jaivin, 207–9. New York: Random House, 1992.

Marx, Leo. "Pastoralism in America." In *Ideology and Classic American Literature*, edited by Sacvan Bercovitch and Myra Jehlen, 36–67. New York: Cambridge University Press, 1986.

Mitchell, W.J.T. *Landscape and Power*. Chicago: University of Chicago Press, 1994.

Mo, Yan. "Bull." *New Yorker*, November 20, 2012, 67–73.

Ninh, erin Khuê. *Ingratitude: The Debt-Bound Daughter in Asian American Literature*. New York: New York University Press, 2011.

Packer, B. L. *Emerson's Fall: A New Interpretation of the Major Essays*. New York: Continuum, 1982.

Pan, Arnold. "Belonging Across Cultures: Immigration and Citizenship in *A Free Life*." *Amerasia Journal* 38.2 (2012): 19–24.

Tao, Qian / Tao Yuanming. "Peach Blossom Spring" and "Two Poems on Returning to Dwell in the Country." Translated by Cyril Birch and William Acker respectively. In *Anthology of Chinese Literature*, edited by Cyril Birch, vol. 1, 167–68, 182–83. New York: Grove Press, 1965.

Whitman, Walt. *Leaves of Grass*. Edited by Malcolm Cowley. New York: Penguin, 1976.

Zhang, Hang. "Bilingual Creativity in Chinese English: Ha Jin's *In the Pond*." *World Englishes* 21.2 (2002): 305–15.

Afterword
Slow and Structural Violence

David L. Eng

On August 6, 1945, the U.S. Army Air Forces detonated "Little Boy" over Hiroshima, Japan. Three days later, on August 9, 1945, they denoted "Fat Man" over Nagasaki, Japan. These two bombs, the former uranium- and the latter plutonium-based, were the only nuclear weapons ever unleashed on a human population. Their use not only marked the advent of the atomic age in world history but also connected the specter of nuclear holocaust indelibly to Asia. Though we imagine atomic destruction today in the language of a "nuclear universalism" that threatens the existence of all of humankind—indeed, every living creature and thing on planet earth—the Asian origins of "ground zero" should not be forgotten.[1]

There are other aspects of this history of atomic devastation—of the "human being after genocide" and nuclear holocaust—that should not be disregarded either.[2] Most of the world's uranium supply is sourced from indigenous peoples' lands. The uranium used for the creation of Little Boy and Fat Man was no exception. Uranium mining for the nuclear arms race during World War II, the Cold War, and beyond has resulted in the poisoning of lands and their inhabitants for millennia to come. It has created what environmentalists have described as new forms of "toxic" or "nuclear colonialism," whose apocalyptic effects stretch far into the future (for example, the half-life of plutonium is 24,000 years) while also remaining little known to current generations. The literary and environmental scholar Rob Nixon describes this process as "slow violence": a violence that "occurs gradually and out of sight, a violence of delayed destruction that is dispersed across time and space, an attritional violence that is typically not viewed as violence at all."[3]

Slow violence challenges the human imagination to envision temporal frames and material effects beyond our comprehension. The nuclear industrial complex is a paradigmatic example of this phenomenon. Although we are barely seventy years into this scientific experiment, this is not to say that the uneven effects of the atomic age have not already been immediately felt by particular populations in particular places. The anthropologist Joseph Masco notes, for instance, that Native Americans in New Mexico on whose lands uranium mining has occurred experience significantly higher rates of cancer than other ethnic groups. This is a startling change from the first decades of this century, when cancer was such a rare occurrence among Native Americans that some specialists thought they were "immune" to the disease. Since the dawn of the nuclear age, however, cancer has become a leading cause of death among Native Americans throughout North America.[4]

Here, let us also recall that many of the internment camps in which Japanese American citizens were detained during World War II by the U.S. government were constructed in the same polluted areas—on native reservations and the dispossessed lands.[5]

The story of the atomic bombings of Hiroshima and Nagasaki, uranium mining on the lands of indigenous peoples, and Japanese internment during World War II (not to mention a long history of Japanese empire in East and Southeast Asia) refocuses our critical attention on the transnational linkages of environmental catastrophe and the uneven histories of environmental degradation and environmental racism.[6] It brings together in a Benjaminian flash a long history of native dispossession in the New World with more recent colonial violence and militarism in the transpacific. It is these forgotten connections among Asia, the Americas, and our ecological life systems that this important book *Asian American Literature and the Environment* impels us to consider. These fleeting connections and stories are not easy to tell. In a neoliberal world system drowned out by streams of data, econometrics, and immediate deliverables, it is perhaps the special responsibility and burden of the literary to imagine a new itinerary for the social, the political, and the ethical concerning slow and structural violence that is only now coming into focus. It is a conversation well worth engaging.

On August 31, 1946, nearly thirteen months after the U.S. Military detonated "Little Boy" over Hiroshima, *The New Yorker* magazine published John Hersey's "Hiroshima," an article recounting the atomic bombing of the city from the perspectives of six survivors. Toward the end of it, Hersey describes the return of Miss Toshiko Sasaki, a clerk in the personnel department of East Asia Tin works, to the devastated city. It is September 9, 1946, just over a month after she had been carried out of the burnt ruins, hovering on the edge of consciousness. Hersey writes,

> Even though the wreckage had been described to her, and though she was still in pain, the sight horrified and amazed her, and there was something she noticed about it that particularly gave her the creeps. Over everything—up through the wreckage of the city, in gutters, along the riverbeds, tangled among tiles and tin roofing, climbing on charred tree trunks—was a blanket of fresh, vivid, lush, optimistic green; the verdancy rose even from the foundations of ruined houses. Weeds already hid the ashes, and wild flowers were in bloom among the city's bones. The bomb had not only left the underground organs of plants intact;

it had stimulated them. Everywhere were bluets and Spanish bayonets, goosefoot, morning glories and day lilies, the hairy-fruited bean, purslane and clotbur and sesame and panic grass and feverfew. Especially in a circle at the center, sickle senna grew in extraordinary regeneration, not only standing among the charred remnants of the same plant but pushing up in new places, among bricks and through cracks in the asphalt. It actually seemed as if a load of sickle-senna seed had been dropped along with the bomb.[7]

The botanical nightmare of "fresh, vivid, lush, optimistic green" covering over the ruins of the destroyed city horrifies and amazes Miss Sasaki, leaving her with "the creeps." The thriving plant life "standing among charred remnants" and "pushing up in new places" is a gruesome affront to the nearly 100,000 people who perished in the flash of the atomic detonation, to their ashes and bones lying just beneath the obscene verdancy.

Hersey's paradoxical image of botanical excess and frenzied life in the face of utter human destruction and death encapsulates a number of key elements concerning the problem of slow as well as structural violence that frame this ground-breaking book on Asian American literature and the environment: namely, the ways in which rural and urban, agrarian and built, environments come together around the figure of the exploited Asian laborer tottering on the edge of precarious life. Coined by the Norwegian mathematician and sociologist Johan Galtung, "structural violence" describes a covert form of violence in which institutional structures harm people by preventing the meeting of their most basic needs for survival. Institutional racism, sexism, and classism are among the most glaring social systems of inequity by which structural violence metes out the unequal distribution of resources, the unequal distribution of life and death, to particular populations and groups. (Michel Foucault would later term a similar conception of state violence and regulation of life and death as "biopower.")[8] For Galtung, structural violence names the systemic and impersonal social conditions that give rise to what are more recognizable individual acts of violence and despair in a world order predicated on the hoarding of resources, premature death, and the ever-widening gulf between rich and poor. Similar to slow violence, structural violence often remains out of sight.

In contrast, Hersey's chilling image of botanical excess in the charred ruins of Hiroshima provides a *visible* coming together of slow and structural violence—of environmental disaster and the figure of Asian death. In the process, it disallows a regnant narrative of American exceptionalism that would seek to represent the colonial pioneer's domination over the pristine wilderness as freedom and mobility, the expansion of U.S. empire as manifest destiny, and Cold War violence as bestowing the gift of freedom on a decolonizing and benighted world. The chapters in this book stretch back from Hiroshima to examine how the plantation system, railroads, agribusiness, and mining industry were made possible precisely through the exploitation of racialized Asian labor under biopolitical regulation of life and death. They also stretch forward from ground zero to consider how violence and militarism connect atomic disaster in Japan to Agent Orange, deforestation, and land mines in the killing fields of Southeast Asia during the Cold War period. They consider not only how a political environment was constructed around Asian immigrants but also how Asian immigrants shaped their environments and played key roles in environmental change. All too often, as the environmental historian Richard White notes, American environmentalists have tended to separate labor and laborers from their vision of nature, while valorizing the wilderness as a site of recreation and personal discovery.[9] The studies in this book expand the field's assumptions about nature as the de facto purview of the environment by highlighting the dissonant ways in which Asian Americans have experienced, apprehended, and represented the various landscapes and spaces in which they have toiled.

Together, these essays problematize the notion of the U.S. frontier as a pastoral retreat and the abiding image of a dominant white masculinity (picture David Henry Thoreau and John Muir) that organizes and limits definitions of the environment as untrammelled nature, obscuring the recognition of slow and structural violence in the field of ecocriticism.[10] Indeed, through their attention to working-class, racialized Asian American labor, they question where the U.S. frontier begins and ends, stringing together a long history of the uneven relationship of social power to the land, framing native dispossession and westward expansion to California, Hawaii, and onward across the transpacific to East and Southeast Asia. They insistently connect violence and environmental disaster transnationally, the military industrial complex to the agribusiness, and growth hormones across human and animal populations with atomic fallout. This book thus advances in crucial ways the call for environmental studies to begin addressing seriously and systematically problems of race, class, and environmental justice.[11] This compelling redefinition of the environment and environmental studies is long overdue.

In a number of recent articles, the postcolonial historian Dipesh Chakrabarty marks a global crisis in climate change by which the human species has emerged as an aggregate geological force on planet Earth, obscuring prior distinctions between natural and human history.[12] Humans, Chakrabarty observes, "now have an agency in determining the climate of the planet as a whole, a privilege reserved in the past only for very large-scale geophysical forces."[13] The advent of what Eugene Stoermer, an American ecologist, and Paul Crutzen, a Dutch Nobel-prize-winning chemist, called the "Anthropocene" describes a period roughly dating back three centuries to the invention of James Watt's steam engine, the ever-increasing consumption of fossil fuels, and concomitant emissions of carbon dioxide that have irreversibly altered the earth's atmosphere for millennia to come. Under the sign of environmental disaster and emergency, the Anthropocene thus marks, as Priscilla Wald observes, "the most recent attempt to tell the story of humankind's planetary impact as an account of unwitting destruction and deferred responsibility."[14]

If natural and human history can no longer be thought apart in the age of the Anthropocene, then what, as John Gamber asks in his introduction to this volume, would be the appropriate parameters of ecocriticism? There are a number of widely divergent responses to this question, and it strikes me that much is at stake in defining the proper ambit of the field. For example, Chakrabarty argues that the Anthropocene era marks a moment in which a human-centered history of difference must give way to a new narrative of "species" under climate change, to a new story of universal humanity, and to a new account of collective human existence with no ontological dimensions. Species functions as a placeholder for shared responsibility, for an uncertain future in which human finitude and extinction loom large:

> The problematic of globalization allows us to read climate change only as a crisis of capitalist management. While there is no denying that climate change has profoundly to do with the history of capital, a critique that is only a critique of capital is not sufficient for addressing questions relating to human history once the crisis of climate change has been acknowledged and the Anthropocene has begun to loom on the horizon of our present. The geologic now of the Anthropocene has become entangled with the now of human history.[15]

While Chakrabarty is undoubtedly correct that environmental crisis is one that confronts humanity as a whole—climate change and global warming cannot simply be reduced to the inequities of capitalist development—it is nonetheless true that we have yet fully to comprehend that human history, its uneven development, and its profoundly uneven effects. An adequate history of capitalism and environmental disaster has yet to be told. In rushing toward a new, universal story about humanity under crisis, we run the risk of bracketing those issues of slow and structural violence that this book so carefully investigates, sidestepping subaltern histories of environmentalism that postcolonial, critical race, cultural, and ethnic studies have recently brought to bear on the field. It strikes me that this book seeks precisely to tell a particular history of capitalism and environmental degradation through the lens of Asian America that still remains widely unknown. It represents a compelling effort to tell those stories of living and dying that remain lost to environmental history.

The unending crises of climate change orient our collective attention away from the past, pushing us forward instead toward a future that demands immediate action in the face of impending disaster. In its presentist stance, this notion of environmental crisis eschews a thorough and critical understanding of how our current state of affairs has come to pass, the inequalities of human agency as well as the unequal impacts on human vulnerabilities that constitute its conditions of possibility. In short, it eschews history in the name of exigency and emergency. Here, it is useful to remember that the state of emergency marking climate change might be, as Walter

Benjamin would remind us, not the exception but the rule.[16] How might the environmental critic tell a story that not only divides but also reconciles the natural history of a species with the human history of geopolitically diverse and culturally disparate populations?

In his most recent work on slow violence and the environmentalism of the poor, Nixon calls for better critical analyses connecting globalization with global warming. He notes that in 2013,

> the world's eighty-five richest people—a group small enough to fit into a double-decker bus, in the unlikely event that they would be inclined to take a bus—had a net worth equal to that of fifty percent of the planet's population, the 3.5 billion poorest people. To take a longer view on disparity, since 1751, a period that encompasses the entire Anthropocene to date, a mere ninety corporations, primarily oil and coal companies, have generated two-thirds of humanity's CO_2 emissions. That's a very high concentration of earth-altering power.[17]

For Nixon, the relationships between globalization and ecocriticism have barely been broached. The Anthropocene for him thus provides a unique opportunity to narrate the story of climate change and environmental disaster as an account of ever-deferred responsibility by a capitalist elite—indeed, the elite of the elite.

The current challenge of climate change calls for a simultaneous analysis and linking of what Nixon terms "the great acceleration" and "the great divergence." Nixon describes the great acceleration as a second stage of the Anthropocene, one dating to the 1950s, as "the exponential increase in human-induced changes to the carbon cycle and nitrogen cycle and in ocean acidification, global trade, and consumerism, as well as the rise of international forms of governance like the World Bank and the IMF."[18] This period is followed closely by the subsequent rise of neoliberal globalization and a widening chasm between the *überrich* and the ultrapoor in the late 1970s, a period Nixon describes, following Timothy Noah, as "the great divergence."

Unlike Chakrabarty who marks a breakdown in the history of capital and climate change, Nixon argues precisely for an exploration of their complicity and convergence. Indeed, the fundamental lapse in the dominant mode of Anthropocene storytelling is the failure to articulate the great acceleration and the great divergence in relation to one another: "We need to acknowledge that the grand species narrative of the Anthropocene—this geomorphic 'age of the human'—is gaining credence at a time when, in society after society, the idea of the human is breaking apart economically, as the distance between affluence and abandonment is increasing. It is time to remold the Anthropocene as a shared story about unshared resources."[19]

If ecocriticism has yet to integrate fully insights from postcolonial, critical race, cultural, and ethnic studies, we are poised with this book to resist the substitution of emergency and crisis for a sustained account of slow and structural violence under the shadows of acceleration and divergence. In the process, we might begin to understand how the stories of climate change that we choose to tell—stories that are now garnering increased attention from a widespread public—will determine what kind of social, political, and ethical opportunities become available and what social, political, and ethical possibilities are foreclosed. We cannot underestimate this mandate, for together environmental disaster and social inequality are the defining failures of our times—perhaps of all time.

NOTES

1. On the cultural politics of nuclear universalism, see Lisa Yoneyama, *Hiroshima Traces: Time, Space, and the Dialectics of Memory* (Berkeley: University of California Press, 1999).
2. I borrow the suggestive phrase "human being after genocide" from Priscilla Wald, referring to the postwar period when the world was forced to come to terms with modern technologies of state violence and bio-politics deployed for the unprecedented destruction of human life. Priscilla Wald, *Human Being after Genocide* (forthcoming).
3. Rob Nixon, *Slow Violence and the Environmentalism of the Poor* (Cambridge: Harvard University Press, 2011), 2.
4. Joseph Masco, *The Nuclear Borderlands: The Manhattan Project in Post-Cold War New Mexico* (Princeton: Princeton University Press, 2006), 140.
5. See Zhou Xiaojing, Chapter 4 in this book.
6. For an exploration of the United States and Japan as parallel multi-ethnic empires, see Takashi Fujitani, *Race for Empire: Koreans as Japanese and Japanese as Americans during World War II* (Berkeley: University of California Press, 2011).
7. John Hersey, "Hiroshima," *The New Yorker*, August 31, 1946, 49–50.
8. See Johan Galtung, "Violence, Peace, and Peace Research," *Journal of Peace Research* 6.3 (1969): 167–91. See Michel Foucault, *"Society Must Be Defended": Lectures at the Collège de France, 1975–1976*, trans. David Macey (New York: Picador, 2003).
9. See Richard White, "'Are you an Environmentalist or Do You Work for a Living?': Work and Nature," in *Uncommon Ground: Rethinking the Human Place in Nature*, ed. William Croon (New York: W.W. Norton and Company, 1996), 171–85. Cited in Robert T. Hayashi, "Beyond Walden Pond: Asian American Literature and the Limits of Ecocriticism," in *Coming into Contact: Explorations in Ecocritical Theory and Practice*, ed. Annie Merrill Ingram, Ian Marshall, Daniel J. Philippon, and Adam W. Sweeting (Athens: University of Georgia Press, 2007), 65.
10. See Dipesh Chakrabarty, *Provincializing Europe: Postcolonial Thought and Historical Difference* (Princeton: Princeton University Press, 2000).
11. See Hayashi, "Beyond Walden Pond," 58–75.
12. See Dipesh Chakrabarty, "The Climate of History: Four Theses," *Critical Inquiry* 35.2 (2009): 197–222, and "Postcolonial Studies and the Challenge of Climate Change," *New Literary History* 43.1 (2012): 1–18.
13. Chakrabarty, "Postcolonial Studies," 9.
14. Priscilla Wald, "From Species to Angels: History as Prophecy in the Age of the Anthropocene," Keynote Address, 2014 International Conference on Narrative, Massachusetts Institute of Technology, March 29, 2014.

15. Chakrabarty, "The Climate of History," 212.
16. See Walter Benjamin, "Theses on the Philosophy of History," in *Illumina-tions*, ed. Hannah Arendt (New York: Schocken Books, 1969), 262–63.
17. Rob Nixon, "The Great Acceleration and the Great Divergence: Vulnerabil-ity in the Anthropocene," *MLA Profession*, http://profession.commons.mla.org/2014/03/19/the-great-acceleration-and-the-great-divergence-vulnerability-in-the-anthropocene/ (accessed April 27, 2014).
18. Ibid.
19. Ibid.

BIBLIOGRAPHY

Benjamin, Walter. "Theses on the Philosophy of History." In *Illuminations*, edited by Hannah Arendt, 253–64. New York: Schocken Books, 1969.
Chakrabarty, Dipesh. "The Climate of History: Four Theses." *Critical Inquiry* 35.2 (2009): 197–222.
———. "Postcolonial Studies and the Challenge of Climate Change." *New Literary History* 43.1 (2012): 1–18.
———. *Provincializing Europe: Postcolonial Thought and Historical Difference.* Princeton: Princeton University Press, 2000.
Fujitani, Takashi. *Race for Empire: Koreans as Japanese and Japanese as Americans during World War II.* Berkeley: University of California Press, 2011.
Foucault, Michel. *"Society Must Be Defended": Lectures at the Collège de France, 1975–1976.* Translated by David Macey. New York: Picador, 2003.
Galtung, Johan. "Violence, Peace, and Peace Research." *Journal of Peace Research* 6.3 (1969): 167–91.
Hayashi, Robert T. "Beyond Walden Pond: Asian American Literature and the Lim-its of Ecocriticism." In *Coming into Contact: Explorations in Ecocritical Theory and Practice*, edited by Annie Merrill Ingram, Ian Marshall, Daniel J. Philippon, and Adam W. Sweeting, 58–75. Athens: University of Georgia Press, 2007.
Hersey, John. "Hiroshima." *The New Yorker*, August 31, 1946, 15–68.
Masco, Joseph. *The Nuclear Borderlands: The Manhattan Project in Post-Cold War New Mexico*, 140. Princeton: Princeton University Press, 2006.
Nixon, Rob. "The Great Acceleration and the Great Divergence: Vulnerabil-ity in the Anthropocene." *MLA Profession*, http://profession.commons.mla.org/2014/03/19/the-great-acceleration-and-the-great-divergence-vulnerability-in-the-anthropocene/ (accessed April 27, 2014).
———. *Slow Violence and the Environmentalism of the Poor.* Cambridge: Harvard University Press, 2011.
Wald, Priscilla. "From Species to Angels: History as Prophecy in the Age of the Anthropocene." Keynote Address, 2014 International Conference on Narrative, Massachusetts Institute of Technology, March 29, 2014.
———. *Human Being after Genocide* (forthcoming).
White, Richard. "'Are you an Environmentalist or Do You Work for a Living?': Work and Nature." In *Uncommon Ground: Rethinking the Human Place in Nature*, edited by William Croon, 171–85. New York: W.W. Norton and Com-pany, 1996.
Yoneyama, Lisa. *Hiroshima Traces: Time, Space, and the Dialectics of Memory.* Berkeley: University of California Press, 1999.

Contributors

Bella Adams is Lecturer in English at Liverpool John Moores University. Her teaching specialism is race in postwar United States. Her publications include *Amy Tan, Asian American Literature*, and essays on Asian American writing and race in the U.S.

Joni Adamson is Professor of English and Environmental Humanities at Arizona State University, where she is a Senior Sustainability Scholar at the Global Institute of Sustainability. She is the author of *American Indian Literature, Environmental Justice, and Ecocriticism* and co-editor of *American Studies, Ecocriticism and Citizenship* and *Keywords for Environmental Studies*. She is past president (2012) of the Association for the Study of Literature and the Environment.

Andrea Aebersold is Assistant Professor of English at Washington State University Tri-Cities. She is editor of *New Directions in Ecofeminist Literary Criticism* (2008) and is currently researching issues of environmental justice in the works of Octavia Butler.

Youngsuk Chae is Associate Professor of English at the University of North Carolina, Pembroke. Her publications include *Politicizing Asian American Literature: Towards a Critical Multiculturalism*, "Neo-Colonial Global Capitalism and Imperial Desire in Lawrence Chua's *Gold by the Inch*," and "Disidentification with the Homogenizing and Commodifying Narratives of Ethnicity in Han Ong's *Fixer Chao*."

King-Kok Cheung is Professor of English at the University of California, Los Angeles. Her publications include *Articulate Silences: Hisaye Yamamoto, Maxine Hong Kingston, Joy Kogawa*; *Words Matter: Conversations with Asian American Writers*; *An Interethnic Companion to Asian American Literature*; "*Seventeen Syllables*"; and *Asian American Literature: An Annotated Bibliography*.

David L. Eng is Richard L. Fisher Professor of English and Professor of Comparative Literature and Asian American Studies at the University of Pennsylvania. His publications include *Racial Castration: Managing Masculinity in Asian America* and *The Feeling of Kinship: Queer Liberalism and the Racialization of Intimacy*.

Stephen L. Field is J.K. and Ingrid Lee Professor of Chinese Language and Literature at Trinity University in San Antonio. His publications include *Ancient Chinese Divination*, "Ruralism in Chinese Poetry: Some Versions of Chinese Pastoral," and "Cosmos, Cosmograph, and the Inquiring Poet: New Answers to the 'Heaven Questions.'"

Lorna Fitzsimmons is Associate Professor and Coordinator of Humanities at California State University Dominguez Hills in Los Angeles. She recently co-edited with John A. Lent *Popular Culture in Asia: Memory, City, Celebrity*; *Asian Popular Culture in Transition*; and *Asian Popular Culture: New, Hybrid, and Alternative Media*.

John Gamber is Assistant Professor in the Department of English and Comparative Literature and the Center for the Study of Ethnicity and Race at Columbia University. He is the author of *Positive Pollutions and Cultural Toxins*. He co-edited *Transnational Asian American Literature: Sites and Transits* and has published numerous articles examining ecocritical issues.

Helena Grice is Senior Lecturer in American Literature at Aberystwyth University, Wales. Her publications include *Asian American Fiction, History and Life Writing: International Encounters*; *Negotiating Identities: An Introduction to Asian American Women's Writing*; *Maxine Hong Kingston*; and *Beginning Ethnic American Literatures*.

Paul Outka is Associate Professor of English at the University of Kansas and 2013 President of the Association for the Study of Literature and Environment. He is the author of *Race and Nature from Transcendentalism to the Harlem Renaissance*.

Cathy J. Schlund-Vials is Director of the Asian American Studies Institute and Associate Professor of English and Asian American Studies at the University of Connecticut. She is the author of *Modeling Citizenship: Naturalization in Jewish and Asian American Writing* and *Resistive Memory: Genocide Remembrance, Justice, and Cambodian American Memory Work*.

Sarah D. Wald is Assistant Professor of English and Environmental Studies at the University of Oregon. She is currently completing a book entitled

The Nature of Citizenship: Race, Citizenship, and Nature in Representations of California Agricultural Labor. She has previously published in *Western American Literature and Food, Culture, and Society.* Her research interests include ecocriticism, critical race theory, Asian American Literature, and Latina/o Literature.

Zhou Xiaojing is Professor of English at the University of the Pacific, where she teaches Asian American literature. Her recent publications include *Cities of Others: Reimagining Urban Spaces in Asian American Literature*; "Arthur Yap's Ecological Poetics of the Daily," in *Common Lines and City Spaces: A Critical Anthology on Arthur Yap*; and "Scenes from the Global South China: Zheng Xiaoqiong's Poetic Agency for Labor and Environmental Justice," in *Ecocriticism of the Global South.*

Wenying Xu is Provost at Jacksonville University. She is the author of *Historical Dictionary of Asian American Literature and Theater*; *Eating Identities: Reading Food in Asian American Literature*; *Ethics and Aesthetics of Freedom in American and Chinese Realism*; and numerous journal articles and book chapters on Asian American literature.

Index